MW00442270

THE
LIGHT
OF THE
TORAH

By

SAMUEL BAVLI

The Light of the Torah
Copyright © 2022 by Samuel Bavli. All rights reserved.

No part of this book may be used or reproduced in any manner
whatsoever without written permission, except in the case of brief
quotations embodied in critical articles or reviews.

Published by Tambora Books.

ISBN: 978-1-7376743-3-7

While working on this book, I sometimes referred
to *Ne'umei Shmuel*, a book by my maternal grandfather
Shmuel Bar-Adon. On more than one occasion,
I had the remarkable feeling that he was reaching across
the decades and speaking directly to me, helping me to
understand and elucidate the text of the Torah. Hence,
I dedicate this book to my children, grandchildren, and future
descendants as yet unborn who may someday read my book
and will know that in writing it, I was thinking of them.

For my children Hillel, David, and Eliana,
and for my grandchildren

Jack

Teddy

Scarlett

George

Sadie

Sophia

Gabe

Reese

Emma

CONTENTS

INTRODUCTION

The Torah, comprising the first five books of the Hebrew Bible, is the fundamental text upon which the Jewish religion is built, and it is the bond that connects the nation of Israel—the Jewish people—to God. Contained within the Torah is a set of laws and moral principles by which we are to live; but the Torah is much more than just a legal and moral code. The Torah is written in the form of a history, from God's creation of the world, up to the death of Moses, just as His people, the nation of Israel, prepared to cross the Jordan River into the Promised Land. And it is precisely this history—this chronicle of events, and the interpretation of those events by the Divine—that illuminates our laws and ordinances, and imprints them upon our national consciousness.

The Torah begins with God's creation of the world, when He separated light from darkness, good from evil, and order from chaos. Significantly, just as Creation began with God's calling forth light out of the darkness, the Torah describes God's initial revelation to the nation of Israel as "the voice from out of the darkness" (Deuteronomy 5:20). It is a voice that would stir our souls and would be our eternal guide, leading us along the path of righteousness, embedding itself in our national character, and directing each of us to reach for holiness.

When the Israelites stood at Mount Sinai preparing to receive the Ten Commandments, God declared that the nation of Israel would be "a kingdom of priests and a holy nation"—the vehicle through which the ethical precepts of the Torah would be brought to a world that was at that time steeped in immorality and injustice. The Torah, starting its historical narrative with the creation of the world and with the history of humankind long before the days of the Hebrew Patriarchs, paints a picture of Israel's role among the nations: not a numerous people, nor a great military power, but a nation founded on the principles of justice, compassion, and the rule of law—a nation that would be an example to the world. And yet, the Torah does not present the founders of the nation as perfect people. Rather, they are described with all their faults and with all their errors. The jealousies and the discord within the families of the Hebrew Patriarchs are described in great detail. The contentiousness and the rebellions that marred the nation's early history are highlighted, and the pagan influences that sorely tempted the Israelites are vividly described and repeatedly condemned. All these elements in the nation's history provide us context to understand the nature of the role that God intended for His people to play upon the stage of history. And the Torah's presentation of its laws and ethical precepts in the course of the historical narrative enables us to understand the context in which those laws and precepts were given.

The Patriarchs and the Foundations of Judaism.

The events of our patriarchs foreshadow the lives of their descendants, and the first book of the Torah, the book of *Bereshit* (Genesis), focuses on the lives of the Patriarchs, including the jealousies and strife within their family, and their relationship and dealings with their neighbors near and far—the Canaanites, the Arameans, the Philistines, and the Egyptians—sometimes cordial, but at other times rocky. There is certainly much to be learned from both the animosities that fractured their families and the external friction that often threatened to either annihilate them or turn them from the path of righteousness.

We learn about Abraham, the first of the Hebrew Patriarchs, who came to know and love the just and merciful Lord Who rules the world. Abraham struggled against the idolatry and the immorality of the neighboring Canaanites. But when God was about to destroy the supremely evil city of Sodom, Abraham argued with God to spare the city. Despite his devotion to and faith in the Lord, he nevertheless did not hesitate to question God's decision. He was successful in worldly affairs; and in time, he became very rich. But, even in a world where corruption and deceit were rampant, Abraham maintained a high ethical standard, as seen in his refusal to share in any profits with the evil king of Sodom (Genesis 14:22–23) and in his dealings with the Hittites when he negotiated the purchase of the cave of Machpela as a burial site for his wife Sarah (ibid., 23:3–16). As the founder and the beacon of the Hebrew tradition—which was destined to germinate into the nation of Israel and the Jewish religion—Abraham stands out as the exemplar of faith in the Almighty and for his steadfast belief in justice, compassion, truth, and reason in dealing both with God and with people.

A critical juncture in the life of Abraham—and of the nation of Israel that would descend from him—occurred when God revealed Himself to Abraham and established a covenant with him and his descendants, promising him the entire land of Canaan as his eternal inheritance.

But possession of the Promised Land would not come immediately, nor would it come without hardship and travail.

Abraham's legacy was transmitted to his son Isaac, and then to Isaac's son Jacob (also known by the name "Israel"); and God reaffirmed His covenant with each of them. All three patriarchs—Abraham, Isaac, and Jacob—were beset by famine in the land, and consequently each had to wander with his family from place to place. All three patriarchs had to endure friction with their neighbors, which reached an ugly extreme when the son of a local Canaanite chieftain raped Jacob's daughter Dina. But, as difficult as relations with the neighboring Canaanites and Philistines may have been, those difficulties were overshadowed by the conflicts within the family—conflicts that threatened to tear the family apart and that eventually resulted in a generations-long exile to Egypt.

The Egyptian Exile.

Jacob's sons, consumed by jealousy, sold their brother Joseph into slavery, to a caravan of merchants bound for Egypt. But divine providence intervened, and, through a series of unlikely events, Joseph rose from slavery to become the viceroy of Egypt. Soon, famine again devastated the region; but, because of Joseph's foresight, and because of Pharaoh's wisdom in recognizing Joseph's talents, Egypt was prepared with plenty of stored food. But Canaan was not prepared. Joseph's brothers went to Egypt to buy food; and later, the entire family moved to Egypt to escape the famine in the land of Canaan.

The pharaoh under whom Joseph served was well disposed to Joseph's family, and he very generously offered them the finest grazing land for their sheep. They found

Egypt to be a land of opportunity; and during the ensuing years, they prospered and multiplied. But their good fortune did not last. A later pharaoh turned against them, regarding them as a dangerous foreign element in his country; and, in a pattern that would repeat itself in many other countries over the centuries through the course of Jewish history, he enacted a series of decrees against the descendants of Jacob, now known as the children—or the people—of Israel.

We see the seeds of antisemitism in Pharaoh's accusations against the Israelites in the first chapter of Exodus, accusations that echo the earlier words of the Philistines toward the patriarch Isaac, and those of Lavan's sons regarding their cousin, the patriarch Jacob. And those poisoned, hate-filled roots came to fruition in later centuries in many countries throughout the world, often using words and phrases similar to those of the Philistines, Lavan's sons, and especially Pharaoh.

As Pharaoh's decrees became increasingly harsh, the Israelites eventually were turned into slaves of the government and were forced into heavy labor. The enslaved Israelites gradually lost their spirit, and many forgot their heritage. Not only their bodies but also their thinking became subject to the national culture of Egypt.

Egyptian bondage served to mold the national character of the nascent nation of Israel, sensitizing its people to the plight of the downtrodden. The history of enslavement in Egypt—and God's redemption of His nation with a strong hand—was an experience never to be forgotten among the people of Israel: it was of such importance that the Torah highlights it fifty times as the basis and rationale for many of the laws and practices that God commanded His nation to obey.

Moses and the Redemption from Egypt.

Moses, who was the scion of a prominent Israelite family, was put afloat in a basket in an effort to save him from Pharaoh's decree to kill all male newborns. Pharaoh's daughter found him and, knowing that she was defying Pharaoh's decree, adopted him as her own son. Significantly, Moses—who was destined to become the instrument through whom God would bring about the redemption of the Hebrew slaves—was brought up as a prince of Egypt: imbued with a deep knowledge and understanding of Egyptian culture, unburdened by a slave mentality, tutored in the ways of nobility and the skills of leadership, and not fearful or cowering when speaking to royalty.

At first, Moses apparently was not aware of his Israelite origin; but when he grew up, he learned—and the Torah doesn't tell us how—that he was in fact an Israelite. He went to see the suffering of his people, and, in an occurrence that suddenly struck Moses with the realization of his true allegiance, he witnessed an Egyptian officer brutally beating an Israelite slave. Moses killed the Egyptian, saving the life of the Hebrew slave but putting his own life in jeopardy. When the authorities learned of Moses's actions, Moses became a fugitive and fled into the eastern desert.

The fallen prince of Egypt found his way to the land of Midian, where he lived for many years, marrying into a Midianite family and becoming a shepherd. Those years served to temper Moses's spirit, to teach him the ways of surviving in the desert, and to give him an appreciation of the life of the common man. These skills, added to those learned in his former life, prepared him for his future role. For soon he would have to confront Pharaoh, the most powerful king on the face of the earth; soon, he would have to lead his subjugated and despondent kin out of Egypt and into the vast and daunting desert. He would have to cleanse their souls of Egyptian idolatry and pagan culture; he would have to rid them of their slave mentality and forge them into a free nation, a nation committed to justice, morality, and holiness—a nation under God. Only then could they be fully redeemed from the bonds of Egypt. But first, Moses had to acquire one more skill—the ability to perceive and communicate the divine message: the faculty known as prophecy.

Moses and Prophecy.

As Moses was leading his father-in-law's sheep through the desert, he came upon Mount Horev—the mountain where God would in the future reveal Himself to the entire people of Israel—and there, on the mountain, he saw a wondrous sight: a bush that was on fire but was not being consumed. He saw an angel within the flames; and as he approached, God spoke to him, declaring that He was the God of Moses's ancestors Abraham, Isaac, and Jacob; that He has seen the suffering of His people in the land of Egypt; that He will redeem them from their bondage and will bring them to the land of Canaan— the land that He promised the Patriarchs as their and their descendants' inheritance. God commanded Moses to return to Egypt and confront Pharaoh, and to lead the Israelites out of Egypt.

Like many other prophets after him, Moses at first was overwhelmed, and he claimed he was not qualified. But in fact, Moses was supremely qualified, and when his prophetic ability matured, he became the greatest prophet of all. Distinct from all other prophets before or since, only he could receive prophecy while fully alert. Only he could have wielded the force and the authority to liberate his people and to unite the twelve tribes of Israel into a single nation in whose midst God's presence dwelled. And only he could ascend the mountain to receive the Ten Commandments and infuse his nation with a steadfast commitment to justice, compassion, and holiness. Thus, it was Moses who led his people through the desert for forty years, to the border of the Promised Land; and it was Moses who, at God's command, wrote the Torah and gave his nation the precepts by which they were to live.

Holiness and Entry into the Promised Land.

At the end of forty years, when the people of Israel stood at the banks of the Jordan River preparing to enter the Promised Land, Moses addressed his nation, recapitulating the history of their journey through the desert, and exhorted them to fulfill God's purpose—to observe the laws of the Torah, to place God's words upon their hearts, and thereby to achieve holiness.

More than other legal codes in the ancient world, the Torah stresses ethical principles. A prominent example of the Torah's emphasis on ethics is seen in its approach to truth and honesty: we are commanded not only to be honest but to avoid even a semblance of dishonesty. This and many other principles come from the good and just God Who made a covenant with the nation of Israel— the Jewish people—when He spoke to the entire nation at Mount Sinai, declaring, "I am the Lord your God, Who took you out of the land of Egypt, out of the house of bondage" (Exodus 20:2). And indeed, it was for the purpose of making that covenant that God brought the Israelites out of Egypt, to mold them into the vehicle through which He would transmit the principles of justice, goodness, and righteousness to the world. And at the end of forty long years in the wilderness of Sinai, God restored His people, the nation of Israel, to the Promised Land, the land that He had promised the Patriarchs Abraham, Isaac, and Jacob, to give to their descendants as an eternal inheritance.

BOOK I

Bereshit **(Genesis)**

The first book of the Bible, *Bereshit*, starts with God's creation of the world and everything in it. But the main focus of the book is neither God's creation of the world nor God's laws (of which there are very few in this first book of the Torah). Instead, the narrative quickly turns to mankind and to mankind's relationship with the Creator. The majority of the book of *Bereshit* is a selected history of the family of Abraham and the following three generations of his descendants, and how that history was orchestrated by divine direction. God chose Abraham to be the progenitor of a nation that would carry God's message to the world and plant the seeds that would, over the course of centuries, steer humanity away from its pagan ways to a social structure based on morality and human dignity. The book of *Bereshit*, then, tells the story of the evolution of Abraham's family into the clan that will later become the nation of Israel, and that family's bond with the holy land that God promises them, the land of Israel.

Bereshit 1:
The Creation Narrative

Why does the Torah present two versions of creation?

"In the beginning, God created the heaven and the earth" (Genesis 1:1). Thus the Torah begins its narrative of God's creation of the world.[1] It is an account of God's power over nature: God commands, and things come into being—light and darkness, heaven and earth, stars and planets, the sun and the moon, the seas and the land, vegetation and animal life, and finally man. Next, there is a verse indicating a transition from the previous narrative that is told from a heavenly perspective, to a narrative that focuses on Man's perspective of the creation: "This is the story of **the heaven and the earth** ... on the day the Lord God made **earth and heaven**" (ibid., 2:4). The account that follows this statement makes no mention of the creation of heavenly bodies, and it glosses over the early history of the earth. Instead, it skips quickly to the role of man on earth and his relationship to God.

Besides the difference in content of the first two chapters,[2] there are also other differences. The creation narrative in the first chapter refers to the Creator by the

---

[1] The first word of the Torah, *Bereshit*, means "In the beginning." The first *sidra* (portion) of the Torah, *Bereshit* (Genesis 1:1 – 6:8}, is named for the first word. Similarly, the entire first book of the Torah is also named *Bereshit*, after the first word. The Torah is divided into 54 *sidrot* (the plural of *sidra*). See *"Sidra"* in the Glossary for more details.

[2] The Torah was not originally divided into chapters. The chapter designations were introduced by Christians in the Middle Ages and then adopted also among the Jews, perhaps in order to facilitate communication. The first three verses of Chapter 2 belong with the preceding chapter, since they are still part of the first creation narrative.

name *Elohim*, which generally is rendered into English as "God." The Hebrew name *Elohim* denotes power or authority. However, in Genesis 2:4, quoted above, the Torah for the first time refers to the Creator by the name YHVH (rendered into English as "the Lord"), a name that connotes mercy or compassion.[3] Thus, in the account of creation that begins with Genesis 2:4, the inversion of the order from "the heaven and the earth" to "earth and heaven" indicates a difference in focus between the two creation narratives—a focus on God's actions in the first and on man's actions in the second narrative. And the use of the name YHVH in the second account of creation changes the focus from God as ruler and master of the universe to God's relationship with His creations, and specifically with humankind.

An additional indication of the difference in focus between the two creation narratives can be seen in designating the names of entities. As Cassuto[4] points out, in the first creation story God gives names to day and night, heaven and earth, and land and sea (Genesis 1:5, 8, & 10) as a token of His sovereignty. Similarly, in the second creation story Adam gives names to each of the animals and birds (ibid., 2:19–20) as an indication of **his** sovereignty,[5] pursuant to God's granting man dominion over the earth.

---

[3] The name YHVH is regarded as exceptionally holy. Therefore, that name is never spoken, and—since Hebrew is generally written without the vowels—over the centuries the pronunciation of that name has been lost. Wherever the name YHVH appears in the Bible, we read another one of God's names—"Adonay"—a name that means "Lord." See "*Va'etchanan* 1: The *Shema*" for further discussion of these names of God.

[4] Rabbi Umberto (Moshe David) Cassuto. Italy and Israel, 1883–1951. See also Description of Sources.

[5] See Cassuto's commentary on the Book of Genesis, in his introduction to The Story of the Garden of Eden (Genesis 2:4 – 3:24), ¶9c (9א).

The two creation stories complement each other and together form a unified whole. Although the two stories are equally God-given, they are told from two different points of view: the first being a history of the heaven and the earth told from a God's-eye view of creation; whereas in the second creation story, God tells the story of creation from a human perspective, detailing what happened at the conclusion of God's work and omitting those details that do not fall within our ken.

Bereshit[1] 2:
Heaven, Earth, and Humankind

Did God regret creating man?

At the completion of God's work of creation, at the end of the sixth day, the Torah tells us: "And God saw all that He had made, and found it very good; and there was evening, and there was morning, the sixth day" (Genesis 1:31).

Let us now jump ahead to the end of the *sidra*[2] *of Bereshit*. God had created Man to be the caretaker of the world; but Man turned to evil, "and the Lord regretted that He had made man on earth" (Genesis 6:6). We know that, unlike a human being, God does not regret or change His mind;[3] and thus, God's regret here is merely an anthropomorphic manner of speaking that should not be taken literally. But I want to focus on what was the object of God's "regret." Some might think that God regretted making humankind. But that evidently is not the case: it does not say that God regretted creating humans, but that He regretted creating humans **on earth**—*i.e.*, subject to the corrupting influences on earth. What God regretted was that He had created man with free will[4] and with an evil impulse.[5]

---

[1] Genesis 1:1 – 6:8.
[2] The word *sidra* refers to one of the 54 "portions" into which the Torah is divided for the purpose of the weekly communal Torah reading. Also, see Glossary.
[3] See Numbers 23:19.
[4] See Malbim's commentary on Genesis 6:6. Also, for a discussion of man's free will, see "*Re'eh* 1: Blessing and Temptation."
[5] See Rabbi Aivo's opinion in *Bereshit Rabba* 27:5.

When God created man, He gave man free will to choose between good and evil. But man—as the Torah informs us just before saying that God regretted making humans on earth—followed his evil inclination and chose to do evil: *vekhol **yetzer** machshevot libo rak ra' kol hayom*—"and all the **inclination** of his thinking is evil all the time" (ibid., 6:5). When God completed His work of creation, He saw that everything was "very good." But the first humans, Adam and Eve, subverted God's plans when they disobeyed Him and ate from the fruit of the Tree of Knowledge. And, in the following generation, Adam's son Cain murdered his brother Abel. As humans proliferated, their evil actions increased, casting a pall on God's design in creating man with free will.

We cannot know God's purpose in creating mankind, but, from the fact that God created us with free will, we can infer that in order to fulfill God's intent, man must **choose** to follow God's commands of his own free will and not because he is compelled to do so. Man had gone astray and rebelled against the divine will. But one man still remained who chose to follow the path of righteousness. And so it was that God called on the prophet Noah to build an ark and give the world a second chance.

Noah:
Noah's Righteousness

Was Noah righteous only compared to the wicked people of his generation?

The Torah portion of *Noah*[1] begins with a perplexing statement: "Noah was a righteous man, wholehearted **in his generations**" (Genesis 6:9). And that phrasing prompts an ages-old dispute about Noah's character. Why does the Torah qualify its praise of Noah? The Talmud presents both sides of the dispute.[2] Does the Torah mean, as Rabbi Yochanan says, that he was righteous only compared to the wicked people of his generation but not compared to those of other generations? Or alternatively, does the Torah mean "in his generation, and how much more so in other generations," as Resh Lakish maintains? As mentioned, this question has been hotly debated over the centuries, and many commentators have offered their opinions; but, as I will show, the weight of evidence favors the opinion of Resh Lakish, as the plain reading of the text of the Torah would suggest.

It is noteworthy that the introductory verse quoted above (Genesis 6:9) does not merely tell us that Noah was righteous and wholehearted, but it concludes by saying that Noah "walked with God"—*et haElohim hit'halekh No'ah.* As Rabbeinu Bachyay[3] points out, the word *hit'halekh—*

---

[1] Genesis 6:9 – 11:32.
[2] Babylonian Talmud, *Sanhedrin* 108a. (See "Talmud" in Description of Sources.)
[3] Rabbeinu Bachyay ben Asher. Spain, 1255–1340. See also Description of Sources.

as opposed to the simpler verb *halakh* (meaning walked, went, or followed)—signifies a quality well beyond merely following in God's ways.[4] The Torah uses the reflexive form *hit'halekh* in the context of walking with God only in reference to Noah, Enoch (Genesis 5:24), and Abraham (Genesis 17:1); and the great righteousness of both Enoch and Abraham is undisputed. Moreover, another line of evidence equating Noah's righteousness with that of Abraham is found in Genesis 17:1, where God tells Abraham to be *tamim* (perfect, complete, whole, or whole-hearted)— the same adjective that the Torah uses to describe Noah in Genesis 6:9.

Returning again to Genesis 6:9, why does the Torah say that Noah was righteous in his **generations**? Why the plural? Addressing this question, Rabbeinu Bachyay comments that before God decreed the Flood, Noah had already lived through several generations, and in all those generations only he was worthy of being saved from annihilation. But Ibn Ezra[5] goes a step further: according to Ibn Ezra, Noah was righteous not only for the generation of the Flood, but also for the generations encompassing the 350 years through which he lived after the flood. As Cassuto puts it, "the purpose of the plural seems to be to glorify Noah: not only was he righteous, but he was wholly righteous; not only was he outstanding in

---

[4] Regarding his assertion that the reflexive form *hit'halekh* refers to a quality well beyond merely following in God's ways, Rabbeinu Bachyay points out that when the Torah commands all of us to follow in His ways— "After the Lord your God you shall go" (Deuteronomy 13:5)—the reflexive form is not used. In that verse, the simpler verb form *telekhu* (you shall go, walk, or follow) is used. The reflexive form, then, says Rabbeinu Bachyay, indicates a level of righteousness well beyond the ordinary.

[5] Rabbi Abraham Ibn Ezra. Spain, 12th Century. See also Description of Sources.

his righteousness among his contemporaries, ... but he was pre-eminent in righteousness relative to all the generations that lived on earth in his days."[6]

But, we may object, if God regarded Noah as outstanding in his righteousness through several generations, why did God, when speaking directly to Noah in Genesis 7:1, refer to Noah as righteous in his generation—not generations— and did not use the word *tamim* (complete, whole, or whole-hearted) as in 6:9? In answer to this question, we can cite the Talmud's explanation[7] that only part of a person's praise is spoken in his presence, but all of it is said in his absence; and Genesis 7:1 is spoken directly to Noah: "Come ... into the ark, for you I have seen to be righteous before me in this generation."[8]

Over the course of the ten generations from Adam to Noah, humans had become increasingly wicked; and in Noah's time, God's dissatisfaction with the way that humanity was conducting itself finally reached a breaking point. In Genesis 6:12, God observes that the earth "was in ruins [*nish'chata*], for all flesh had ruined its way upon the earth." Cassuto analyzes the use of the word *nish'chata* by comparing the use of the word in Jeremiah 18:4.[9] There, God sends the prophet Jeremiah to a potter's house, and

---

[6] Cassuto's commentary on the Book of Genesis, translated from the Hebrew by Israel Abrahams (U. Cassuto, *A Commentary on the Book of Genesis, Part Two*, pp 49–50).

[7] See Babylonian Talmud, *Eruvin* 18b.

[8] See Cassuto, ibid., p 50.

[9] Cassuto's comparison of the word *nish'chata* (which Prof. Abrahams translates as "corrupt") in Genesis to its use in Jeremiah is found on p 53.

Cassuto also points out the contrast between Genesis 1:31 and Genesis 6:12. In the former verse, God sees all that He has made, and it is very good; but in the latter verse, it is corrupt. Cassuto says, "The world as it emerged from the hands of the Creator was exceedingly good, but now, because of man's conduct, it was corrupt." (See Cassuto, ibid.)

the pot that he was making was ruined (*nish'chat*). God tells the prophet that we are in God's hand just as the ruined pot is in the potter's hand: the potter can reduce the ruined pot to a shapeless mass and completely remake it to his liking. Similarly, in Noah's time, God was resolved to annihilate mankind and to form a new human race. Let us have no doubt that God had considered annihilating all living beings on the face of the earth, as He says, "I shall wipe out Mankind, which I have created, from the face of the earth: both man and beast, and creeping things, and fowl of the sky ...; but Noah found favor in the eyes of the Lord" (verses 7–8). And it was Noah's righteousness that delivered mankind from complete extinction.

Lekh Lekha 1:
Who Was Lot?

Was Lot a good man or a bad man?

At the beginning of the portion of *Lekh Lekha*,[1] God commands Abram to leave his home and his family and go to the land that God will show him. "Abram went as the Lord had commanded him, and Lot went with him" (Genesis 12:4). Lot, whose father had died young, was Abram's nephew, and probably Lot looked up to his uncle Abram as a father figure. But who was Lot in reality? Was he a good man or a bad man? Did he go with Abram because he wanted to learn from him and emulate his ways, or was Lot motivated by selfish reasons? We are told that after arrival in the land of Canaan, Abram became rich (see Genesis 13:2), and "also Lot, who had gone with Abram, had sheep and cattle and tents" (ibid., verse 5). So, was Lot motivated only by financial profit? Did he go with Abram solely because he sensed that his uncle was a good businessman, and he expected to get rich if he stuck by his uncle?

The Zohar[2] opines that Lot went with Abram on his journey because he wanted to learn from his uncle; but unfortunately, says the Zohar, he didn't learn very much.[3] Yet even worse, Lot's presence appears to have been a deterrent to Abram's prophetic development, because it appears that God did not speak to Abram again while Lot

---

[1] Genesis 12:1 – 17:27.
[2] See Description of Sources.
[3] Zohar I:78b.

was with him: the next time that God speaks to Abram, the Torah goes out of its way to say that it was "after Lot had separated from him" (ibid., verse 14), and Rashi[4] comments that it was because God wouldn't speak to Abram as long as that wicked man was with him. Moreover, where did Lot go after he left Abram? He went to live in Sodom—a city known for its evil ways—because it was financially profitable for him.

Certainly there is much reason to think of Lot as a person who was inclined to evil. And yet, as we see in the following *sidra*, when the angels came to Sodom in the guise of humans, Lot offered them hospitality at the risk of his life.[5] Thus, even though Lot had not learned the majority of his uncle's virtues, he did incorporate into his own behavior Abram's most prominent virtues: the qualities of hospitality and kindness to others.[6] Lot certainly had his very significant faults; but in his behavior with the angels, he showed the underlying goodness of his character that justified his being saved from the destruction of Sodom. The angels may have been sent to save Lot largely for the sake of his uncle Abram, but Lot passed the angels' test, and in the end he merited being saved for his own sake as well.

According to rabbinic tradition, Lot's display of kindness was not a one-time event but intrinsic to his character: *Pirkei Rabbi Eliezer*[7] relates that one of Lot's daughters had previously brought food surreptitiously every day to a certain poor man, ignoring the law in Sodom forbidding

---

[4]   Rabbi Shlomo Yitzchaki. Troyes, (France), 1040–1105. Also, see Description of Sources.

[5]   See Genesis 15:1–6 and 9–10; and *Pirkei Rabbi Eliezer*, Chapter 25.

[6]   See Zohar I:105a.

[7]   See Description of Sources.

charity on pain of death. When the authorities found her out, she was put to death. According to this *midrash*,[8] then, kindness was so deeply ingrained in Lot that he transmitted it to his daughter, even in the midst of wicked Sodom.[9]

So, in conclusion, who was Lot? Was he a good man or a bad one? It seems that, like many of us, he was both—a conflicted character, an enigma. But despite his grievous faults, despite his moral lapses, Lot merited to become an ancestor of King David, and ultimately of the Messiah.[10]

---

[8] See "*Midrash*" in Glossary.
[9] *Pirkei Rabbi Eliezer*, Chapter 25.
[10] Lot was the father of Moav, whose descendant Ruth became the great-grandmother of King David.

Lekh Lekha[1] 2:
Of Worms and Caterpillars, Of Weakness and Of Strength

Why is Israel compared to a worm?

In the *Haftarah*[2] of *Lekh Lekha*,[3] Isaiah says, *Al tire'i tola'at Ya'akov* (Isaiah 41:14), the usual interpretation of which would be, "Do not fear, O worm Jacob." In this view, Israel is seen as weak, just as a worm is weak and vulnerable; but Israel will prevail, because God will aid them and will vanquish Israel's enemies. Certainly, this interpretation is consistent with the prophet's foregoing language: "For I am the Lord your God who grasps your right hand and says to you, 'Do not fear: I will help you'" (ibid., verse 13). But the Zohar has a very different interpretation that in many ways is more elegant:

The Zohar interprets the word *tola'at* not as a worm but as a caterpillar.[4] The caterpillar spins a silk cocoon and disappears from sight; it seems to die. But soon it reappears in a new form, able to soar above the earth. Thus, the Zohar sees the caterpillar as a symbol not of Israel's weakness but of her rebirth—a rebirth enabled by Israel's adherence to the divine spirit, to the Tree of Life. And this interpretation also is consistent with the context of that prophesy of Isaiah,

---

[1] Genesis 12:1 – 17:27.
[2] The *Haftarah* is an excerpt from one of the prophetic books, read in the synagogue each week at the end of that week's Torah portion. Also, see Glosssary.
[3] The *Haftarah* of *Lekh Lekha* is Isaiah 40:27 – 41:16.
[4] See Zohar I:178a, at top of the page.

in which Isaiah prophesies the rebirth of Israel in future days: "They who trust in the Lord shall renew their strength; they shall grow a wing like eagles;[5] they will run and will not tire" (Isaiah 40:31); and "You whom I drew from the ends of the earth and called from its distant corners" (ibid., 41:9)—prophesying the return of the Jewish people to their land after their exile and dispersion. And so, despite the prophecies of Israel's defeat and destruction, Isaiah tells Israel not to despair, because God is with them; and he foretells that Israel, whose status as a nation will be eclipsed, nevertheless shall someday rise again.[6]

Isaiah's prophecy of Israel's rebirth mirrors Abram's prophesy in the Torah portion of *Lekh Lekha*.[7] In that Torah portion, a carrion bird descends, and, as the sun is about to set, Abram has a vision of darkness and dread falling upon him. God speaks to him, saying that his descendants will be strangers in a foreign land and will be enslaved and tormented for four hundred years but will then emerge with great wealth and will return to their own land.[8] And this prophesy that was given to Abram— which came true with his descendants' exile to Egypt and their eventual exodus and establishment as the nation of Israel—finds its counterpart in Isaiah's prophesy of Israel's rebirth after the nation's later exile.

---

[5] This refers to a popular belief that eagles regain their youthful strength when molting, as in Psalms 103:5.

[6] In this essay, I am using the name "Israel" to mean all the people who are descendants of our patriarch Jacob (who was also known by the name "Israel"), as in Isaiah 41:14, quoted above.

[7] This observation is not mentioned in the Zohar but is my own.

[8] See Genesis 15:11–16.

Vayera 1:
Whose Son Was Ishmael?

What did Ishmael do to incur Sarah's wrath?

There is much to discuss regarding the portion of *Vayera*,[1] which is filled with significant, perplexing, and emotionally charged events in the lives of our patriarchs. But in this essay, I will focus on just one thing: the mind-set of Sarah that led her to demand the expulsion of Hagar and Ishmael from Abraham's household.

"Sarah saw the son of Hagar the Egyptian woman, whom she had borne to Abraham, *metzachek*. And she said to Abraham, 'Drive out this slave-woman and her son, for this slave-woman's son shall not inherit with my son, with Isaac'" (Genesis 21:9–10). The Torah leaves unclear exactly what Ishmael had done to incur Sarah's wrath. The crucial word here—*metzachek*—is variously translated as "laughing," "mocking," or "playing." Indeed, the word could mean any those things, but in some contexts it also carries the connotation of sexual play or sexual intercourse.[2] Rabbinic commentaries speculate that Ishmael was mocking Isaac (and perhaps spreading a rumor that Isaac was not Abraham's son), or that Ishmael was sexually promiscuous, or that

---

[1] Genesis 18:1 – 22:24.

[2] For examples of where the word *metzachek* refers to sexual intercourse or sexual play, see Genesis 26:8 and Genesis 39:17. (The same verb in Exodus 32:6 in connection with the revelry celebrating the Golden Calf is cited by *Midrash Rabba* to show that the word *metzachek* may connote idolatry; but in that verse, it could equally well have a sexual connotation.)

he was practicing idolatry.[3]   The preponderance of
evidence supports the interpretation that he was sexually
promiscuous; but whatever it was that Ishmael had done,
note that Sarah's anger was focused not only on Ishmael
himself but perhaps as much or more on his mother,
saying: "Drive out this slave-woman and her son."

One reason why Sarah might have wanted Hagar
expelled together with Ishmael could be that Ishmael was
still a child, not old enough to care for himself. But if his
sin was sexual promiscuity, he couldn't have been a mere
child. Moreover, if Hagar was to be expelled only because
Ishmael needed her, Sarah probably would not have
mentioned the mother first and Ishmael second.

Another more likely possibility is that Sarah believed
Ishmael had learned his bad behavior from his mother.
If Ishmael's offense was sexual promiscuity, perhaps the
Torah's labeling Ishmael's mother as "the Egyptian woman"
(ibid., verse 9) and referring to Ishmael as "her son" was
meant to emphasize Hagar's origin from an idolatrous
nation whose sexual mores were very different from those of
Abraham's family. Alternatively, if Ishmael's offense was that
he was mocking Isaac, perhaps Hagar had actually put him
up to it. In either case, we can understand why Sarah might
have attributed Ishmael's behavior to his mother's teaching.

---

[3] For alternative explanations of what Ishmael may have done to incur
Sarah's wrath, see *Midrash Rabba*, Sforno, and Rashi on Genesis 21:9. In fact,
there may have been multiple reasons for Sarah's wanting to expel Hagar
and multiple reasons for her wanting to expel Ishmael. One additional
reason that *Midrash Rabba* mentions is that Ishmael had argued with Isaac
about their inheritance, saying that he and not Isaac was the firstborn. The
latter part of Sarah's statement—"for this slave-woman's son shall not inherit
with my son"—supports that view, since it not only addresses the inheritance
but also stresses that Ishmael was the son of a slave and therefore not worthy
of any inheritance.

A third reason for Sarah's demand to dismiss Hagar and Ishmael is the history of Sarah's strained relationship with Hagar. Let us not forget that years earlier, after trying unsuccessfully for many years to get pregnant, Sarah had asked Abraham to have a child by her slave Hagar, and the child would be considered as Sarah's offspring. But when Hagar got pregnant, she began to taunt Sarah, and Sarah retaliated by oppressing Hagar.[4] Although that period of unpleasantness was now far in the past, it is likely that it had continued to seethe all those years beneath the surface, and Ishmael's offense—whatever it may have been—served to reignite the former discord, and Sarah's antipathy toward Hagar.

Note that Hagar, in giving birth to Ishmael, was to be merely a surrogate womb, and Ishmael was to be considered Sarah's son. But did Sarah ever really think of Ishmael as her own? The Zohar points to Sarah's labeling him as "this slave-woman's son" as evidence that Sarah did not consider him to be her own son. But Abraham had a completely different view of Ishmael. Thus, the Torah continues, "The matter was very distressing to Abraham, on account of his son" (Genesis 21:11). To Sarah, Ishmael was Hagar's son, a foreign element in her home. In contrast, however, Abraham did not think of Ishmael as a foreign element; to Abraham, Ishmael was very much his own.[5] But, the Zohar concludes, Sarah's assessment of Ishmael was correct. And how do we know this? Because in the end, God told Abraham to listen to Sarah.

---

[4] See Genesis 16:1–6.
[5] See Zohar I:118b.

Vayera[1] 2:
The *Akedah*

What was God's purpose in testing Abraham in the Akedah?

And how does the Akedah relate to Rosh Hashanah?

The story of the *Akedah* (Genesis 22:1–24) is one of the most difficult sections of the Torah to understand, and one of the most troubling. And it is the section that the rabbis chose to be read on the second day of *Rosh Hashanah*. Why, we may ask, was that story chosen for the reading on *Rosh Hashanah*? How does the *Akedah* relate to *Rosh Hashanah*? The usual explanation is that the *Akedah* occurred on *Rosh Hashanah*, and that the *shofar*—the ram's horn—that we blow on that holiday is reminiscent of the ram that Abraham sacrificed at the end of the *Akedah*, in place of his son Isaac (ibid., verse 13). While those explanations are correct to a degree, the association of the *Akedah* with *Rosh Hashanah* goes much deeper.

The Torah begins the story of the *Akedah* (the binding of Isaac) by telling us that God tested Abraham—*nissa et Avraham*. This was the tenth and final test with which Abraham would be confronted, but it is the only one that the Torah actually labels as a test. Why did God test Abraham? Since God is all-knowing, didn't He know in advance what Abraham would do?

Indeed, as Ramban[2] says, the test is only a test from

---

[1] Genesis 18:1 – 22:24.
[2] Rabbi Moses ben Nachman. Spain, 1194–1270. See also Description of Sources.

the standpoint of the person who is tested, because God knows in advance what the outcome will be. Therefore, says Ramban, the purpose of the test is to translate a person's potential into practice: that is, to strengthen the person's character, enabling him to realize his own spiritual potentialities.

This final test of Abraham was not only the most difficult one, but, as mentioned, it was the only one that the Torah specifically calls a test. Abravnel[3] asks why the Torah did not apply the word "test" to any of the other nine tests. His answer is that the primary purpose of each of the other tests was something other than to test Abraham, and only as a side effect did it constitute a test. For example, when God commanded Abram (as he was called at that time) to leave his home and his family and go to a land that God would show him, the primary purpose was to have Abram take up residence in Canaan, the land that God would bequeath to Abram's descendants. But in the case of the *Akedah*, says Abravnel, the **primary** purpose was as a test of Abraham's love of and devotion to the Lord.

Why, we may ask, did God choose to subject Abraham to such a horrendous test? To answer that question, we must understand the religious outlook of the age and the locale in which Abraham lived. Child sacrifice was prevalent throughout the Near East, in the worship of Baal, Moloch, Kemosh, and other pagan deities. It was practiced in Tyre and Sidon, in Moav, and in Canaan where Abraham lived. In fact, sacrificing one's child to a god was seen as the supreme act of devotion that would bestow that deity's greatest favor upon the person bringing the sacrifice. But Abraham's God had never hitherto

---

[3] Don Isaac Abravnel (or Abarbanel). Portugal, Spain, Corfu, and Italy, 1437–1508. See also Description of Sources.

demanded such a sacrifice, and it is therefore likely that the following doubt lurked in Abraham's mind: What if my God demanded of me that I sacrifice my beloved son? Would I be able to do it? The purpose of this tenth and most difficult test to which God subjected Abraham was not to prove Abraham's devotion in the eyes of God. Rather, the purpose of the test was to prove to Abraham that his religious devotion and love of God was as strong as that of his neighbors to their false gods—so strong that he wouldn't hesitate to do whatever God asked of him—even to sacrifice his beloved son Isaac. The test served to strengthen Abraham's devotion to God; and, after passing the test and being commanded not to sacrifice Isaac, Abraham showed his devotion by immediately sacrificing the ram in place of his son and naming the mountain *YHVH Yir'eh* (the Lord will see).

Sforno[4] reiterates Ramban's view that Abraham's test served to translate his potential inner power of faith into practice. Moreover, Sforno adds that in doing so, Abraham accomplished the goal of imitating his Creator, by which He provides goodness to the world through the actual and not only the potential.

Sforno's view, then, accords with the prevailing rabbinic interpretation of the word *nissa* (tested) in the opening verse of the *Akedah* (Genesis 22:1) to signify not only God's testing of Abraham but also elevating him spiritually. Various *midrashim*, as well as later commentators, draw an association between the word נסה (*nissa*—"tested") and the homonymous word נשא (spelled differently but also pronounced *nissa*, meaning "elevated"), implying that the test of the *Akedah* was a means of elevating Abraham's spiritual level. In passing the test of the *Akedah*, Abraham

---

[4]   Rabbi Ovadia Sforno. Italy, 1475–1550. See also Description of Sources.

proved to himself the depth of his faith and his love and reverence of God, and thereby elevated his soul, bringing him closer to his Creator. That is also the essence of our objective on *Rosh Hashanah*, which is the day on which God began the creation of the world, the day on which God judges the world, the day on which God judges each of us. On *Rosh Hashanah*, we blow the *shofar* to wake us from our spiritual slumber, to recall the sound of the *shofar* that enveloped us in our encounter with the divine at Mount Sinai (see Exodus 19:19 and 20:15), and to elevate our souls to communicate with our Creator. On *Rosh Hashanah*, we read the story of the *Akedah* as an exemplar to strengthen our devotion and enable our thoughts to lift our prayers heavenwards.

Chayei Sarah:
Isaac and the Power of One

What was unique about our patriarch Isaac?

Most of the Torah portion of *Chayei Sarah*[1] is concerned with the story of Isaac, the middle one of our three patriarchs. In many respects, Isaac is more enigmatic than either his father Abraham or his son Jacob, in no small part because the Torah gives us fewer clues to his character. And yet, at least three unique features of Isaac's character stand out.

Of the three patriarchs, Isaac is the only one who was monogamous. The Torah tells us that Rebecca was carefully selected to be Isaac's wife because of her kindness and welcoming character, and that Isaac loved her (see Genesis 24:67). But love alone would be an insufficient reason for Isaac not to take a second wife, or at least a concubine. In those days, it was normal for any man who could afford it to take multiple wives; but Isaac did no such thing, even when his wife was barren. So how should we explain Isaac's having only one wife?

In the previous *sidra*—*Vayera*—we saw the discord in Abraham's family that resulted from his having a second wife.[2] And perhaps Isaac refrained from taking a second wife because he saw how fractured Abraham's family had become. He had seen how his mother Sarah was distressed, and he had seen the effects of her distress on his father. It was his love for his wife together with the bond with his

---

[1] Genesis 23:1 – 25:18.
[2] See "*Vayera* 1: Whose Son Was Ishmael," above.

parents that prevented him from taking a second wife, or even a concubine. Isaac and his wife Rebecca were a unit not to be sundered by the presence of another.

A second point stands out in Isaac's history. All three of our patriarchs wandered from place to place. Abraham lived in Mesopotamia, then in Canaan, and to escape a famine he went to Egypt for a time. Jacob also went to Egypt for the last years of his life. But Isaac never left the Promised Land. In fact, like his father before him, Isaac was about to go to Egypt to escape a famine; but "The Lord appeared to him and said, 'Do not go down to Egypt; dwell in the land that I will tell you. Reside in this land, and I will be with you'" (Genesis 26:2–3). And so he did: he lived in only one land all his life—the land that God had promised to him and his descendants.[3] Indeed, it may well be Isaac's steadfast residence in the Promised Land that cemented the bond between that land and Isaac's future descendants, the nation of Israel— the Jewish people.

Isaac's third unique characteristic concerns the nature of his soul. The *Neshama*—the God-given soul—was originally blown into Adam's nostrils when he was created (see Genesis 2:7); and since that day, each person's soul descends from the upper world (the spiritual world) to enter that person's body at birth.[4] But the *Neshama*'s true home is in the upper world, and one part of every righteous person's soul stays connected to the upper world even while it inhabits the body in the physical world.[5]

---

[3] When a famine struck, Isaac went to live among the Philistines, in Gerar. But that territory, although it was occupied at that time by the Philistines, was still part of the Promised Land.

[4] See Zohar I:76b–77a (*Sitrei Torah*) for the descent of the *Neshama* from the upper world to our world.

[5] See Zohar I:60a (*Tosefta*).

Isaac, however, at the age of 37 underwent an experience that would change his life forever:[6] in fulfillment of God's command, his father Abraham—with Isaac's compliance—placed him on an altar and prepared to sacrifice him. Both Abraham and Isaac passed this test of faith, and at the last moment an angel stopped Abraham from slaughtering his son; but Isaac did not escape unscathed. Tradition tells us that in the final moments of his ordeal, Isaac's *Neshama* fled his body. The *Neshama* returned immediately,[7] but it was only the part of Isaac's soul that normally connects to the spiritual world that came back to animate his body.[8] The other portion of his soul did not return. Thus, Isaac had only one portion of his soul, not two as he had before. And, I propose, that perhaps the absence of the worldly component of Isaac's soul explains his inability in later years to perceive the corrupt nature of his elder son Esau.

In conclusion, then, Isaac was a man of steadfast devotion. Unlike other men of his era, Isaac had only one wife. Unlike his father and his son, he did not leave the Promised Land but lived all his life in one land. Unlike almost all people of his time, Isaac worshipped only one God; and in consequence of his subjecting himself to God's will, the worldly portion of his soul departed, leaving him possessed of only the heavenly portion of his *Neshama*.

---

[6] The consensus of rabbinic opinions is that Isaac was 37 years old when he was placed on the altar. (See *Shemot Rabba* 1:1 and *Pirkei Rabbi Eliezer*, Chapter 31.) However, that opinion is not unanimous. For example, in the Babylonian Talmud, *Yevamot* 61b, *Tosafot* opines that Isaac was 26 years old at the *Akedah*. And, in Ibn Ezra's opinion, Isaac was "almost 13 years old" at the time of the *Akedah*. (See Ibn Ezra on Genesis 22:7.)

[7] See *Pirkei Rabbi Eliezer*, Chapter 31, for the statement that Isaac's *Neshama* fled his body when he was almost sacrificed, and returned immediately.

[8] See Zohar I:60a (*Tosefta*) for the statement that after Isaac's *Neshama* left his body on the altar, only the higher portion of his soul returned to him.

Toldot 1:
Portents of Expulsion

How does Isaac's expulsion foretell future expulsions?

In the *sidra* of *Toldot*,[1] there is a famine in the land of Canaan, and the patriarch Isaac goes to the land of the Philistines (see Genesis 26:1).[2] Many years earlier, Isaac's father Abraham made a treaty with Avimelekh the Philistine king, which was to be binding on their sons and grandsons, and which included an acknowledgement of Abraham's property rights to certain wells (ibid., 21:22–32). While living among the Philistines, Isaac becomes rich and powerful. The Philistines become very jealous of him (ibid., 26:13–14), and they fill all of his father's wells with earth (ibid., verse 15).

Avimelekh[3]—the Philistine king in Isaac's time—like so many future rulers throughout Jewish history, turns a blind eye to his people's mischief. Stopping up Abraham's wells was clearly an act of jealousy, since it was wanton destruction from which the perpetrators derived no benefit. And yet, despite the treaty with Abraham, the Torah gives us no evidence that Avimelekh objects to his people's filling of the

---

[1] Genesis 25:19 – 28:9.

[2] The Philistines were one of the "Sea Peoples" that invaded Canaan. The Promised Land included territory that, during the lifetimes of the Patriarchs, was occupied by the Philistines. Also, see "Phillistines" in Glossary.

[3] Note that the Philistine king Avimelekh who made a treaty with Abraham may not be the same person as Avimelekh who was king of the Philistines in the time of Isaac. Avimelekh may be a title rather than a name, or alternatively, a name that was commonly used among royalty— *e.g.* Avimelekh I, Avimelekh II, *etc.*

wells. In fact, the 16th Century commentator Rabbi Moshe Alsheikh[4] speculates that Avimelekh was embarrassed to tell Isaac to leave his domain, and that therefore Avimelekh actually told his people to fill the wells so that Isaac would decide on his own that it would be best for him to leave. But Isaac does not leave, and eventually the king expels Isaac:[5] *Lekh me'imanu, ki 'atzamta mimennu me'od*—"Go away from us, because you have become much mightier than we" (ibid., verse 16).

Interestingly, the stated reason for the expulsion—*ki 'atzamta mimennu me'od* (see above)—is very telling. It is essentially the same reason that Pharaoh will give many years later for enslaving and oppressing the Israelites: the people of Israel are **rav ve'atzum mimennu**—"too numerous and mightier than we" (Exodus 1:9). However, both in the words of Avimelekh and in those of Pharaoh (which I put in bold-face), there is an additional overtone. The word *mimennu*, in both Avimelekh's and Pharaoh's statement, can mean "than we" as it is usually translated in this verse; but that word can equally well mean (and often does mean) "from us"; and this is the interpretation of Avimelekh's words that the *Midrash Rabba*[6] chooses to adopt: "..., because you have become very great **from us**."[7] The *Midrash Rabba* continues: "Doesn't all the might that you have obtained come from us? Previously you had only one flock [of sheep], but now you have

---

[4] Rabbi Moshe Alsheikh was a major Torah commentator who lived in Safed (Israel) in the 16th Century. See also Description of Sources.

[5] When Avimelekh expels Isaac in Genesis 26:16, it appears to be only an expulsion from the city of Gerar and not from the entire kingdom, because we see in verses 17–21 that Isaac relocates to other parts of the Philistine kingdom.

[6] See Description of Sources.

[7] *Bereshit Rabba* 64:6.

many flocks."[8]   Moreover, this reading of Avimelekh's phrasing is identical to the explicit assertion of Lavan's sons: "Jacob has taken all that belongs to our father, and it is from our father's possessions that he has made all this wealth" (Genesis 31:1)—an assertion that is later echoed by Lavan himself when he confronts Jacob (see ibid., verse 43).

In claiming that "you have become rich from us," Avimelekh is discounting Isaac's hard work in sowing the land, digging wells, and planting seeds.   Moreover, he is discounting God's hand in blessing Isaac, as God says: "Live in this land, and I will be with you, and I will bless you" (Genesis 26:3).   Unfortunately, the sentiment expressed in the words of Avimelekh and of Lavan's sons is not unique to them, but has been repeated by countless mouths throughout the generations.   It is the fruit of jealousy, and a desire to dismiss the value of hard work, ingenuity, and individual achievement, and to deprive people of the fruits of their labor.

After Avimelekh expels Isaac from his city, Isaac goes to live in the desert, and he re-digs the wells that his father had previously dug and that the Philistines stopped up.   But each time he digs a well, the Philistines claim that well, and Isaac has to move on (see Genesis 26:17–21).   This pattern also foreshadows events that will befall Isaac's descendants

---

[8]   The 19th Century commentator Malbim echoes the interpretation of the *Midrash Rabba*.   He says, "*Ki atzamta mimennu*—that is to say, by means of us you have become great, that you are taking the abundance that belongs to us."

Regarding Pharaoh's statement (Exodus 1:9) that the people of Israel are **rav ve'atzum mimennu** (see above), the commentary *Or HaChayyim* interprets the phrase *rav ve'atzum mimennu* to mean that they have become great **from us**—similar to the interpretations of Avimelekh's statement given by *Midrash Rabba* and Malbim.

throughout Jewish history: The Jews come to a new land; they grow and prosper; but then they are expelled, in many cases also being forced to abandon their property and their savings. They move from place to place, trying to find a hospitable environment. And sometimes the country that expelled the Jews later asks them to return, as is the case with Avimelekh (ibid., verses 26–28). As the rabbis have noted, the events of our patriarchs foreshadow the lives of their descendants.

Toldot 2:
Tales of Jealousy and Hatred

How is the Philistines' jealousy of Isaac connected to Esau's jealousy of Jacob?

The *sidra* of *Toldot*[1] contains two tales of jealousy: one directed at the patriarch Isaac, and the other at his son Jacob. In this essay, I will focus mainly on the second story, but I will conclude my discussion with an interesting parallel connecting the two stories.

Isaac's twin sons, Esau and Jacob, were in many ways opposite personalities. Esau is described as a man of the field (Genesis 26:27) and a hunter (ibid., 26:28 and 27:3), whereas Jacob is a tent-dweller (ibid., 26:27). One day, Esau returns from the field tired and hungry, and he demands that Jacob give him some of the lentil soup that he has been cooking. Jacob offers his brother a portion of the soup, in exchange for Esau's birthright. Esau readily agrees to that exchange, indicating that the birthright is meaningless to him. (See Genesis 25:31–35.)

In order to understand Esau's attitude toward the birthright, we must first understand what the birthright was. The birthright was the right of the firstborn to become the spiritual head of the family after his father's demise, but it entailed no material benefits. As the Torah portrays him, Esau was completely rooted in the physical world, with no regard for spiritual values; thus it should not surprise us that he considered the birthright to be of no value to him.

---

[1] Genesis 25:19 – 28:9.

In contrast to the birthright, the blessing that Isaac later gave Jacob (thinking that he was Esau) before he died was focused on material things; and consequently, Esau became jealous of Jacob and hated him. But interestingly, it was not the blessing alone that irked Esau: as Esau says, "he has cheated me now twice; he took my birthright, and now he has taken my blessing" (Genesis 27:36). If the birthright was of no value to Esau, why does he now link those two events? As Malbim[2] explains in his commentary on Genesis 27:36, Esau considered the taking of both the birthright and the blessing to be mutually contradictory. He thought that by taking the birthright, Jacob chose to be focused on the spiritual, and therefore he had no business being also interested in worldly matters. In Esau's mind, the two were mutually exclusive.[3]

So Esau hated his twin brother. But this was no ordinary hatred: *Vayistom Esav et Ya'akov*—"And Esau was consumed with hatred against Jacob" (ibid., 27:41). The word *vayistom* is not the usual word for hatred. It indicates a special type of hatred that fills the mind of its bearer and becomes an obsession.[4] But that word is very similar to another word that is found much earlier in *Toldot*. While living among the Philistines, Isaac became rich and powerful. The Philistines became very jealous of him (ibid., 26:13–14), and they filled all his father's wells with earth—*sitmum Pelishtim, vayemal'um 'afar* (ibid., 26:15). Note that the word used in Esau's case derives from the

---

[2]   Malbim was an important biblical commentator of the 19th Century. See Description of Sources.
[3]   For Malbim's full discussion of Esau's attitude toward his birthright, see his commentaries on Genesis 25:29 & 31, and 26:41.
[4]   For a discussion of the connotation of the word *vayistom* in Genesis 27:41, see Malbim's commentary on that verse. See also Onkelos's Aramaic translation of that verse.

verb root *satom* (שׂטם), whereas the word used for filling the wells derives from the verb *sathom* (סתם). The two spellings are different from each other, but the pronunciation is very similar. (In modern Hebrew, the pronunciations are identical, but in ancient Hebrew they were slightly different, the ת probably pronounced like the English th, as in the word "thing.")

Perhaps the use of two such similar-sounding words is not a coincidence. The context in both cases is jealousy: the Philistines were jealous of Isaac when he became wealthy and powerful, and Esau was jealous of Jacob when Jacob took his blessing. Also, the two words have somewhat similar connotations: in the first case, the Philistines filled the wells with earth; while in the latter case, Esau filled his mind with hatred of his brother. Thus, the word *vayistom*, used to describe Esau's hatred, serves to link the two stories of jealousy and hatred.[5]

---

[5] Note that the verb *vayistom* serving as a link between the two tales of jealousy and hatred is not attributable to Malbim, but is my own observation.

Vayetze:
Angels Ascending and Descending

*How did God protect Jacob against the heathen sorcerer,
Lavan?*

The *sidra* of *Vayetze*[1] has two main themes: the quest to
beget children who will continue a person's heritage, and
the struggle of two opposing views of how the universe is
governed. On the one hand, the monotheistic view holds
that there is one God, Who rules the universe according
to a clearly defined set of principles that He created;
versus the polytheistic view that posits multiple gods and
goddesses, with no set standard of good and bad, but
each deity having his or her own vacillating whims, and
with demands that may in fact conflict with the demands
of other gods. Although *Vayetze* seems to give more
attention to the first of these two themes (the quest to
beget children), I believe that it is the second one—the
conflicting views of how the universe is governed—that is
the main focus of the *sidra*, and it is this theme that I will
address in the present essay.

Vaytze begins and ends with Jacob encountering the
Divine, and with Jacob erecting a monument invoking
God. But sandwiched between these two bookends, Jacob
encounters Lavan the conniver, the polytheist, the master
of sorcery.[2]

---

[1] Genesis 28:10 – 32:2.

[2] For more about Lavan's being a sorcerer, see "*Vayishlach*: I Have
Sojourned with Lavan." Sorcery is a viable practice in the pagan
conception; but in the Torah, sorcery and its practitioners are anathema.

At the start of the *sidra*, Jacob dreams of a ladder standing on the ground, with its head extending to the heavens, and angels of God are going up and down the ladder (Genesis 28:12). From atop the ladder, the voice of God then calls to Jacob and says, "I am YHVH, the God of your father Abraham, and the God of Isaac; the land upon which you are lying I will give to you and your descendants" (ibid., verse 13). And God pledges that He will be with Jacob wherever Jacob will go, and will protect him. When Jacob arises in the morning, he erects a monument, saying, "How awe-inspiring is this place; this is none other than the house of God, and this is the gate of heaven" (ibid., verse 17). Jacob makes a vow, saying that if the Lord will protect him and return him safely to his father's house, then the Lord will be his God (ibid., verses 20–21). And Sforno comments that Jacob here is asking the Lord to guard him from idolators who would rise up against him.

Jacob leaves the land of Canaan and arrives in Haran,[3] where he encounters his future wife Rachel and her father Lavan. At first, Lavan appears gracious and welcoming, but over time he finds multiple ways to cheat Jacob. When Jacob has had enough of Lavan's treatment and requests Lavan's permission to take his wives and leave, Lavan refuses to release him, saying, "I have learned by sorcery that the Lord has blessed me on account of you" (ibid., 30:27). So, even acknowledging the God of Jacob, Lavan continues to engage in heathen practices.

After many years working for Lavan, Jacob finally sneaks away with his family. His wife Rachel steals her father's idols, either in order to get her father to stop

---

[3] Haran was a city in the kingdom of Aram.

worshipping them (as *Bereshit Rabba* suggests), or perhaps because she fears that he will use the idols to harm Jacob through sorcery. Lavan, along with his kinsmen, chases after Jacob and catches up with him after seven days (Genesis 31:23). He angrily accuses Jacob of stealing his daughters and leading them away like captives (ibid., verses 26–27). And, to top off his accusation, Lavan concludes, "Why did you steal my gods?" (ibid., verse 30). Even without his idols, Lavan believes in his own power, and there is reason to think that perhaps he had in mind to kill Jacob;[4] and yet, he also fears the power of Jacob's God. He says: "I have the power to do you harm; but the God of your fathers last night said to me, 'Be careful lest you speak to Jacob either good or ill'" (ibid., verse 29). Lavan is wary, but he can't resist making the implied threat in saying "I have the power to do you harm."

Jacob counters Lavan's threat by invoking the power of the Almighty, not merely by using God's usual name but by invoking God in a way that is meant to instill fear in Lavan's heart: "Had not the God of my father—the God of Abraham and the Terror of Isaac—been with me, you would have dispatched me now with nothing" (ibid., 31:42). Jacob here refers to God by a unique appellation,

---

[4] Lavan's statement, in verse 29, that he has the power to do Jacob harm is suggestive, although not conclusive, that Lavan meant to kill Jacob. Also, Rashi, based on Onkelos's translation, interprets *Arami 'oved avi* in Deuteronomy 26:5 to mean that Lavan wanted to kill Jacob, and the Passover Haggadah adopts that interpretation. It should be noted, however, that both Ibn Ezra and Sforno reject that interpretation of Deuteronomy 26:5. Nevertheless, the fact that Lavan chased after Jacob not all by himself but with a retinue of his kinsmen, and Lavan's statement in Genesis 31:29 saying that he has the power to harm Jacob, are strong evidence of Lavan's evil intentions regarding Jacob.

"the Terror of Isaac," signifying God as the wielder of Justice and of retribution.[5]

Lavan backs down and asks for a truce. And, complementing God's promise to Jacob and Jacob's erecting a monument near the beginning of the *sidra*, here near the end of *Vayetze* Jacob and Lavan together erect a monument to testify to their treaty (ibid., verse 52). Lavan, true to his heathen nature, in making his treaty invokes multiple gods: "The God of Abraham and the god of [Abraham's brother] Nahor will judge between us." And then, he also invokes the gods of Abraham and Nahor's father (*i.e.* Terah), perhaps in an effort to find common ground with Jacob by invoking a common ancestor. But Jacob pointedly rejects that formulation, and instead he swears "by the Terror of his father Isaac" (ibid., verse 53).

Lavan and Jacob go their ways, and thus ends the standoff between the two, between the heathen sorcerer and the man of God. But the Torah has not yet finished the tale. No sooner does Jacob take his leave of Lavan than the Torah says that "angels of God encountered him. And Jacob said when he saw them, 'this is a camp of God'; and he called the name of that place *Machanayim* [paired camps]" (Genesis 32:1–2). The dual form of the word *Machanayim* could indicate the camp of Jacob and the camp of angels, or alternatively it could indicate (as the *Midrash* interprets it) that a group of angels who had hitherto accompanied Jacob were leaving while another group of angels came to accompany him to the Promised Land. Thus, the final two verses of *Vayetze* parallel Jacob's

---

[5] "The Terror of Isaac" (or "The Dread of Isaac") is found nowhere else in the Torah. An alternative explanation of "the Terror of Isaac" is a reference to Isaac's experience at the *Akedah*, as Ibn Ezra mentions. For more about the divine names, see "*Re'eh*: What's in a Name?"

dream near the start of the *sidra*, in which some angels were going up and others were going down the ladder. And, just as Jacob's vision at the start of the *sidra* is an indication of God's oversight and protection, so too does the camp of angels at the end signify God's continuing protection of Jacob on his journey.

Vayishlach:
I Have Sojourned with Lavan

*Why did Jacob's message to Esau start with
"I have sojourned with Lavan"?*

At the beginning of the portion of *Vayishlach*,[1] Jacob sends
messengers to his brother Esau in an attempt to make
peace and to dissuade Esau from attacking him. Jacob
instructs the messengers to begin his message saying,
"I have sojourned with Lavan and have tarried till now"
(Genesis 32:4). What is the significance of that statement?

In his well-known commentary on this verse, Rashi
interprets: *Im Lavan harasha' garti, vetaryag mitzvot
shamarti*—"I have sojourned with Lavan and have kept the
commandments, and I have not learned from his evil ways."
Indeed, this interpretation may contain a worthy lesson for
us, Jacob's descendants; but such a statement would make
no impression on Esau, since Esau wouldn't care whether
Jacob observed God's commandments. Why, then, would
Jacob see fit to begin his message to Esau with such words?

Lavan was a powerful man, and at one point he even
says to Jacob, "It is in my power to do you harm" (Genesis
31:19). In fact, the Zohar points out that Lavan was known
as a master sorcerer who would not allow anybody to get the
better of him.[2] And yet, the Zohar stresses, Jacob had escaped
from Lavan's clutches! Let that fact be a warning to Esau.

The Zohar continues with a second interpretation,
focusing on the words "and have tarried till now." In fact,

---

1 Genesis 32:3 – 36:43.
2 Zohar I:166b. See also Zohar I:161a, regarding Lavan's being a sorcerer.

Jacob had lived with Lavan for twenty years, and, as Jacob says in the following verse, from his work with Lavan he had amassed great wealth: cattle, donkeys, sheep, slaves, and maidservants. Let Esau wonder whether in all that time Jacob had also acquired from Lavan the knowledge of sorcery. Let that also be a warning to Esau.

Jacob may have intended either or both of these two veiled threats in his message to Esau; but we may postulate yet another possibility: perhaps Jacob's words, "I have sojourned with Lavan and have tarried till now" (Genesis 32:4), were meant as an offering of peace, and are words intended to assuage Esau's feelings of jealousy. Although Rashi's statement about Jacob's keeping the commandments and not learning Lavan's evil ways (see above) stands out in the memory of most people who have had a Torah education, there is another part of Rashi's commentary on that verse that is generally overlooked or forgotten. Commenting on the word *garti* ("I sojourned"), Rashi says: "I did not become a prince or somebody important, but I remained a sojourner—an alien"; I am a nobody, and you have no reason to hate me on account of your father's blessing that he gave me, saying, "Be an overlord to your brothers," because clearly, it did not come true for me. And, Rashi then adds his enigmatic statement that Jacob lived with Lavan but kept the commandments and didn't learn Lavan's evil ways. Perhaps what Rashi implies but leaves unsaid is that, in remaining true to God's commandments, the **birthright**—*i.e.* the spiritual leadership of the family—was fulfilled, but their father's **blessing** was not fulfilled for Jacob.[3]

---

[3] Note that, although Esau faulted his brother for taking both his birthright and his blessing (see Genesis 27:36), it was only on account of their father's blessing that Esau hated Jacob (ibid., verse 41). See also my discussion in "*Toldot* 2: Tales of Jealousy and Hatred."

But as it turns out, Jacob's message—whether intended as a veiled threat or as an offer of peace—does not have the desired effect; and after receiving the message, Esau continues to advance toward Jacob, backed up by a retinue of four hundred men (Genesis 32:7), and "Jacob feared greatly" (verse 8). It is only after Jacob heaps upon Esau lavish presents—a multitude of sheep, goats, camels, and donkeys (verses 14–21)—and bows before Esau seven times (ibid., 33:3) that Esau relents and makes peace with his brother (verse 4). Esau at first declines Jacob's presents, saying, "I have much, my brother; keep what you have" (verse 9); and Rashi, citing *Midrash Rabba*, says that Esau's saying "keep what you have" indicates that Esau is here admitting Jacob's right to their father's blessings. But Jacob insists that Esau accept the present, and he says, "Please accept my blessing ..." (verse 11), significantly, using the word *birkhati*—"my blessing"—referring to his offering to Esau.[4] Esau then accepts Jacob's present, and he even offers to travel together with Jacob. But Jacob declines, and the two brothers go their separate ways (verses 11–17).

---

[4] Rashi, in commenting on verse 11, does not equate Jacob's offering to Esau with their father's blessing that he gave to Jacob, nor does any other commentator to my knowledge. And, in fact, Rabbi Elijah Mizrachi (Constantinople, 1455–1525) says that "blessing" is a term that is used in reference to a peace offering. Nevertheless, I find it significant that Jacob here refers to his offering as "my blessing."

Vayeshev 1:
The Sun, the Moon, and the Dream

What did the sun and the moon symbolize in Joseph's second dream?

At the beginning of *Vayeshev*,[1] Joseph, son of Jacob, dreams two dreams foretelling his destiny: that he will someday rule over his eleven brothers. He tells the first dream to his brothers and incurs their animosity. He tells the second dream to his brothers, and they despise him even more. Then he repeats the second dream to his father in the presence of his brothers: the sun, the moon, and eleven stars are bowing down to Joseph. Jacob immediately rebukes his son. How could this possibly be? "Will I and your mother and brothers come to grovel before you on the ground?" As Jacob portrays it, the whole thing sounds ridiculous. And moreover, Joseph's mother is dead! The dream obviously makes no sense. Jacob, in an effort to make light of the dream and to make peace among his children, mocks Joseph's dream. And yet, the Torah, says, Jacob kept the matter in mind (Genesis 37:11). Jacob believed the dream; and therefore we must assume that Jacob understood that the correct interpretation of Joseph's dream was not as he portrayed it to his sons.

What, then, is the true symbolism of Joseph's dream? As we have seen, the moon cannot represent Joseph's mother Rachel. Rashi, quoting *Midrash Rabba*, says that the moon actually represents Jacob's concubine Bilha, who had raised Joseph as though she had been his mother. But

---

[1] Genesis 37:1 – 40:23.

I have never found that explanation very satisfying. I feel the symbolism of Joseph's dream must be more robust.

In an effort to discover the *peshat* (*i.e.* the plain meaning) of Joseph's second dream, I believe we must take a whole new approach, completely abandoning Jacob's proposed interpretation. After all, Jacob did not believe that interpretation either, and he only advanced it in an effort to make peace. I think the key to interpreting Joseph's dream is to realize that the moon does not symbolize Joseph's mother; and if that is the case, perhaps the sun does not symbolize Joseph's father. Rather, I propose that the sun of Joseph's dream represents a mighty nation. In the ancient world in the time of our patriarchs, there was one nation whose might was legendary, whose culture was famed throughout the world, whose prosperity was the envy of all nations—a nation whose chief deity was the sun god, whose king was said to be the offspring of the sun god, and whose countless monuments prominently displayed an image of the sun: Egypt. Surely any person living in those times, if asked what nation he would associate with the sun, would unhesitatingly pick Egypt.

But if the sun is Egypt, and the eleven stars are Joseph's eleven brothers, who, years in the future, are destined to come as supplicants before Joseph the Viceroy of Egypt, then what does the moon in Joseph's dream represent? I believe the moon represents Jacob, the father of the Jewish nation. In later prophetic literature, the moon symbolizes Israel. Sometimes the nation of Israel wanes, and her face is darkened; but she always returns in the fullness of time, just like the moon. Thus, Jacob, the father of our nation, is the moon of Joseph's dream; and he, too, is destined to go to Egypt at Joseph's behest. Perhaps Jacob himself did not understand the dream fully, but he knew it was not just an empty dream but a prophecy, and that it would someday be fulfilled.

Vayeshev 2:
Joseph and His Brothers

Did Joseph's brothers really sell Joseph into slavery?

In the *sidra* of *Vayeshev*,[1] our patriarch Jacob favors his son Joseph over his other children. When Joseph tells his brothers about two dreams he has dreamt foretelling that he will someday rule over them, he incurs their hatred; and soon after, they plot to kill him. But Reuben, the oldest of the brothers, has second thoughts and convinces the others not to kill Joseph (Genesis 37:21–22). Instead, according to the usual view, the brothers sell Joseph into slavery. But is that interpretation correct? Did the brothers really sell Joseph? Perhaps not. In the view of Rashi's grandson Rashbam,[2] the most straightforward reading of the text of the Torah suggests otherwise.

As the Torah tells it, the brothers capture Joseph, throw him into a pit, and sit down to eat, apparently while deliberating exactly what to do with him (Genesis 37:24–25). While they are eating, they see a caravan of Ishmaelites coming, and Judah proposes that they sell Joseph to the Ishmaelites instead of killing him (ibid., verses 26–27). But now, the Torah says, "Midianite merchants passed by; they hauled Joseph out of the pit, they sold him to the Ishmaelites for twenty pieces of silver, and they brought Joseph to Egypt" (ibid., verse 28). So, who sold Joseph? "They." And who are "they"? The most straightforward

---

[1] Genesis 37:1 – 40:23.
[2] Rabbi Shmuel ben Meir. France, c. 1085 – c. 1158. See also Description of Sources.

way to read that verse in isolation of the rest of the story is to assume that "they" refers to the last plural noun mentioned: the Midianite merchants. In that case, the Midianites were the ones who sold Joseph, and not the brothers. According to Rashbam, then, the entire scenario was as follows:

While the brothers were eating, at some distance from the pit, and waiting for the Ishmaelite caravan that they had seen in the distance, a group of Midianite merchants happened by—coming from a different direction—and they spotted Joseph in the pit. The Midianites pulled Joseph out of the pit, and they were the ones who sold Joseph to the Ishmaelites, perhaps without the brothers' knowledge (and likely before the Ishmaelite caravan approached the spot where the brothers sat waiting for them). The Torah then tells us that Reuben returned to the pit and was surprised to find Joseph gone (ibid., verse 29). But maybe all the brothers were surprised to find Joseph gone, and the text only singles out Reuben because he intended to rescue Joseph and return him to his father (see verse 22), and therefore Reuben hurried to the pit to get there before his brothers.

In support of Rashbam's interpretation, when Joseph relates his history to Pharaoh's butler and baker many years later, he does not say that he was sold into slavery; rather, Joseph says, "For I was stolen, indeed stolen, from the land of the Hebrews" (Genesis 40:15). And yet, we may object that when Joseph reveals himself to his brothers, he says, "I am Joseph your brother, whom you sold to Egypt" (ibid.. 45:4). Rashbam addresses this objection, saying that Joseph attributes the sale to his brothers because they were the indirect cause of his being sold. This is a reasonable explanation, especially since—

even in the usual interpretation—the brothers did not directly sell Joseph to Egypt but were only the indirect cause of that event. Let us not forget, however, that it had been the brothers' intention to sell Joseph; and therefore, considering their intention and their being the indirect cause of Joseph being sold, the accusation was justified.

So why does the Torah say ambiguously "**they** sold him" in Genesis 37:28 (see above)? Why doesn't the Torah make it clear who actually sold Joseph? In answer, we may say that perhaps, even assuming that Rashbam is correct, and Joseph's brothers did not actually commit their intended act, the Torah nevertheless holds the brothers morally responsible and therefore is purposely vague about who actually sold Joseph.

In the end, though, God has the final say, as He always does. As Joseph puts it, "You intended evil for me, but God intended it for good, in order to bring about today's result: the survival of a multitude of people" (Genesis 50:20). And so it was.

Miketz:
Interpreting Pharaoh's Dream

How did Pharaoh know that Joseph interpreted his dream correctly?

In the *sidra* of *Miketz*,[1] Pharaoh dreams two troubling dreams. In the first dream, he sees seven fat cows and seven emaciated cows, and the emaciated cows devour the fat cows. The second dream has the same theme, but features fat and emaciated stalks of wheat. Pharaoh summons his sorcerers and bids them interpret his dreams, but he is not satisfied with their interpretations. Somehow he feels that they have not hit the mark. But what specifically is the basis for Pharaoh's skepticism, and how does he know that Joseph's interpretation is correct?

The *Midrash* presents a number of interpretations that Pharaoh's sorcerers may have given him.[2] However, the *Midrash* does not tell us the reason, based on the language of the Biblical text, why Pharaoh would have rejected those interpretations. I believe that a careful reading of *Miketz* tells us Pharaoh's reason for rejecting his sorcerers' interpretations, and also the reason that he was willing to accept Joseph's words.

When Pharaoh relates his dreams to the sorcerers, pay attention to the unusual phrasing of the text: "Pharaoh told them his dream, but there was none who could interpret them for Pharaoh" (Genesis 41:8). Note the sudden switch from singular to plural: Pharaoh told them his

---

[1] Genesis 41:1 – 44:17.
[2] See *Bereshit Rabba* 89:7.

dream (singular), but there was none who could interpret **them** (plural) for Pharaoh. Why the sudden change from singular to plural? What is the Torah telling us? I believe the Torah is saying that Pharaoh knew his two dreams were one—that both dreams had the same meaning; but his sorcerers were viewing them as two separate dreams with two separate meanings, and that was the basis for Pharaoh's unwillingness to accept their words.

In contrast, when Pharaoh finished telling his dreams to Joseph, the first words out of Joseph's mouth were, "Pharaoh's dream is one" (Genesis 41:25). Immediately, Pharaoh knew that Joseph understood the import of the dream, and therefore he was willing to trust Joseph's interpretation.

Vayigash:[1]
Jacob Refuses to Be Consoled

Did Jacob ever believe that Joseph was dead?

In *Vayeshev*, Joseph's brothers present their father with Joseph's blood-covered garment, and Jacob immediately declares, "A vile beast has devoured him; Joseph has been torn apart" (Genesis 37:33). Jacob then tears his own clothing and mourns his son for a long time, refusing to be consoled (ibid., verses 34–35). The *Midrash* comments that a person accepts consolation when he mourns somebody who has died but not when mourning one who is alive and only believed to be dead.[2] But did Jacob really believe Joseph to be dead?

Years later, in the portion of *Vayigash*, Joseph's eleven brothers stand before the viceroy of Egypt—who, unbeknownst to them, is really Joseph—and try to counter his demand that Benjamin, the youngest of the brothers, remain as a slave in Egypt. Judah, who feels most responsible for Benjamin (see Genesis 43:9 and 44:32), steps forward and tells the viceroy how attached their father is to Benjamin,[3] the only remaining son of Jacob's beloved wife Rachel: "Your subject, our father, said to us, 'You know that my wife bore me two children. But one

---

[1] Genesis 44:18 – 47:27.
[2] *Bereshit Rabba* on Genesis 37:35.
[3] The Zohar points out that it had to be Judah rather than any of the other brothers who came forward to approach Joseph to object to Joseph's demand that Benjamin remain as a slave in Egypt, because it was Judah who had pledged himself responsible for Benjamin (see Genesis 44:32). Zohar I:206b.

went away from me, and I said, he has been torn apart; and I have not seen him since. If you also take this one away from me and a disaster befalls him, you will send my hoary head in grief down to the nether world'" (ibid.. 44:27–29). Notice that Jacob does not say that Joseph is dead. Instead, he tells how he had stated his conclusion from the evidence presented to him: "I said, he has been torn apart." But did Jacob believe the words that he had spoken? Not likely: "I have not seen him since" does not sound like the phrasing he would have used had he believed his son was dead. Jacob's words, "I said," reflect his acknowledgement of the apparent conclusion from the evidence, but his phrasing suggests that in the depths of his heart he continued to believe that the evidence was wrong and that Joseph still lived.

And yet, after Joseph reveals himself to his brothers and they return to Canaan to tell their father that Joseph is alive, Jacob at first does not believe them (ibid., 45:26). This, too, is understandable. After 22 years of telling himself that Joseph is dead despite his intuitive feeling to the contrary, it could not be easy to cast away all doubt and immediately accept this new story. What if the new story were later proven false? Jacob has to be sure before accepting such a far-fetched tale: not only is Joseph still alive, but he is the viceroy of Egypt! So, of course, Jacob doubts. It is only when Jacob sees the wagons that Joseph has sent to bring him to Egypt that Jacob's spirit revives (ibid., 45:27), and he finally allows himself to believe in his mind what his heart has known all these many years.

Vayechi:
Judah and the Scepter of Royalty

What did Jacob's enigmatic blessing of his son Judah mean?

In the Torah portion of *Vayechi*,[1] our patriarch Jacob blesses his children before his death. He begins by saying, "Assemble, and I will reveal to you what will befall you in the latter days" (Genesis 49:1).[2] The *Midrash* tells us that Jacob wanted to reveal what will happen at the end of days, but it was concealed from him.[3] Nevertheless, Jacob's words do hint at things to come, although couched in cryptic language. In the present discussion, I will focus on the prophecy that Jacob foretold for Judah, his third son.

Although not the oldest of the brothers, Judah appears always to have been their leader. Many years earlier, when the brothers wanted to kill Joseph, it was Judah who spoke up and persuaded them not to kill Joseph.[4]

---

[1] Genesis 47:28 – 50:26.

[2] My translation of the Hebrew *ve'aggida lakhem* as "I will reveal to you" follows the interpretations of the Zohar and Ibn Ezra. The verb *lesapper* simply means to tell, but, the Zohar says, *lehaggid* connotes revealing an element of wisdom or revealing a fact that was previously concealed or not known to the listener, as in Genesis 3:11, or especially in Job 11:6. (See Zohar I:234b, I:249a, II:80a, and III:50b). Ibn Ezra also says that *lehaggid* refers to "a new matter that has not been mentioned previously." (See Ibn Ezra on Exodus 19:9.)

[3] See *Bereshit Rabba* on Genesis 49:1.

[4] First, Reuben persuaded his brothers to throw Joseph in a pit instead of killing him. Reuben had intended to then return Joseph to their father unharmed; but, while Joseph was in the pit and Reuben was absent for a short while, the other brothers apparently still considered killing Joseph, and Judah—perhaps unable to dissuade them—proposed that they sell him into slavery instead. See also "*Vayeshev* 2: Joseph and His Brothers," above.

And when, many years after Joseph's abduction, the brothers confront the viceroy of Egypt who demands that they bring him their youngest brother Benjamin, it is Judah who takes responsibility for Benjamin's safe return to his father. Therefore, it is not surprising that Jacob begins his blessing to Judah saying, "Judah, your brothers will acknowledge you," and "your father's sons will bow to you" (Genesis 49:8). But Jacob goes still further: "The scepter shall not depart from Judah, nor the ruler's staff from between his legs, until Shiloh shall come, and the reverence of nations be his" (ibid., verse 10).[5] And indeed, the kingship in Jerusalem did reside in the House of David, a descendant of Judah, for about four hundred years. But what are we to make of other rulers of Israel who were not of the tribe of Judah? And what does Jacob mean when he says "until Shiloh shall come"?

As to my first question, Ramban addresses that issue. Ramban points out that Jacob's phrasing, "The scepter shall not depart from Judah," leaves open the possibility that there will be a king from another tribe first; but once the kingship devolves to Judah's descendants, it will not depart from them. Thus, King Saul, the first king of Israel, was a legitimate ruler; but once David became the next king, kings from other tribes could not be legitimate rulers of Israel. In particular, Ramban states that the Hasmonean rulers (who ruled several centuries later)— being *kohanim* and thus not from the tribe of Judah—

---

[5] Jacob's allusion to "the ruler's staff between his legs" accords with the frequent description of Assyrian and Babylonian kings holding in the right hand a staff of authority that rests between the ruler's legs. There is also a later statue of Darius the Great of Persia sitting on his throne and holding a staff resting on the floor between his legs.

sinned by declaring themselves king, and therefore all of the sons of Matityahu who ruled as kings "fell by the sword of their enemies."[6]

Ramban then addresses the kingship of Yerav'am, from the tribe of Ephraim, who ruled over the ten northern tribes two generations after King David. It is true that he was crowned by a prophet and therefore must be regarded as a legitimate ruler; but Yerav'am was crowned in order to be a thorn in the side of the Judean monarchy (see I Kings 11:39). That role, says Ramban, was to be temporary, and the crowning of subsequent monarchs of the Ten Tribes was not in accordance with God's wishes, as evidenced by the prophet Hosea's statement, "They have established kings, but not from Me" (Hosea 8:4).

Now we come to my second question: what does Jacob mean when he says "until Shiloh shall come"? Indeed, the phrase 'ad ki yavo Shiloh ("until Shiloh shall come") has perplexed commentators and translators through the ages. Many have proposed that Shiloh refers to the Messiah, but the reason for calling the Messiah by that name is not adequately explained. Others have said that Shiloh refers to Moses, who ruled the Israelites for forty years after the Exodus from Egypt. And Ramban theorizes that Shiloh refers to King David's son Shlomo (Solomon). Many modern translations take "Shiloh" to be a contraction of shai lo (i.e., a tribute or offering to him) and translate the phrase 'ad ki yavo Shiloh as "so that

---

[6] Matityahu, a kohen, initiated the Jewish revolt against the Seleucid Greeks who were then in control of Judea in 167 BCE. His son Judah the Maccabee then led the revolt, finally defeating the Seleucid army. After the Seleucids were expelled from Jerusalem, Judah's brother Simon declared himself king. Since the family of Matityahu were known as "Hasmoneans," the kings who descended from him are known as the Hasmonean dynasty.

tribute shall come to him".[7]   Or, alternatively, it could be translated as "until he comes to Shiloh."   I find none of these interpretations especially convincing.   Instead, I want to propose yet another interpretation of "until Shiloh shall come."

The first two kings of the Davidic dynasty, David and Solomon, ruled in Jerusalem over a united nation.   But when Solomon's son Rechav'am (Rehoboam) began his rule, rebellion broke out, and ten of the twelve tribes of Israel seceded, forming a separate nation with Yerav'am (Jeroboam) of the tribe of Ephraim as their king. Yerav'am was not just a man selected by popular acclaim or because of his prowess as a military commander; he was crowned king of the ten tribes by a prophet of God named Ahiah the Shilonite—i.e. Ahiah from Shiloh (see I Kings 11:29–38).   Perhaps, then, Jacob's prophecy means that the sole kingship of the descendants of Judah will be interrupted when the man from Shiloh shall come, resulting in the secession of the Ten Tribes and the splitting of Israel into two nations.   In that case, the king to whom the reverence of nations will come (see Genesis 49:10) may refer to King Solomon (as Ramban proposes), who was the last king of a united Israel (before the secession of the ten northern tribes). King Solomon, who was held in high repute in the ancient Near East, made alliances with several nations, and the kings of other nations sent emissaries to learn from his wisdom (see 1 Kings 5:14).

A final question: will the Ten Lost Tribes return and the entire nation of Israel be reunited?   That is a matter

---

[7]   For example, see the Jewish Publication Society's Torah translation of 1962.

of controversy.[8] Ezekiel's prophecy (see Ezekiel 37:15–28), which is the *Haftarah* of *Vayigash*, suggests that the Ten Lost Tribes will return and will be reunited with the Jewish people, under a descendant of the Davidic line.

---

[8] The Talmud presents two opinions: Rabbi Akiva says the Ten Tribes will not return, whereas Rabbi Eliezer says they will return (in the Messianic age). See Mishnah *Sanhedrin* 10:3.

BOOK II

Shemot (Exodus)

The book of *Shemot* continues where the book of *Bereshit* leaves off. It begins by naming the sons of Jacob and tells us that they and their children who went down to Egypt numbered seventy souls.

After the deaths of Joseph and his brothers, a new king arose, who enslaved and oppressed the Israelites. We learn of the Israelites' suffering and how God sent the prophet Moses to deliver them from slavery. Moses led his nascent nation to Mount Sinai, where God established a covenant with them, and gave them a set of commandments engraved on two stone tablets. The Israelites, however, rebelled against God and worshipped a golden calf, thus dissolving the covenant. But God, in His mercy, forgave the nation, inscribed the commandments on a second set of tablets, and directed the building of a sanctuary that allowed them to regain their former spiritual status, so that once again God's Presence dwelled in their midst.

Shemot 1:
The Birth of Moses

What do Moses and Noah have in common?

Following the death and mummification of Joseph at the end of *Vayechi*, the book of *Shemot* (Exodus)[1] resumes the story of the sons of Jacob (who was also known as Israel) and begins with a statement identical to that of Genesis 46:8: "These are the names of the sons of Israel who came to Egypt ..." (Exodus 1:1). The Torah then tells us that the descendants of Jacob who went to Egypt totaled seventy souls, that they were very fertile, and they multiplied and "swarmed,"[2] so that the land was filled with them (Exodus 1:5 & 7). Pharaoh is alarmed, thinking of the Israelites as a foreign element who would side with Egypt's enemies in the event of war. And so, Pharaoh devises a plan of action to thwart this putative threat. He subjects the Israelites to forced labor and has his taskmasters work them brutally. And when, despite those measures, the Israelites continue to multiply, Pharaoh tells the midwives to kill all male newborns among the Israelites. But at least two midwives defy Pharaoh's order and refuse to kill the Israelite babies. So Pharaoh decrees that all male babies be drowned in the Nile (ibid., 1:22).

---

[1] The word *Shemot* ("the names of") is the second word of the book, but it is the first **significant** word. In keeping with the common Hebrew practice, the *sidra* of *Shemot* (Exodus 1:1 – 6:1) is named after the first significant word, as is also the entire book of *Shemot*.

[2] For the significance of this wording, see my discussion in "*Bo* 2: Symbolism and Parallelism in the Plagues of Egypt."

Notwithstanding Pharaoh's decree, a Levite woman named Yocheved[3] bears a male infant and seeks to hide him from Pharaoh's enforcers. But after three months, she realizes it would be impossible to hide the baby much longer, and she puts him afloat on the river among the reeds, in a *teva* (a box or chest) made of reeds and rendered watertight with pitch and bitumen.[4] Before long, an Egyptian princess goes to bathe in the river and sees the *teva* among the reeds; and, on opening the box, she finds a crying infant. She immediately realizes the infant must be an Israelite; nevertheless, in defiance of Pharaoh's decree, she has mercy on the child. "And he became a son to her, and she called his name Moshe [Moses] ..." (Exodus 2:10).

Cassuto points out that the word *teva* is used in the Torah in only two contexts: here, and in the *sidra* of *Noah*. And, Cassuto says, this is no coincidence. By using the same word, the Torah is drawing a parallel between the two events: "In both cases there is to be saved from drowning one who is worthy of salvation and is destined to bring deliverance to others."[5] In the Flood, Noah saved the human race; whereas in the book of *Shemot*, Moses saves the people of Israel.

The word *teva* is apparently a loan-word, closely resembling an ancient Egyptian word meaning a box or

---

[3] Neither Yocheved nor her husband Amram is named in Exodus 2:1–2, where the birth of Moses is told. But the names of both of Moses's parents are given later, in Exodus 6:20.

[4] An interesting parallel: Moses's mother puts the infant Moses afloat in a *teva* "among the reeds" (*ba-suf*) on the banks of the Nile. And, years later, when Moses leads his newly-formed nation out of Egypt, the final confrontation with Pharaoh occurs at the splitting of the sea that the Torah calls *Yam Suf*—"The Sea of Reeds."

[5] See Cassuto's commentary on the Book of Genesis, translated from the Hebrew by Israel Abrahams (U. Cassuto, *A Commentary on the Book of Genesis, Part Two*), p 59.

a chest. Like Moshe's *teva*, Noah's *teva* was not shaped like a boat that was designed to be navigated by mariners; instead, it had a flat bottom and moved along the surface, driven by the wind and by the water currents.[6] In both cases, the *teva* floated on the surface of the water, carried by the currents and the wind. And in both cases, the destiny of the *teva* was left in God's hands.

---

[6] Cassuto, ibid., pp 59–60. Cassuto notes that the Torah's statement, "the ark went on the face of the waters" (Genesis 7:18) in reference to Noah's ark, would not be the way to describe the motion of a ship. Also, "The ark came to REST ... upon the mountains of Ararat" (ibid., 8:4) suggests that the bottom of Noah's ark was flat, making it possible for it to rest on the ground, unlike the hull of ship.

Shemot[1] 2:
The Burning Bush

Was it God or an angel who spoke to Moses
from the burning bush?

"And an angel of the Lord appeared to him in a flare of fire from within the bush; and he saw the bush was burning in the fire, but the bush was not consumed" (Exodus 3:2). Thus begins Moses's first experience with prophecy. Intrigued by the unusual phenomenon, Moses turns from his path. God calls to him from within the bush (ibid., verse 4), and He says: "I am the God of your father, the God of Abraham, the God of Isaac, and the God of Jacob" (verse 6). And Moses hid his face, because he was afraid to look. But, we may ask, what did Moses actually see; and was the entire prophecy delivered by an angel, or was it God Himself who spoke to Moses? Unfortunately for our understanding, the details are clouded in mystery, and there are at least as many answers to these questions as there are commentators.

Ibn Ezra opines that in this entire episode—that is, both in verse 2 and in verse 4—it was only an angel who spoke to Moses. He points out that the name *Elohim*, which signifies power or authority,[2] does not always refer to God Himself but is sometimes used to refer to an angel, as Jacob says after wrestling with the angel: "... for I have

---

[1] Exodus 1:1 – 6:1
[2] The word *elohim* is also used in the Torah in a secular sense, as in Exodus 22:7 & 8, where it refers to a court of law. Also, see *Elohim* in Glossary.

seen *Elohim* face to face" (Genesis 32:30). Therefore, in Ibn Ezra's opinion, when the Torah says that "*Elohim* called to him from within the bush" (Exodus 3:4), it means that God spoke to Moses through an angel, just as in verse 2. But most commentators do not agree with Ibn Ezra. Indeed, Ramban points out that after Moses approached the burning bush and heard the Lord speaking to him, Moses hid his face; and, Ramban comments, he wouldn't have hidden his face from a mere angel.

So, if the Lord was going to speak to Moses from within the burning bush, what was the purpose of having him first see an angel, especially since the angel apparently did not say anything? In answer to that question, several commentators say that since this was Moses's first prophecy, and he was not yet used to prophecy, God wanted to break him in gradually. Therefore, first Moses saw only an unusual phenomenon—a bush that was on fire but was not being consumed. Next, he saw an angel within the flame. And only after that did the Lord actually speak to him.

In order to explain the reason for God's not speaking to Moses from the start, Rabbeinu Bachyay draws an analogy to a person who has been in a dark house for a long time. If he suddenly goes out into bright sunlight, the light would be blinding. Similarly, God used a stepped approach to prepare Moses for his first prophecy. The burning bush served to attract Moses's attention, and once Moses turned to see, God sent an angel. Only after that did the Lord speak to him. Rabbi Moshe Alsheikh comments that it was not appropriate for God Himself to prepare Moses for prophecy, and thus the angel's function was to make Moses attuned to the divine and to cause him to separate himself from mundane matters before God spoke to him. Thus Moses, whose level of prophetic power would ultimately exceed that of all other prophets,[3] had his initial introduction to prophecy by means of an angel.

Sforno notes that Moses's prophetic power was not yet as great at this time as it would be later on, as indicated by the statement that "he was afraid to look at God" (Exodus 3:6); whereas after his prophetic power matures, the Torah says of Moses, "the likeness of the Lord he beholds" (Numbers 12:8).[4] Moreover, after Moses saw the angel in the burning bush, God warned him to approach no closer (Exodus 3:5): Moses was not yet ready to approach the divine presence; whereas much later, when the people of Israel stood at Mount Sinai to receive the Ten Commandments, the Torah tells us (ibid., 20:18) that Moses approached the thick fog within which was the presence of God.[5]

We see, then, how Moses very rapidly ascended the prophetic ladder—from his initial vision of an angel in the burning bush to his ability to perceive the voice of God speaking to him from within the bush. He had not yet reached the level that he would eventually achieve some months later, when he and his nation would stand at Mount Sinai to receive the Ten Commandments. But even now, Moses had already risen to a prophetic level exceeding that

---

[3] For a discussion of how the prophecy of Moses differed from that of all other prophets, see Moses Maimonides, *Mishneh Torah, Hilkhot Yesodei HaTorah* 7:6, and also his book *The Guide for the Perplexed* II:45 at the end of the chapter. In his opinion (and many Biblical commentators disagree with him), Moses was the only prophet to whom God spoke directly; in the case of all other prophets, in his opinion (and again, many Biblical commentators disagree with him), even when those prophets said that God spoke to them, it was always through an angel.

Also, for a discussion of the different levels of prophecy, refer to Maimonides's *The Guide for the Perplexed* II:45.

[4] See Sforno on Exodus 3:2.
[5] See Ramban on Exodus 3:5.

of other prophets. Indeed, he needed to achieve that high level, since his mission was different from that of other prophets. Moses was to confront and threaten Pharaoh, perhaps the most powerful ruler on earth at that time, and to extract the Israelites from slavery in Egypt, thus creating a new nation under God's providence. To accomplish such a mission, Moses needed to receive his orders directly from God, and not through an angel or any intermediary.

Thus ends Moses's introduction to prophecy and the start of his prophetic mission.

Va'era[1] *1:*
Master of the Universe

How did God's revelation in the burning bush differ from His revelation to the Patriarchs?

In the previous *sidra*—*Shemot*—God sends Moses back to Egypt to demand that Pharaoh release the Israelites from his land; but Pharaoh responds by increasing the Israelites' workload and their suffering. And the *sidra* of *Shemot* ends with Moses complaining to God: "Why have You caused harm to this nation? Why have You sent me? ... And You have not rescued Your nation" (Exodus 6:22–23). But God answers, "... you will see what I will do to Pharaoh." And, as the *sidra* of *Va'era* begins, God continues with an enigmatic statement: "I am YHVH. I was revealed to Abraham, to Isaac, and to Jacob as *El Shaddai*, but as my name YHVH I was not known to them.'" (Exodus 6:2–3.)[2]

What does this mean? On the surface, it appears that God is telling Moses a new name that was hitherto unknown to the patriarchs and their descendants. But that can't be the correct interpretation, for God had already identified Himself to Abraham by the name YHVH (see Genesis 15:7). In the present essay, I will try to clarify the import of these opening verses of *Va'era*.

---

[1] Exodus 6:2 – 9:35.

[2] This *sidra* is named for its first significant word, *va'era*, which I have translated here as "I was revealed." This follows the Aramaic translation of Onkelos, a Roman (thought to be a relative of the emperor Titus) who converted to Judaism and is thought to have lived from 35 to 120 CE. See also Description of Sources.

The introductory statement, "I am YHVH," is a proclamation of authority. Similarly, when establishing His covenant with Abraham, God begins by saying, "I am *El Shaddai*" (Genesis 17:1). And when Pharaoh confers upon Joseph a new title and position of authority, he begins by saying, "I am Pharaoh" (ibid. 41:44).

But God's statement of "I am YHVH" is much more than just a proclamation of authority, and much more than an identification of a name by which He is to be called. In the Torah, a name is not merely a label that is used to identify someone. A person's name expresses the essence of that person's character. However, God is so much beyond our understanding and experience that we can say nothing about His nature or His essence; and it is primarily through His actions in our world that we are able to know anything about Him. Therefore, since God Himself is unknowable, He also has no name; and thus, all the names by which God is known to us are actually names given to the actions through which He manifests Himself in the world of our experience.[3]

Notice that, in God's establishing His covenant with Abraham (in Genesis 17:1), He refers to Himself as *El Shaddai*. This is the name that refers to God as the maker of the covenant with the patriarchs and their descendants, the nation of Israel. It is God Who made an eternal promise to the people of Israel that He will be with them and that He will give them the entire land of Canaan as their inheritance (Genesis 17:7–8), a promise first given to Abraham and later reaffirmed to Isaac and to Jacob as the heirs to that covenant (ibid., 21:13, 26:3, and 35:12).

---

[3] See *Midrash Rabba* on Exodus 3:6. For more about the divine names, see "*Re'eh*: What's In a Name?"

Indeed, it was primarily through the covenant that our patriarchs Abraham, Isaac, and Jacob experienced the Almighty.

As mentioned, the Patriarchs knew the name YHVH, but they did not have first-hand experience with the implication of that name—the God of Israel, Who is faithful to His word—because His promise to give them the entire land of Canaan was not fulfilled in their lifetimes. Now, addressing Moses, God again reaffirms the covenant that He made with the Patriarchs to give them the land of Canaan, and He declares that He has heard the groans of the Israelites. He identifies himself to Moses as YHVH, the Lord Who fulfills His promises,[4] Who brings His word into fruition.[5] And he commands Moses to tell the people of Israel that He, the Lord (**YHVH**), will bring them out of Egypt, will deliver them from bondage, and will bring them to the land that He has promised them (Exodus 6:4–8).

The name YHVH also signifies God as the source of all being,[6] He Who is above the natural order, God the Master of the Universe. Soon the Israelites will witness miracles wrought by God, the Master of Creation, Who is not bound by the laws of nature; for He is the source of all that is and all that ever will be. In fact, Moses himself will not live to see his nation's entry into the Promised Land; but it is through Moses that God initiates the process that will result in the final fulfillment of His promise.

---

[4] See Rashi on Exodus 6:2.
[5] See Sforno on Exodus 6:2.
[6] The name YHVH is derived from the verb of being, as is the name *Eh'yeh*, which God told Moses at the burning bush (Exodus 3:13–14). Thus, although the name YHVH is used in reference to His quality of mercy and of being true to His word, the primary meaning of the name YHVH is the source of all existence. Also, see Glossary.

Va'era 2:
Hardening of Pharaoh's Heart

When God hardened Pharaoh's heart,
did Pharaoh still have free will?

In the *sidra* of *Va'era*,[1] God tells Moses to speak to Pharaoh
and command him to release the Israelites from his land
(Exodus 6:10–11). But soon after, God says that He "will
harden Pharaoh's heart," and Pharaoh "will not listen to
you" (ibid., 7:3–4). How can this be? Doesn't Pharaoh—
like all men—have free will?[2] And if Pharaoh sinned,
doesn't he have the right to repent? As God says to the
prophet Ezekiel, "I do not wish the death of the wicked, but
that the wicked person change his ways and live" (Ezekiel
33:11). Finally, how can God punish Pharaoh for not
allowing the Israelites to leave if God Himself prevented
Pharaoh from doing so?

In answer to these questions, Ramban gives two
explanations and says that both are correct. In his
first explanation, he says that Pharaoh's sins against the
Israelites were so egregious that, after God gave him five
warnings that he failed to heed, Pharaoh then deserved to
be punished for the evil that he had already committed
in enslaving and oppressing the Israelites, and to have
the path to repentance withheld from him. For his
second explanation, Ramban says that the punishment in
the first five plagues came as a result of Pharaoh's own

---

[1]   Exodus 6:2 – 9:35.
[2]   For a discussion about free will, see "*Re'eh*: Blessing and Temptation."
See also "*Nitzavim*: The Power of Repentance."

stubbornness. In each case, it says, "Pharaoh's heart strengthened" (Exodus 7:13, 7:22, 8:15, and 9:7) and "Pharaoh hardened his heart" (ibid, 8:28), meaning that Pharaoh strengthened **his own** resolve and became more obstinate. God did not interfere with Pharaoh's free will at first, and in each case it was Pharaoh's own decision to resist God's will. But after the first five plagues, Pharaoh could no longer bear the suffering that resulted from his stubbornness, and he was inclined to yield because of the intensity of the plagues and not because of any willingness to submit to God's command or to repent his wrongdoing. Only then, Ramban says, did God intervene and strengthen Pharaoh's spirit to withstand the punishments.

Sforno's interpretation is akin to Ramban's second explanation, except that Sforno does not make a distinction between the first five and the last five plagues. In Sforno's view, God always wants an evil person to repent, but He did not want Pharaoh to give in only as a result of his growing weary of the plagues and his inability to withstand the punishment. God wanted Pharaoh to see God's power, to realize that God is the master over nature, and to submit to God's will. What God wanted from Pharaoh was his recognition of God's power and his sincere repentance. Therefore, God "hardened" Pharaoh's heart in the sense of giving him the fortitude to endure his punishments. Nevertheless, the door to true repentance was always open.

Bo 1:
A Clash of Deities

How did Pharaoh attempt to test the power of his god against the God of Israel?

Early in the Torah portion of *Bo*,[1] Moses and Aaron stand before Pharaoh and threaten him with a plague of locusts of a magnitude such as Egypt has never seen before. As Moses and Aaron exit, Pharaoh's subjects ask Pharaoh to reconsider and allow the Israelite men to leave Egypt and worship their God, saying, "Do you not yet know that Egypt is lost?" (Exodus 10:7.)

Moses and Aaron are recalled, and Pharaoh says, "Go and worship YHVH your God." But when Pharaoh then asks who will be going with Moses, Moses answers, "With our young and our old we will go; with our sons and our daughters, with our sheep and our cattle we will go, for it is YHVH's pilgrimage festival for us" (ibid., 10:9). And to this statement, Pharaoh replies with apparent sarcasm (verse 10): "Then may YHVH be with you, even as I will send you forth with your children; see that *Ra'a* [evil] is before your faces!"

What is the meaning of this cryptic reply? Specifically, what is this *Ra'a* that Pharaoh says will confront the Israelites. The commentators and translators all struggle with Pharaoh's intention. According to the Aramaic translation of Onkelos (as interpreted by Ramban), Pharaoh's meaning was that the evil action that the

---

[1]   Exodus 10:1 – 13:16.

81

Israelites were about to undertake would return to strike them.[2] Rashi says he agrees with Onkelos's interpretation, but then offers an alternative explanation: *Ra'a* in verse 10:10 should not be taken simply to mean "evil"; rather, says Rashi, *Ra'a* is the name of a star, and that star is an omen of blood and death that, Pharaoh claims, will work against the Israelites. Rabbeinu Bachyay agrees with both of the above interpretations and adds that the heavenly body called *Ra'a* is actually the red planet Mars. And Sforno, who generally seeks the most straightforward explanation consistent with the language of the Torah text, interprets Pharaoh's reply to mean, "You are headed for evil consequences."

To me, none of these explanations is fully satisfying, and I want to propose a different interpretation. None of the traditional commentaries look at Pharaoh's statement from Pharaoh's point of view, in the context of Egyptian culture. This is Pharaoh speaking—Pharaoh, king of Egypt—regarded among his people as a god on earth, who claims his father to be the sun god Ra. Thus, the word *Ra'a* in verse 10:10 may not be the Hebrew word for evil, but rather a transliteration of the name of the Egyptian sun god; and Pharaoh's reply may therefore be viewed as a challenge to the Israelites, pitting his deity against ours: "Then may YHVH be with you, when I will send you forth with your children; you will see that Ra [my god] opposes you!" In other words, let your God be with you, and we shall see how much

_____

[2] Another commentator who interprets *Ra'a* in verse 10:10 to mean "evil" is Bekhor Shor (France, 12th Century); but Bekhor Shor puts a different twist on it. According to him, what Pharaoh meant was, "The evil that you are planning to do—to escape from my country altogether—is apparent on your faces."

good that does when my god is against you. And God later answers Pharaoh's challenge in the ninth plague—darkness—wherein He demonstrates His power over Ra, the Egyptian sun god.

Bo[1] 2:
Symbolism and Parallelism in the Plagues of Egypt

How did the plagues mirror the Egyptians' treatment of the Israelites?

As a matter of justice, we generally expect that the punishment fit the crime. And so it was with the "plagues" with which God punished Egypt. The ten plagues, which are detailed in the two *sidrot* of *Va'era* and *Bo*, struck at the land, the economy, the lives of the people of Egypt, and the gods that they worshipped. In short, the plagues punished Egypt in every facet of the nation's existence, just as the oppression of the Israelites over the span of several generations destroyed the spirit of the people of Israel and every facet of their lives.

Some of the plagues were directed against the Egyptian gods, in order to demonstrate that those deities have no power and are not real gods. Therefore, the first plague turned the Nile to blood, and the second plague was a swarm of frogs throughout the land: the Egyptians worshipped the Nile as a god, and the frog-goddess Heket was a goddess of fertility. The ninth plague (darkness) demonstrated God's power over the chief god of Egypt— Ra, the sun god.[2] And, of course, the tenth plague showed God's power over life and death. But other plagues

---

[1] Exodus 10:1 – 13:16.
[2] See "*Bo* 1: A Clash of Deities" for Pharaoh's challenge pitting the power of Ra against that of Israel's God.

exhibited parallels to aspects of Pharaoh's oppression of the Israelites.

The prelude to the oppression is told at the beginning of *Shemot*: "And the people of Israel were fruitful, and they swarmed and multiplied, and they became very great; and the land was filled with them" (Exodus 1:7). It is likely that these were the very words that Pharaoh or his advisors used, and it is upon this description of the Israelites that Pharaoh then based his alarm and his actions to oppress the Israelites.[3] And so, just as Pharaoh had described the Israelites as "swarming" over the land, God punished Egypt measure for measure, bringing the plague of frogs: "And the Nile **will swarm** with frogs" (ibid., 7:28), and the frogs will cover the land. The Torah pointedly describes the plague of frogs (the second plague) using the same verb that was previously used to describe the people of Israel. Similarly, just as previously it had been said about the Israelites that "the land was filled with them" (ibid., 1:7), in the eighth plague (locusts), the locusts "covered the face of the land" so the land could no longer be seen (ibid., 10:5 & 15).

Among the chief labors with which the Israelite slaves were burdened was the making of bricks. As Cassuto points out,[4] in addition to sun-dried bricks, fired bricks were also commonly used in 19th Dynasty Egypt. The soot

---

[3] The initiation of Pharaoh's oppression of the Israelites is related in Exodus 1:9–11. Of note, Pharaoh's statement in verse 9 may not mean that the Israelites are "too numerous and mightier than we" (as it is usually translated), but may actually mean that the Israelites have become numerous and mighty **from us**—*i.e.* they have taken from us; they have taken what rightfully belongs to us, and they are parasites on our land. See "*Toldot* 1: Portents of Expulsion." Thus, the seventh and eighth plagues destroyed all the produce of the land.

[4] See Umberto Cassuto, *A Commentary on the Book of Exodus*, pp 112–113.

generated in the firing of the bricks would cling to the walls of the kiln in which the bricks were fired; and it was this soot that God commanded Moses to throw heavenward to initiate the sixth plague (boils). Thus, symbolically, Egypt was punished for the hard labor that they had imposed upon the Israelite slaves.

In all of these instances, we have seen, then, how God did indeed punish Egypt measure for measure, or, as the prophet Ovadia put it, "Just as you have done, so it will be done to you; what you deserve will befall you" (Ovadia 1:15).

Beshalach 1:
The Splitting of the Sea and the Art of Leadership

When is it time to pray, and when is it time to act?

The *sidra* of *Beshalach*[1] begins less than a week after the Exodus from Egypt. The newly-freed Israelite slaves are camped by the sea, and the Egyptian chariots are bearing down upon them (Exodus 14:2 and 14:9–10). What does Moses do? He prays.[2] But, perhaps surprisingly, God tells Moses that it is not the time for prayer: "Why do you cry out to Me? Speak to the people of Israel, and have them go forward! And you, lift up your staff, stretch out your hand upon the sea, and split it" (ibid., verses 15–16).

Or HaChayyim[3] asks: isn't prayer the proper response when people are in distress? He answers that the Israelites had been idol worshippers, just like the Egyptians, and therefore at this time they did not have any merit and were not yet worthy. The sea had not yet split, and the Israelites had to obtain merit by going forward into the sea, thus actively demonstrating their faith in God.

We see, then, how God was seeking to train the Israelites to have faith in Him. But in addition, just as importantly, God was seeking to train Moses as a leader. Until now,

---

[1]   Exodus 13:17 – 17:16.
[2]   The Torah does not explicitly say that Moses prayed, but Rashi comments that God's question of "Why do you cry out to me?" implies that Moses prayed to God.
[3]   A Torah commentary by Rabbi Chayyim ben Moshe ibn Attar (Morocco, Italy, and Israel, 1696–1743).

Moses had served as a prophet, delivering God's message to Pharaoh and demonstrating God's power. Now, however, Moses was called upon to lead a nation of former slaves, and to free not just their bodies—but their hearts and minds as well—from the shackles of Egyptian bondage.[4] Moses must still be God's spokesman and must train his people to trust in the Lord. But he must also be a man of action, a leader who acts with firm resolve and inspires the confidence of his people. God tells Moses to end his entreaties, and act!

Later in *Beshalach*, at a place called Rephidim, the Israelites are short of water; they grow rebellious, and Moses fears that they will stone him. God says to Moses (Exodus 17:5), "Pass before the nation, take with you some of the elders of Israel, and take in your hand your staff with which you struck the Nile, and go!" Several commentators, including the *Midrash Tanchuma*[5] and Rashi, say that God is telling Moses to go before the people to demonstrate to Moses that they will not stone him. But Sforno and *Or HaChayyim* both say that God tells Moses to go before the people to demonstrate that he has empathy and is doing his best to address their needs. God is teaching Moses the art of being the leader of a nation, and the importance of showing his concern, thereby reassuring his people.[6]

Forty years later, in Joshua's first year as successor to Moses and leader of his nation, God gives the new leader

---

[4] Josephus says that Moses, prior to discovering his Israelite roots, was an Egyptian general who conquered Ethiopia. (See Flavius Josephus, *The Antiquities of the Jews*, Book 2, Chapter 10.) Therefore, if Josephus is correct, Moses did in fact have leadership experience, but that was many years in the past. Moreover, leadership of a trained, disciplined army is quite different from leadership of a newly-liberated, unruly, and at times rebellious nation of former slaves; and God had to train Moses for his new role.

[5] See Description of Sources.

[6] See "*Beshalach* 2: God in Our Midst" for further discussion of the episode at Rephidim.

similar guidance in the art of leadership. After a resounding victory at Jericho, Joshua suffers his first defeat at the hands of his enemies, and he cries out to God: "Ah, Lord God, why did You lead this nation across the Jordan only to deliver us into the hands of the Amorites, to be destroyed by them?" (Joshua 7:7.) And God answers him: "Get Up! Why do you prostrate yourself?" God wants Joshua to show leadership and act decisively to punish the sin that led to God's allowing the Amorites to rout the Israelite attackers.[7] But, Rashi comments, God's intention in saying "Get up!" is also a lesson in leadership: You, Joshua, stayed back in camp and did not go out with the attacking force. And, Rashi emphasizes, God previously had said to Moses that Joshua will "go out before them and come in before them" (Numbers 27:17–18). Moreover, He had said to Joshua, "You will bring the Israelites to the land that I have vowed to give them, and I will be with you" (Deuteronomy 31:23). In other words, Rashi says, God's words imply: if you go before them, they will prevail; but if you don't go before them, I will not be with you, and they will not prevail.[8]

---

[7] In Joshua Chapter 6, when the Israelites conquer Jericho, Joshua delivers God's command prohibiting anybody from taking any booty. But that order is disobeyed (Joshua 7:2), and God attributes the Israelites' subsequent defeat at the hand of the Amorites to the Israelites' disobeying the order. Note that, even though the text in verse 7:2 says that a certain individual named 'Akhan took from the spoils of Jericho in contravention of God's order, that verse begins by saying that "the Israelites violated the proscription," implying that there was general complicity with 'Akhan's insubordination.

[8] See Rashi on Joshua 7:10. Rashi's point is that the Israelites can prevail only if Joshua will act as a leader by going before his people, because Deuteronomy 31:23 links God's support to Joshua's going before the people. Significantly, however, God's initial mention of Joshua going before the nation occurs in Deuteronomy 3:28, when He first tells Moses to appoint Joshua as his successor: *vehu ya'avor lifnei ha'am hazeh*—"and he will pass before this nation." Those are almost exactly the same words that God uses when telling Moses to pass before his people at Rephidim. And this parallelism supports Sforno's—and contradicts *Midrash Tanchuma's*—interpretation of the purpose of Moses passing before the people at Rephidim.

So we see—here at the shore of the sea, later at Rephidim, and in various other places—how God shows Moses, and later Joshua, how to be a man of action and a leader of the nation, who will instill trust in his people.

Beshalach 2:
God in Our Midst

After seeing God's miracles, how could the Israelites ask whether God was in their midst?

After redemption from bondage in Egypt, the Israelites repeatedly complained to Moses. But in the *sidra* of *Beshalach*,[1] the complaining became especially egregious. Within the last few months, the entire nation had borne witness to the ten plagues with which God punished Egypt, culminating in the Exodus. In the few weeks following their departure from Egypt, they had seen the miraculous splitting of the sea and the defeat of Pharaoh's army; they had experienced the Lord's hand in sweetening the bitter waters of Mara (Exodus 15:23–25); and they had been the recipients of the Manna that fell daily from heaven to sustain them (ibid., 16:13–21). And yet, despite all of these displays of the Lord's compassion for His people, the Israelites continued to complain.

But the people's complaints at Rephidim, the place that Moses later named *Massa Um'riva* (Testing and Disputation), were entirely different, as we can tell from five lines of evidence: first, as I will detail below, the motivation for the complaints in this case was not as urgent as on previous occasions; second—and more importantly—unlike in the previous cases, at *Massa Um'riva* the people questioned, "Is the Lord in our midst or isn't He?" (Exodus 17:7). Third, Moses's level of exasperation at the nation's complaints

---

[1] Exodus 13:17 – 17:16.

was far greater than with any of their previous complaints: "Moses cried out to the Lord, saying, 'What shall I do with this nation? Very soon, they will stone me!'" (ibid., verse 4). Fourth, the attack of the Amalekites, which the Torah relates immediately after (ibid., verse 8), was punishment for the people's questioning whether the Lord was in their midst.[2] And finally, forty years later, in Moses's farewell address as the nation was about to enter the Promised Land, Moses singled out this one rebellious act of all the rebellious acts that they had committed, and admonished his people: "Do not test the Lord your God the way you tested Him at *Massa*" (Deuteronomy 6:16).

Immediately upon their arrival at *Massa Um'riva*, the Israelites did not merely complain but commenced to argue with Moses, demanding water (Exodus 17:1–2). There is no indication that at that time they were yet out of water; only somewhat later (verse 3) does the Torah actually say that they were thirsty, and then they complained to Moses but did not argue with him. Thus, regarding the statement, in Exodus 17:1, that on their arrival "there was no water to drink for the nation," the 19th Century commentary *Haketav Vehakabbalah*[3] remarks that they had enough water if they were to ration, but there was no water there to replenish their reserve; and it was only later, in verse 3, that they actually ran out of water.

Notice that in Exodus 17:2, when the people demand *Tenu lanu mayyim venishteh*—"give us water to drink"—the

---

[2] For the explanation that the attack by Amalek was punishment of the Israelites for questioning whether the Lord was in their midst, see Zohar II:64b and III:129a, and also Rabbeinu Bachyay's commentary on Exodus 17:7.

[3] *Haketav Vehakabbalah* (*i.e.* "The Text and the Tradition") is a prominent commentary on the Torah written by Rabbi Ya'akov Tzvi Mecklenburg (Germany, 1785–1865).

verb "give" is in plural and is addressed to Moses and Aaron (or alternatively, perhaps to Moses and God). But in verse 4, when the people ask "Why did you bring us up out of Egypt to kill us in the desert?" the verb "bring" is in singular, directed at Moses alone. Therefore, Rabbi Moshe Alsheikh comments that the people were saying it was Moses's idea to take the Israelites out of Egypt, and that it was not God who had commanded Moses to do so. In consequence, Moses thought, the people were about to stone him. But Moses was wrong. And so, the *Midrash Tanchuma* says,[4] God told Moses to pass before the people (verse 5) and see whether they would stone him.[5] They did not. Nevertheless, the Israelites **were** testing God, and their reason for doing so was that they doubted His presence in their midst (verse 7). But, after all the miracles that God had so recently performed for them, how could they doubt His presence?

To answer that question, we must consider that the Israelites had just been released from bondage in Egypt, where they had lived for several generations. Egyptian gods had a physical form, and they had earthly dwellings. Therefore, Abravnel points out in his commentary on Exodus 25:8, to these newly-emancipated people, the concept of a non-physical deity whose spirit was among them even though He had no physical dwelling was totally alien: if God was in heaven, then He was far distant, and, in their conception, He could not be also in their midst.

---

[4] See *Midrash Tanchuma, Beshalach* §22.

[5] Sforno and *Or HaChayyim* give an alternative interpretation of God's command that Moses pass before the people (Exodus 17:5). In their view, God told Moses to do so in order to show his concern and to show that he was doing all he could to satisfy their need for water. See "*Beshalach* 1: The Splitting of the Sea."

Therefore, Abravnel says, to dispel that false notion, God soon thereafter commanded Moses to build a Tabernacle:[6] "And they shall make Me a Tabernacle, and I shall dwell in their midst" (Exodus 25:8). Thus, the Tabernacle became the palpable evidence of God's providence, and His presence in the midst of the nation of Israel.

---

[6] It should be noted that there is controversy regarding whether God ordered the building of the Tabernacle in response to the sin of the Golden Calf (Rashi's opinion), or whether He had already ordained the Tabernacle prior to that sin (Ramban's opinion, and see also Zohar III:30b). In either case, Abravnel's opinion regarding God's reason for ordering the building of the Tabernacle is still valid: in the latter case, as the only reason for the Tabernacle; and in the former case, as an additional reason.

Yitro[1] *1:*
The Voice Out of the Darkness

What was the nature of Moses's speech impediment,
and when was it cured?

The Torah tells us that when God first spoke to Moses in the
desert and commanded him to return to Egypt and deliver
God's message to the enslaved Israelites, Moses responded,
"I am not a man of words ... for I am heavy of mouth
and heavy of tongue" (Exodus 4:10). And later, when God
sent him to speak to Pharaoh, Moses objected, again citing
his speech impediment (ibid., 6:12). Later prophets also
claimed to be unable to deliver God's message: Isaiah
claimed that he was of impure lips (see Isaiah 6:5), and
Jeremiah said he was too young (see Jeremiah 1:6). But
Moses apparently had some sort of speech impediment,
the nature of which the Torah never clarifies. Various
commentators have speculated that perhaps he could not
enunciate certain letters; or perhaps he had a stutter or
a stammer. Perhaps he was born with the speech defect,
or perhaps he burned his tongue during infancy; or
perhaps he had no physical impediment but a fear of
public speaking. We will never know for certain.

But, while the Torah highlights Moses's speech defect,
and we see repeatedly that Moses's brother Aaron served
as his mouthpiece when he confronted Pharaoh, nowhere
does the Torah tell us how or when Moses was cured of
his speech problem. In fact, there is not even any mention

---

[1]   Exodus 18:1 – 20:23.

that he was cured. And yet, through the forty years in the desert, Moses seems to have had no trouble speaking. He apparently no longer needed Aaron to speak for him, and often he was able to speak forcefully and eloquently, even in times of great stress. Therefore we may ask, when and how was Moses cured of his speech defect?

The Zohar considers this question and concludes that Moses was cured of his speech impediment when God spoke to the people of Israel at Mount Sinai; and Moses's cure was intimately connected with how God related to His nation, the nation of Israel, as I will now discuss.

Two centuries earlier, when Jacob hesitated to go to Egypt, God said to him, "Do not fear to go down to Egypt ... I will go down with you to Egypt, and I will bring you back as well ..." (Genesis 46:3–4). The *Shekhina*—God's presence in our midst—went with Jacob to Egypt and was always present among the Israelites during their Egyptian exile. But during the long years of bondage, the *Shekhina* remained completely silent. The silence was only broken when, after many years of slavery, God revealed himself to Moses in the burning bush and sent Moses back to Egypt to be His voice. Moses was the transmitter of the Voice of the divine will, but the Voice was still muted, and Aaron spoke for Moses. The *Shekhina*, though ever-present, chose to remain concealed among us yet awhile longer; and therefore there was no reason yet for Moses's speech impediment to be cured. But when Israel arose from bondage, left Egypt, and stood before the Lord at Mount Sinai, the time had come to break the silence. We were now free in body, and it was time to begin the process of freeing us from the slave mentality.[2] At Sinai, all of Israel

---

[2]   For a continuation of this theme, see "*Yitro* 2: The Ten Commandments."

heard the voice of the *Shekhina* speaking to them. The people's bond with God was reaffirmed, and the time had come to cure the impediment that had prevented Moses from wielding his voice to fully transmit the words of God to the fledgling nation.[3] He was now *Moshe Rabbeinu*, Moses our teacher, who would be both our spiritual and secular leader through the forty difficult, formative years in the desert.

---

[3] For the Zohar's discussion of Moses's speech impediment being cured when God revealed Himself at Mount Sinai, see Zohar II:25b. My interpretation above is loosely based on that of the Zohar.

Yitro[1] 2:
The Ten Commandments

What sets the first two statements
of the Decalogue apart from the other eight?

After generations of the Israelites' oppression and bondage
in the land of Egypt, Moses declares to the Israelite slaves
that God has heard the cries of His people, has sent
Moses to redeem them from slavery, and will bring them
to their own land, where they will live in freedom. After
hearing such news, we might have expected the people to
be overjoyed and to sing and dance in the streets. But
instead, the Torah tells us that when Moses delivered God's
message, "they didn't listen to Moses, out of lack of spirit,
and hard labor" (Exodus 6:9). In other words, their many
decades of slavery had so crushed their spirit that even the
thought of freedom was far beyond their comprehension.

But the Egyptians had done more than only break the
spirit and the desire for freedom of the Israelite slaves:
Egyptian culture had contaminated their views and attitudes,
so that many of the Israelites also had adopted the social
mores and the pagan religious practices of the Egyptians.[2]

---

[1] Exodus 18:1 – 20:23.

[2] The fact that the Torah (in Leviticus 18:2) warns not to follow the practices
of Egypt, a land from which the Israelites had already departed, suggests
that many Israelites had adopted Egyptian customs and mores; and in
Leviticus 17:7, God forbids sacrificing to the demons after which they had
been straying. Moreover, Joshua, in his final speech, tells his people to worship
God wholeheartedly, "and remove the gods that your forefathers worshipped
across the river and in Egypt" (Joshua 24:14). And Ezekiel recalls that God
told the Israelites not to be contaminated with the Egyptian idols, but they
did not discard or abandon those idols (Ezekiel 20:7–8). Also, see Zohar
II:170a–b regarding idolatrous and immoral practices among the Israelites.

Therefore, in preparation for giving the Israelites a new set of principles and practices, God first had to begin by rooting out the influence of Egyptian customs and the slave mentality that prevailed among His newly emancipated nation. Various commentators have pointed out that the first five statements of the Decalogue[3] comprise commandments between man and God, whereas the latter five are laws between man and man; but the first two statements of the Decalogue—which, all commentators agree, the people heard directly from God—have a special role. Indeed, the entire nation heard the voice of God speaking to them when they stood at Mount Sinai, as it says: "You yourselves saw that from the Heavens I spoke with you" (Exodus 20: 19).[4] But the experience was overwhelming. Fear overcame them, and they asked Moses to convey God's words to them (Exodus 20:17).[5]

It was important that they hear the voice of God speak at least the beginning of the Decalogue, "in order that the nation will hear when I speak to you, and they will have faith in you forever" (Exodus 19:9). In other words, the entire nation had to experience at least a taste of Moses's prophecy, so that they will have faith that the laws Moses would later transmit to them in God's name were indeed from God.

---

[3] The Ten Commandments are often referred to as "The Decalogue," which is a more accurate appellation. The "Ten Commandments" are called in Hebrew *Aseret Hadibrot*—"The Ten Statements." They are actually ten *dibrot* (statements), not ten *mitzvot* (commandments), and they consist of fourteen *mitzvot* (or thirteen according to some commentators).

[4] See also Exodus 20:1, and Deuteronomy 4:12 & 5:19.

[5] For the opinion that the entire nation heard only the first two statements of the Decalogue directly from God, see Babylonian Talmud, Tractate *Makkot* 23b–24a, *Shir HaShirim Rabba* 1:13 (on the word *yishakeini*), and Maimonides's *The Guide for the Perplexed* II:33. However, Ramban and Rabbeinu Bachyay maintain that all the people heard not only the first two statements but the entire Decalogue directly from God.

The Decalogue begins with the statement, "I am the Lord your God, Who took you out of the land of Egypt, out of the house of bondage" (Exodus 20:2).[6] The opening declaration—"I am the Lord your God ..."—taken together with the second statement—"You shall have no other gods beside Me" (ibid., verse 3)—was meant to remove the Israelites from the pagan mindset. And the latter portion of the opening declaration—"... Who took you ... out of the house of bondage" (verse 2) was meant to emphasize that they were now free people, and to liberate them from their slave mentality.

After generations of enslavement, the Israelites had ceased to think of themselves as individuals. Despair, lack of self-esteem, and hopelessness had set in. But significantly the Decalogue was addressed not to the nation as a whole, but to each person individually: "I am the Lord your God, Who took **YOU** [**singular**] out of the land of Egypt, out of the house of bondage." It was God, King of Universe, Who was speaking to them! And He was addressing His words to each of them individually! This was the first step in liberating the people's minds from bondage. And it was the first step in leading them to take responsibility for their own actions. It was only after liberating their

---

[6] Most Jewish commentators regard the first verse of the Decalogue (Exodus 20:2) to be a *mitzvah* (commandment), even though it is not phrased in the form of a command. Thus, Maimonides lists belief in God as the first and most fundamental of all the *mitzvot* (see his *Sefer HaMitzvot, mitzvah* 1), citing this verse as the source of that *mitzvah*. Ramban agrees that the first statement of the Decalogue is a *mitzvah* (see his commentary on Exodus 20:2). However, Abravnel regards that first statement as a preamble and not a *mitzvah*. Thus, in Abravnel's view, the ten statements of the Decalogue contain thirteen *mitzvot* (commandments), and not the fourteen that other Jewish commentators count. Christian commentaries generally consider Exodus 20:2 as a preamble and count verse 3 as the first Commandment of the Decalogue.

minds from the tyranny of Egyptian culture and Egyptian bondage that they would be prepared to accept the other laws that God was about to give them.

The first two statements of the Decalogue served to reorient the people's mindset, distancing them from the culture of Egypt and extirpating the slave mentality that still haunted the newly-emancipated nation.

Mishpatim[1]:
Double Jeopardy

What does the Jewish law have to say about double jeopardy?

The Fifth Amendment of the Constitution of the United States forbids trying a person again for the same crime after he has already been acquitted (or convicted), a situation known as "double jeopardy." This constitutional guarantee derives from English common law. A similar provision exists also in Jewish law,[2] a provision that the Talmud derives from a verse in the Torah, in the portion of *Mishpatim*.[3]

The Torah says, "Keep distant from falsehood; do not execute the blameless or the innocent, for I will not acquit the wicked" (Exodus 23:7). Regarding this verse, the Talmud comments: after a person is convicted, if someone brings exonerating evidence, how do we know that the case must be re-tried? Because it says, "Do not execute the blameless." And how do we know that if a person is found innocent, but subsequently someone brings evidence of guilt, we do not re-try the case? Because the Torah says, "Do not execute ... the innocent" (ibid.)—that is, someone whom the court has declared innocent.[4]

---

[1] Exodus 21:1 – 24:18.
[2] See Moses Maimonides, *Mishneh Torah, Hilkhot Sanhedrin* 10:9.
[3] Babylonian Talmud, *Sanhedrin* 33b.
[4] It is assumed that the Torah does not insert unnecessary phrasing, and therefore "the innocent" is not identical to "the blameless." This leads to the interpretation that "the blameless" refers to one who is truly blameless, whereas "the innocent" refers to one whom the court has declared innocent.

But, you may object, in the latter case we are letting a guilty person go free. Isn't that a miscarriage of justice? In answer to this objection, Rashi, in his commentary on the Torah, points to the conclusion of the above verse: "for I will not acquit the wicked." Although the court has acquitted the culprit, God does not acquit him, and God will execute the judgement that he deserves.[5]

---

[5] Rashi on Exodus 23:7.

Teruma:
The Tabernacle

Why did God command the building of a Tabernacle?

In the *sidra* of *Teruma*,[1] God commands Moses to build a Tabernacle: *Ve'asu li mikdash, veshakhanti betokham*—"And they shall make Me a sanctuary, and I will dwell among them" (Exodus 25:8). But why would God want the Israelites to make Him a sanctuary in which to dwell? What could be the purpose of making a physical structure in which God would dwell? As the prophet Jeremiah says, "Indeed, I fill both Heaven and Earth, says the Lord" (Jeremiah 23:24). Moreover, as King Solomon said when he built the Temple in Jerusalem, "Even the heavens and the heavens of the heavens cannot contain You" (1 Kings 8:27). So what could be the purpose of building a physical structure for the Lord?

In order to give an answer, first we must consider the chronology underlying God's command. Rashi, following his general principle that the Torah is not written in chronological order, says that God's command to construct the Tabernacle was actually given after the sin of the Golden Calf,[2] and thus the Tabernacle was an expiation of that sin and a sign of God's forgiveness. But there is no obvious reason why the Torah would present the two events out of sequence. Moreover, Ramban disputes Rashi's underlying premise that the Torah is not written chronologically. As Ramban says elsewhere, "In my opinion, the entire Torah

---

[1]   Exodus 25:1 – 27:19.
[2]   See Rashi on Exodus 31:18.

is in chronological order," except where explicitly stated otherwise.[3] Thus, assuming the Torah's account is indeed in chronological order, then the command to construct the Tabernacle comes at an earlier time—*i.e.*, soon after God's revelation to the entire nation on Mount Sinai, while the Israelites were still camped at the foot of the mountain. In that case, we cannot say that the Tabernacle was an atonement for the sin of the Golden Calf, and we must look elsewhere for the motivation for constructing that sanctuary.

In the *sidra* of *Beshalach*, the Israelites complained to Moses, saying, "Is the Lord in our midst or isn't He?" (Exodus 17:7). As discussed in my commentary on *Beshalach*,[4] of all the many complaints with which the people harassed Moses, this one was the most egregious—so much so, that Moses singled it out to admonish his nation during his farewell address (Deuteronomy 6:16). In fact, the entire nation of Israel had witnessed with their own eyes God's miracles in Egypt and at the splitting of the sea; but in the absence of a physical sanctuary, the people questioned whether God's presence was still among them. As I also discussed in *Beshalach*, Abravnel, in his commentary on Exodus 25:8, says that the concept of a non-physical deity whose spirit was among them even though He had no physical dwelling was totally alien to these people who had lived all their lives in Egypt, where each god had his own temple that housed both his image and his spirit. Therefore, Abravnel says, God commanded Moses to build a sanctuary that would be a palpable evidence of God's presence in the midst of the nation.

---

[3] See Ramban's commentary on Leviticus 16:1.
[4] See "*Beshalach* 2: God in Our Midst."

But, in Ramban's view,[5] the Tabernacle was not built only as a concession to dispel a false notion about God's presence as Abravnel explains it. According to Ramban, God had intended the building of a sanctuary "from the beginning." God's speaking the Ten Commandments at Mount Sinai constituted a covenant with the nation of Israel; and, Ramban says, God specified the conditions of the covenant: "And now, if you listen to my voice and keep my covenant, then you will be for Me a treasure among all the nations, ... and you will be for Me a kingdom of priests and a holy nation" (Exodus 19:5–6). Keeping that covenant would make the Israelites worthy to have God's presence manifest among them just as it was at Sinai. Thus, the Tabernacle would enable the Israelites to continue feeling God's presence among them as they traveled through the desert just as they had felt it at Mount Sinai.

Interestingly, Cassuto resolves the disagreement between Rashi's view (see above) that God commanded the building of the Tabernacle as an expiation of the sin of the Golden Calf and Ramban's view that God's command to build the Tabernacle preceded that sin.[6] According to Cassuto, God commanded the construction of the Tabernacle, which symbolized God's presence among the people, immediately after establishing the covenant with Israel by speaking the Ten Commandments at Mount Sinai. But the Israelites then dissolved the covenant when they worshipped the Golden Calf; and for that reason, when Moses descended the mountain with the two tablets upon which those Commandments were inscribed, he threw the tablets that

---

[5] For Ramban's view of the reason for God's command to construct the Tabernacle, see his commentary on the first verse of *Teruma* (Exodus 25:1).

[6] See Umberto Cassuto's commentary on Exodus, in the section on "The Making of the Calf," in the *sidra* of *Ki Tissa*.

bore witness to the covenant, and shattered them at the foot of the mountain. Only after God forgave the people was the covenant reinstated, the Ten Commandments were re-inscribed on a new set of tablets, and permission was given to proceed with the erection of the Tabernacle.

Sefer HaChinukh[7] gives an additional explanation of the reason for the Tabernacle. It says that God does not need a house in which to reside, because even all the heavens cannot contain him; nor does He need it for His honor. Rather, He wanted people to build Him a house of worship for the betterment of their persons. A person is purified by his actions: performing acts of devotion to God help to purify a person's thoughts and his heart.[8]

In summary, the building of the Tabernacle was ordained for our sake and not for God's. It was a concession to human nature, which is rooted in the physical world.[9]

---

[7] *Sefer HaChinukh* is a book about the 613 *mitzvot* of the Torah, published anonymously in the 13th Century. See also Description of Sources.

[8] See *Sefer HaChinukh*, *mitzvah* #95.

[9] See also "*Vayak'hel*: The Sanctity of Time Over Space."

Tetzaveh:
Moses is Singled Out

What did God see in Moses that was so special?

The portion of *Tetzaveh*[1] begins with three commands that
God gives to Moses: 1) You shall command the people of
Israel to bring you pure olive oil to light the candelabra
in the Tabernacle (Exodus 27:20–21). 2) You shall appoint
your brother Aaron and his sons to be priests for Me
(ibid., 28:1). 3) You shall speak to each skilled artisan
whom God has filled with the spirit of wisdom, and have
them make priestly garments for Aaron and his sons, for
glory and for splendor (ibid., verses 2–3). Each of these
three commands is phrased differently from the previous
commands that God gave Moses regarding the construction
of the Tabernacle, and we will now discuss the significance
of the phrasing and what it tells us about the common
thread that runs through the three commands.

Each of these first three commands in *Tetzaveh* starts
with the apparently superfluous word *Ve'atta*—"And you."[2]

---

[1] Exodus 27:20 – 30:10.

[2] The commands that God gave Moses regarding the construction of
the Tabernacle begin with the word *Ve'asita*—"And you shall make"—as in
Exodus 27:1, 2, 3, 4, and 9, and again in 28:2. Unlike in English, the
pronoun (you) is incorporated in the grammatical form of the word *ve'asita*.
But the three commands at the beginning of the *sidra* of *Tetzaveh* start with
the word *Ve'atta*—"And you," which appears to be superfluous. Thus, in
Exodus 27:20, instead of *Ve'atta tetzaveh* ("And you shall command"), God
could have used the imperative verb *Tzav* ("Command"), as in Leviticus 6:2.
Similarly, in Exodus 28:1, *Ve'atta hakrev* ("And you, bring close"), the word
hakrev is already an imperative, and *Ve'atta* could have been omitted. And
in the third command, *Ve'atta tedabber* ("And you shall speak") could have
been phrased as the imperative *Dabber* ("Speak"), or as *Vedibbarta* ("And you
shall speak"), without the additional explicit use of the pronoun *atta* (you).

108

Ramban and Sforno both comment that the significance of this additional word is that these three acts were to be performed by or directly supervised by Moses. In contrast, other acts such as the construction of the Tabernacle itself, of the vessels to be used, and of the altar to be placed in the Tabernacle, were all delegated to the artisans and their assistants; and Moses oversaw those activities only indirectly. So, we may ask, why did God want Moses to have hands-on involvement in these three matters?

As I discussed in my commentary on *Teruma*, the building of the Tabernacle was either a concession to the people in response to their doubting whether God's spirit was in their midst (according to Abravnel), or an atonement for the sin of the Golden Calf (according to Rashi). But, just as God's creation of the universe began with the creation of light, the lighting of the candelabra in the Tabernacle, using exceptionally pure olive oil, symbolizes our link to God, the source of all creation. The *kohanim*—the priests—represent the people of Israel before God, and they transmit and bestow God's blessings upon His people. The appointment of the *kohanim* flows directly from God, Who chose them to minister to the people. Therefore, God wanted Moses himself to oversee these matters directly.

But still, we may ask, why must it be Moses? Doesn't God later tell Moses that He will fill Bezalel "with God's spirit, with wisdom, with understanding, and with knowledge" (ibid., 31:2–5)? Why, then, shouldn't Bezalel be in charge of these three matters just as he is to supervise all the other aspects involved in building the Tabernacle and fashioning its vessels?

I believe the answer lies in the enigmatic verse that concludes God's instructions to Moses regarding Aaron and his sons: "And you shall do for Aaron and his sons

thus, according to all that I have commanded you"—
Ve'asita leAharon ul'vanav kakha, kekhol asher tziviti otakha
(Exodus 29:35). That last word, *otakha*, is not found
anywhere else in the Torah; and, as Ibn Ezra notes, it
is a hybrid word composed of *otakh*—a normal word for
"you" when addressing a woman, or of addressing a man
when "you" is the last word of a clause—combined with
the word *otkha*—the usual word for "you" when addressing
a man. Why employ this unusual hybrid word *otakha*? It
appears that the word is used primarily for the rhyme:
kakha rhymes with *otakha*. But this is not poetry, so what
is the purpose of a rhyme here? Why not simply use the
word *otakh*, which would be the usual form of that word in
the Torah at the end of a clause?

I believe that the purpose of the rhyme is to emphasize
the conclusion of the instructions regarding the *kohanim*,
and to highlight the importance of this task with which
Moses is charged. Moreover, Ibn Ezra provides an
additional clue. Instead of just telling us that the word
otakha is compounded from *otakh* and *otkha*, Ibn Ezra
quotes an example of a phrase in which God uses the
usual word *otkha*: *ki **otkha** ra'iti*—"because you I have
seen." It may seem strange that Ibn Ezra sees fit to give
an example of the usual form of address (*otkha*), which is
used innumerable times in the Torah. Therefore we must
consider the reason why Ibn Ezra selected that particular
example.[3] The phrase that Ibn Ezra quotes is taken from

---

[3] Ibn Ezra's commentary often relies on grammar and syntax of the
text in arriving at his interpretations. Also, he was fond of riddles; and
sometimes, as is the case in the verse discussed above (Exodus 29:35), his
commentary does not state his full intended interpretation but presents
the discerning reader with a puzzle to be solved. See also Description of
Sources.

the words that God addresses to Noah after He resolves to bring a flood to annihilate all of humankind; and He tells Noah that only he and his immediate family will be saved, because it is only Noah whom God has seen to be righteous in his generation. (See Genesis 7:1.) I think that Ibn Ezra selected specifically that verse as his example of the use of the very common word *otkha* in order to tell us that just as Noah was the only righteous person who was worthy of being saved when God destroyed the world, so now Moses is the only one whom God would save when He proposes to wipe out all the Israelites after the sin of the Golden Calf (in the next *sidra*), and to re-create the nation starting from Moses (see Exodus 32:10). It is Moses's unique righteousness and elevation of spirit that motivated God to single out Moses for execution of these three most sublime tasks.

Ki Tissa:
The Sin of the Golden Calf

Does God care what people think of Him?

The portion of *Ki Tissa*[1] tells of the great sin that the Israelites committed shortly after witnessing God's presence and hearing the words of the Ten Commandments spoken at Mount Sinai. Soon after the awesome event at Mount Sinai, God commands Moses to ascend the mountain, where, over the span of forty days and forty nights, He will teach Moses the Torah and will present Moses with the stone tablets upon which God Himself will inscribe the text of the Ten Commandments (ibid., 24:12–13 and 18).

But while Moses is on the mountain receiving the Torah, the Israelites grow anxious at his long absence and demand the construction of an idol, the Golden Calf. God informs Moses of his nation's grievous sin (ibid., 32:7–8) and says, "Leave me to rage against them, and I will destroy them; and I will make you a great nation" (ibid., verse 10). God is here testing Moses, asking his permission as it were, to see how Moses will answer. And Moses passes the test brilliantly.

Instead of merely pleading for God's mercy and forgiveness for his people, as we might have expected Moses to do, his immediate response is to ask, "Why, Lord, should You rage against Your nation that You took out of the land of Egypt with great might and with a strong hand? Why should Egypt say, 'With evil intent He took

---

[1]   Exodus 30:11 – 34:35.

them out, to kill them in the mountains and to wipe them off the face of the earth?'" (ibid., verses 11 and 12.)

At first blush, this seems to be a strange argument to make, and various questions may be raised. But I will focus specifically on two issues. First, in asking God why He is raging against His nation for turning away from Him and worshiping an idol, isn't Moses downplaying the magnitude of the grave sin of idolatry, as he appears to be doing? And second, Moses's reference to what the Egyptians will say if God were to annihilate the Israelites seems to make no sense: why should it matter so much to God what people think of His intentions, that He would change His course of action on that account?

In answer to the first question, Abravnel, quoting and expanding upon the *Midrash Rabba*, remarks that after living for so many years in a land where idolatry was prevalent, God knew it was natural for the Israelites to turn to idols. Why, then, should God be so furious when they revert to the practices to which they are accustomed? Moses does not downplay the sin of the Golden Calf; instead, he cites human nature and emphasizes that breaking the force of ingrained practices is a difficult and gradual process.

Now we come to the second question, and we can affirm that God indeed does care what people think of Him. We do not know exactly for what purpose God created the human race, but we know He must have had a purpose in mind. And the nation of Israel was to be "a kingdom of priests, and a holy nation" (Exodus 19:6), to bring the awareness of the Lord to the nations of the world, and thus to bring to fruition God's purpose in His creation of mankind. But if, after demonstrating His awesome power when He brought His people out of slavery in Egypt, God were now to annihilate them in the mountains, such an act would diminish His repute among the nations and would therefore severely set back His intended purpose for humankind.

Thus, contrary to what we might have expected, the argument that Moses gives in defense of the Israelites is exactly the correct defense. It is the argument that serves to enhance the Lord's standing among the nations and will enhance the spread of holiness throughout the world.

Finally, to drive home these arguments against killing off the Israelites, Moses rejects God's offer of starting over—and creating a new nation from Moses—by reminding God of the promises that He made to the patriarchs Abraham, Isaac, and Jacob when He swore to them that He would make a great nation from them. Thus, Moses, through his improbable three-pronged argument, shows why annihilating the Israelites and starting over would be wrong for God to do, not merely from a sense of mercy but from the point of view of justice and of achieving God's purpose of spreading holiness throughout the world. And indeed, Moses did succeed in averting the decree pronounced against his nation (Exodus 32:14).

Vayak'hel:
The Sanctity of Time Over Space

Why didn't the construction of the Tabernacle supersede the laws of the Sabbath?

On the tenth day of the month of *Tishrei*, Moses descended Mount Sinai with the second set of tablets. It was *Yom Kippur*, and God had forgiven His people for the sin of the Golden Calf. Now, as the Torah portion of *Vayak'hel*[1] begins—perhaps on the day following *Yom Kippur*[2]—Moses assembles the entire nation for the purpose of instructing them about the building of the Tabernacle, the *Mishkan*: "These are the words that God has commanded you to perform" (Exodus 35:1). The consensus of commentaries is that the "words" to which Moses here refers are the instructions for building the *Mishkan*. But in the very next verse, the Torah follows up with a seemingly unrelated statement: "Six days shall work be done"; but the seventh day, *Shabbat* (Sabbath), is holy, a day of rest during which work must not be done. In fact, the law regarding the Sabbath was already given twice previously: in the Ten Commandments (Exodus 20:8–11), and in Exodus 31:12–18. So why is it repeated here, apparently as a *non sequitur*?

Rashi and Ramban both comment that the prohibition of work on the seventh day is placed here in order to

---

[1] Exodus 35:1 – 38:21.

[2] Regarding the timing of the beginning of *Vayak'hel*, see Rashi and Ramban on Exodus 35:1. Rashi says flatly that it was on the day after *Yom Kippur*. Ramban, however, apparently is not so certain: he says only that "it is conceivable" that this was the day following Moses's descent from the mountain (which occurred on Yom Kippur).

dispel the notion that work on construction of the *Mishkan* would supersede *Shabbat*;[3] but they do not explain why we might have thought that it would. Abravnel answers that because the *Mishkan* testifies to God's presence among His people, we might have thought that the work of building the *Mishkan* would supersede all else, and would especially supersede resting on the seventh day. Moreover, Abravnel says, perfection is brought about by action and not by refraining from action, and action bears witness to faith more than does refraining from action. Therefore, he says, the Torah here reiterates the prohibition of work on the seventh day, to affirm that construction of the *Mishkan* does not set aside the prohibition of work on *Shabbat*.[4]

But, we may ask, why indeed shouldn't construction of the *Mishkan*—the physical representation of God's presence among us—take priority over resting on the seventh day of the week? What is the underlying philosophical reason that the Torah decrees the priority of the *Shabbat*? Abraham Heschel answers that from the perspective of the Torah, time trumps space;[5] and, as Heschel points out, the first

---

[3] Rashi opines that the word *akh* (but) in Exodus 31:13—"**But** my Sabbaths you shall keep"—is there to forbid work on the Sabbath for constructing the Tabernacle. Ramban, on the other hand, maintains that the word *akh* in that verse implies no such thing, and that the prohibition of work on the Sabbath for construction of the Tabernacle can be learned only from the beginning of *Vayak'hel* ("Six days shall work be done ... " in Exodus 35:2) as discussed above.

[4] Abravnel's statement that the prohibition of work on the seventh day is reiterated here because we might have thought that work on the *Mishkan* supersedes *Shabbat* is given in his commentary on Exodus 35:2. But the reason we might have thought in the first place that it would supersede *Shabbat* is given in his commentary on Exodus 31:12.

[5] Abraham Joshua Heschel (1907-1972) was a rabbi, theologian, and philosopher. He was the descendant of distinguished Chasidic rabbinic dynasties. Also, he was a good friend of my father's; and in my youth, my parents and I often visited him and his family at his home. His ideas presented here are found in the Prologue to his book *The Sabbath*. See also Description of Sources.

reference to holiness in the Torah occurs at the conclusion of creation (in Genesis 2:3). "How extremely significant is the fact that it [holiness] is applied to time: 'God blessed the seventh *day* and made it *holy*.'" [Italics here are Heschel's.] This, Heschel says, is a radical departure from the conceptions of the pagan religions that were prevalent. In other religions, we would have expected that God would first establish a holy place, such as a holy mountain. (For example, the Greeks had Mount Olympus.) But in the Bible, holiness in time takes priority over holiness in physical space.

Although God did ordain the building of the Tabernacle, in which His presence would be manifest, that was done for our sake and not for His.[6] As the *Sefer HaChinukh* says, God does not need a house in which to reside, because even all the heavens cannot contain him (1 Kings 8:27); nor does He need it for His honor. Rather, He wanted people to build Him a house of worship for the betterment of their persons. The *Mishkan*, and later the Temple in Jerusalem, was a concession to human nature, which is rooted in the physical world. But, in keeping with the priority of the holiness of time over that of physical space, the holiness of the seventh day and the prohibition of work on that day superseded the holiness of building the *Mishkan*. Moses anointed and sanctified the *Mishkan* (Exodus 40:9); but it was God Himself who blessed and sanctified the Sabbath day (Genesis 2:3).

---

[6] For a discussion of the purpose of building a physical structure in which God's presence would "dwell," see my commentary on *Teruma* above ("*Teruma*: The Tabernacle").

Pekudei:
The Fulfillment of the Redemption

*Why didn't the book of Exodus end
with the revelation at Mount Sinai?*

The *sidra* of *Pekudei*[1] concludes the book of *Shemot* (Exodus) with the anointing of Moses's brother Aaron as High Priest, the ordination of Aaron's sons as priests (*kohanim*), and the completion of the building of the Tabernacle. Following the completion of the Tabernacle, the divine Presence fills the Tabernacle, fulfilling God's promise in Exodus 29:43 and 29:45, to dwell in the midst of the people of Israel. But, we may ask, why does the book of *Shemot*—the book that tells of the Egyptian exile and the redemption therefrom—end with God's Presence filling the Tabernacle and not with the revelation at Mount Sinai? Isn't God's revelation on Mount Sinai and His speaking of the Ten Commandments to the entire nation the climax of the redemption?

Ramban, in his introduction to the book of Exodus, points out that the book begins with the names of all the Israelites who went down to Egypt, showing that the subject of this book is the Egyptian exile. Moreover, Ramban says that the Israelites' exile was not finished until they returned to the spiritual level of their forefathers. When they left Egypt, he says, "even though they had left the house of bondage, they were still considered as exiles." And even after the revelation at Mount Sinai, they still had not returned to the spiritual level of the Patriarchs. According to Rashi,

---

[1]   Exodus 38:21 – 40:38.

in former times, the divine Presence—the *Shekhina*—was manifest in the tents of the righteous.[2] Indeed, consistent with Rashi's statement, in the Torah we see each of the Patriarchs frequently conversing with God; and the *Midrash Rabba* says that the Patriarchs were the chariot of the Lord, *i.e.* they were the vehicle through which God's presence in the world became manifest.[3] Moreover, when the patriarch Jacob is about to leave the Holy Land to go to Egypt, God reassures Jacob that He will make Jacob into a great nation there, that He will go with Jacob to Egypt, and He will also return with him (see Genesis 46:3–4). The divine Presence, in fact, remained among the Israelites all through their exile in Egypt, but it was concealed for many years. So much so, that even after all the miracles that God had wrought in bringing His people out of Egypt, in splitting the sea and in vanquishing Pharaoh's army, the Israelites still questioned, "Is the Lord in our midst or isn't He?" (Exodus 17:7).

Thus, Ramban says, it was only after God had the Israelites build the Tabernacle and allowed His presence to be manifest among them that they were restored to the spiritual level of their forefathers. Only then could they be fully considered to be redeemed, and therefore the book of Exodus—the book devoted to the Israelites' exile and their redemption—ends with the completion of the Tabernacle and with the divine Presence filling the Tabernacle, signifying the completion of the redemption.

---

[2] Rashi, in his commentary on the Babylonian Talmud (*Shabbat* 55b) says that before the building of the Tabernacle, the divine Presence dwelled in the tents of the righteous. While Rashi's statement was made in a context discussing the patriarch Jacob and his family, it is a general statement pertaining to all righteous people before the building of the Tabernacle. Perhaps Rashi was also thinking of Job as another example. See Job 29:4.
[3] In *Bereshit Rabba* 47:8, Resh Lakish says that the Patriarchs are the chariot (of the Lord).

BOOK III

Vayikra (Leviticus)

Just as the second book of the Torah, the book of Exodus, takes up where the first book leaves off, the book of *Vayikra* takes up where the book of Exodus leaves off. The book of Exodus concludes with the completion of the Tabernacle and God's Presence enveloping it. Now, *Vayikra* opens with God instructing Moses in the laws pertaining to worship in the newly-completed Tabernacle, including the laws regarding burnt offerings and the sacred priestly functions.

But purity and holiness are not only matters for the priests—the *kohanim*. As God said at the time of the giving of the Decalogue, the entire people of Israel was to be a holy nation (Exodus 19:10). Indeed, the theme of holiness is pervasive throughout the book of *Vayikra*, and the laws of holiness affect both the physical and the spiritual life of each individual. We, who were created in God's image, are to emulate God: "Be holy, because I, your God, am holy" (Leviticus 19:2). And through the sanctification of human life, we are better able to approach the divine.

Vayikra[1]:
The Lord Calls to Moses

How did God's call to Moses from within the Tabernacle parallel the revelation at Mount Sinai?

As we have seen in the portion of *Teruma*, God commanded the Israelites to build a Tabernacle, which was to be a place where God's presence would be manifest in the midst of the people (Exodus 25:8). In the final verses of the book of Exodus, the Torah tells us that the construction of the Tabernacle was completed, but Moses could not enter, "because the cloud dwelled upon it, and the Presence of the Lord filled the Tabernacle" (Exodus 40:35). The third book of the Torah, *Vayikra* (the book of Leviticus), now begins where the book of Exodus left off, with the Lord calling to Moses from within the Tabernacle.

Cassuto suggests that the Tabernacle was to be a quasi-Mount Sinai that would accompany the people of Israel in their wanderings through the desert and would serve as a physical sign of God's presence among them. Therefore, Cassuto says, the language describing the Lord's presence in the Tabernacle exactly parallels the revelation on Mount Sinai.[2]

---

[1] Leviticus 1:1 – 5:26.

[2] See Cassuto's commentary on Exodus 40:34. It should be noted also that Ramban, and especially Rabbeinu Bachyay, in their commentaries on that verse, mention the similarities between God's Presence in the Tabernacle and His revelation at Mount Sinai. But Cassuto goes much further in portraying the similarity of the awe-inspiring experience of God's presence in the Tabernacle with the revelation at Mount Sinai. And Cassuto's analysis of the poetic structure of Exodus 40:34 and of the Torah's similar phrasing in regard to Mount Sinai (ibid., 24:15–16) leads him to describe the Tabernacle as a mobile Mount Sinai that would accompany the Israelites in the desert after they left Mount Sinai.

Upon completion of the Tabernacle (also known as the Tent of Meeting), the Torah tells us, "And the cloud covered the Tent of Meeting, and the Presence of the Lord filled the Tabernacle" (Exodus 40:34). Similarly, regarding God's revelation at Mount Sinai, it says, "And the cloud covered the mountain. And the Presence of the Lord dwelled on Mount Sinai" (ibid., 24:15–16). Moreover, just as at Mount Sinai, Moses could not enter the cloud in which the Lord's Presence was manifest until God called to him (Exodus 24:16–18, and see also 19:16 & 20), similarly, when the cloud enveloped the Tabernacle, Moses could not enter until God called to him: *Vayikra el Moshe, vay'dabber YHVH elav me'ohel mo'ed*—"And He called to Moses, and the Lord spoke to him from the Tent of Meeting" (Leviticus 1:1).

But, we may ask, how did God's calling to Moses change Moses's ability to enter the cloud? Did the cloud change in some way to allow Moses to enter; and if so, what was the nature of the change? Rabbeinu Bachyay maintains that the call was not merely a **permission** to enter; but rather, it was a **sign** that it was safe for Moses to enter the Tabernacle. And similarly on Mount Sinai, God's call to Moses was an indication that it was safe for him to ascend the mountain. So, if God's call to Moses was not merely giving permission to enter, then what change had occurred to make it safe for Moses to enter?

Ramban, in his commentary on Exodus 40:34, suggests that the Lord's Presence was contained within the cloud but was distinct from the cloud.[3] And Rabbeinu Bachyay, basing

---

[3] Ramban, like Rabbeinu Bachyay, says that when God called to Moses, he was able to enter the Tabernacle. But Ramban also raises an alternative possibility: that God called to Moses from within the Tabernacle, but Moses remained just outside while God spoke to him. And, Ramban says, this interpretation is consistent with the text, ". . . and the Lord spoke to him from the Tent of Meeting" (Leviticus 1:1). Nevertheless, such an interpretation would not be consistent with the parallelism between the Tabernacle and God's revelation on Mount Sinai (to which both Ramban and Bachyay refer, in their commentaries on Exodus 40:34); and thus, Ramban's

himself on Ramban's interpretation, opines that prior to calling Moses, the Lord's Presence was diffused throughout the Tabernacle, but once the intense manifestation of His Presence no longer enveloped the entire Tabernacle but came to rest between the two cherubim (in the Holy of Holies), it was safe for Moses to enter the cloud, and it was only then that the Lord called to him.[4]

primary interpretation remains that Moses did enter the Tabernacle after God called to him. Rabbeinu Bachyay, on the other hand, would not even consider Ramban's alternative interpretation: he says emphatically that a person standing outside the Tabernacle would hear nothing.

[4] Rashbam, in his commentary on Exodus 40:35, cites two verses to show that God spoke to Moses in the Tabernacle from between the two cherubim (Exodus 25:22 and Numbers 7:89); and he then concludes that only after God concentrated His presence to that location did He call to Moses to enter the cloud.

Tzav[1]:
The Sacrificial Laws

God has no need of animal sacrifices.
Why, then, does the Torah mandate animal sacrifices?

The Torah portions of *Vayikra* and *Tzav* are entirely devoted to the laws pertaining to the burnt offerings that were to be brought in the Tabernacle, and the laws pertaining to the *kohanim*—the priests—who were charged with conducting the service in the Tabernacle. But why, we may ask, would God command us to kill an animal and offer it up to him? Certainly, our reason dictates that God has no need for such an offering! And indeed, Isaiah seems to indicate that God doesn't need our sacrifices (see Isaiah 1:11). Moreover, in the *Haftarah* of *Tzav*, the prophet Jeremiah declares that God did not command us regarding sacrifices when we left Egypt (Jeremiah 7:22). Why, then, does the Torah mandate these sacrifices, and in fact seem to place so much emphasis on them?

To us, in modern times, this question seems very reasonable. In today's world, prayer substitutes for burnt offerings to God,[2] and it is now many centuries since animal sacrifice has ceased to be commonly practiced in the world. But we must understand that to the ancients, animal sacrifice was a way of life, and it was prevalent throughout human history. In the Torah, we see sacrifice of animals in the days of the first men on earth (see Genesis 4:4);

---

[1] Leviticus 6:1 – 8:36.
[2] For a discussion of prayer substituting for burnt offerings, see "*Ekev:* Worship of the Heart."

and again, Noah sacrificed multiple animals as soon as he left the ark after the great flood (ibid., 8:20). We also know from the literature of other nations that animal sacrifices to their gods were the usual form of worship. In fact, human sacrifice was practiced in the worship of the Canaanite god Ba'al, and of the pagan gods of other nations; and the sacrifice of an animal may sometimes have been regarded as a stand-in for a human sacrifice. People wanted to demonstrate their submissiveness and devotion to their deities and thus to gain the favor of their gods. Additionally, in pagan religions the sacrifices were often regarded as an offering of food to the gods. But the Torah strives to distance us from the practices and the mind-set of idolators. So why did God not forbid animal sacrifice and command us to worship Him only through our verbal prayers and through our deeds?

Moses Maimonides[3] addresses this issue in *The Guide for the Perplexed*. In his view,[4] animal sacrifice has no intrinsic value to God; but it is impossible to expect people to go from one extreme to the other and abruptly to discontinue everything to which they have been accustomed. Since animal sacrifice was such an integral part of human practice and such an accepted mode of worship with which the Israelites had been brought up since childhood in Egypt, it would have made no sense to them to institute a form of worship that completely excluded animal sacrifice. And so, God gave us laws of animal sacrifice, but with severe restrictions: only certain animals could be sacrificed for certain purposes, and only in the specified way, and only in one specified place—*i.e.* the Tabernacle, or eventually in the

---

[3] Spain and Egypt, 1138–1204. See also Description of Sources.
[4] See *The Guide for the Perplexed* III:32.

Temple in Jerusalem. Also, Maimonides points out that the ram was worshipped by the Egyptians, that the Chaldeans worshipped demons in the form of goats, and that cows are considered holy in India.[5] Therefore, Maimonides opines, God had us sacrifice those animals specifically, in order to show that we deny the divinity of those animals.[6]

In contrast to Maimonides's opinion in *The Guide for the Perplexed*, Ramban vehemently asserts that, far from being merely a concession to human nature, the sacrifices have intrinsic value, and that God's acceptance of "the fragrant odor" of Noah's sacrifice (Genesis 8:21) is consistent with this view. And, Ramban says, we see that animal sacrifice since earlier times was not only a pagan practice, since Noah sacrificed to God, and at that time there were no idolators in the world. Animal sacrifices were brought in atonement for sins, or as an expression of gratitude to God as Noah did. Ramban points out that the Hebrew

---

[5] See *The Guide for the Perplexed* III:46.

[6] Although Maimonides doesn't say so explicitly, it would follow logically from his discussion in *The Guide for the Perplexed* III:32 (discussed above) that when the Holy Temple in Jerusalem is eventually rebuilt in Messianic times, there will be no animal sacrifices. However, in *Mishneh Torah, Hilkhot Melakhim* 11:1, Maimonides says that in Messianic times the Temple will be rebuilt, and there will again be burnt offerings as there were in olden days. This statement is very perplexing, since it seems to undermine his reasoning in *The Guide*. If animal sacrifices were not commanded for their own value but were merely an accommodation to the mindset of the Israelites of ancient times, then why would God want to return to the practice in Messianic times, long after humanity has advanced beyond that way of thinking? I am not certain how Maimonides would have resolved this contradiction between his two statements.

One further question regarding the opinion of Maimonides in *Mishneh Torah*. There is a *midrash* saying that "all the sacrifices will be abolished, except that the thanksgiving offering will not be abolished." (See *Midrash Tanchuma, Emor* §14, and *Vayikra Rabba* 27:12.) Did Maimonides mean that all the burnt offerings will take place in Messianic times, or only the thanksgiving offering, as mentioned in those two *midrashim*? He does not say.

word *korban* (a burnt offering) is derived from the root *karev*, meaning to bring close; and thus, he says, the burnt offerings that were brought in the Tabernacle, and later in the Holy Temple in Jerusalem, served to bring us closer to the Lord our God.

So here we have two diametrically opposite views of the rationale for animal sacrifice in the Torah. Unfortunately, there is nothing in the text of the Torah, or of the prophetic books of the Bible, that would conclusively prove one or the other of these views. And even those verses that some in modern times have cited as evidence[7] that the prophets were opposed to animal sacrifices, show no such thing. Rather, the prophets condemned the empty sacrifices and prayers that were offered to God while continuing to behave in ways contrary to basic morality. As Isaiah puts it, "Do not continue to bring empty offerings .... Your hands are filled with blood" (Isaiah 1:13 & 15). Instead, Isaiah tells the people to cleanse themselves, set aside their evil ways, and devote themselves to justice (ibid., verses 16–17). And supporting Jeremiah's statement that God made no mention of sacrifices when He took us out of Egypt, Radak points out, the first thing with which God charged us after our final rescue from Egypt (with the splitting of the sea) was not the sacrifice of animals but that we should do what is right and keep His commandments (Exodus 15:26). Furthermore, the Ten Commandments themselves do not mention sacrifices; and, Radak, says, it was only after the Israelites sinned—by worshipping the Golden Calf—that God gave us the laws of sacrifices.[8]

---

[7] Such as Isaiah 1:11, Jeremiah 7:21–22, and Amos 5:22.

[8] For Radak's comments about the laws of sacrifices being given only after the Israelites sinned, and about there being no mention of sacrifices before that, see his commentary on Psalms 40:7 and on Jeremiah 7:22.

In conclusion, then, the reason God gave us the laws of animal sacrifice remains a mystery. Nevertheless, as Maimonides says in his *Mishneh Torah*, "It is appropriate for a person to reflect upon the laws of the holy Torah and to understand their meaning insofar as he is able; but regarding a matter for which he finds no rationale and does not understand the cause, it should not be inconsequential in his eyes," and he should treat such laws with respect. Even laws whose reason we cannot comprehend must be observed, as the Torah commands us: "And you shall keep all My statutes and all My laws, and you shall do them" (Leviticus 20:22).[9] Maimonides then lists several categories of statutes for which we do not understand the reasons; and last among such statutes, he lists the laws of animal sacrifice.

---

[9] For Maimonides's statement regarding observance of statutes whose reasons we don't understand, see *Mishneh Torah, Hilkhot Me'ila* 8:8.

Shemini:
An Alien Fire

What was the sin of Aaron's sons,
and what was the fire from heaven that consumed
them?

In the portion of *Shemini*,[1] Nadav and Avihu, the sons of
Aaron the high priest, "each took his pan, put fire in it,
placed incense upon it, and offered an alien fire before the
Lord, which He had not commanded them" (Leviticus 10:1).
In response, a fire descended from Heaven and consumed
them in punishment for their transgression (ibid., verse 2).
These two verses have perplexed commentators through
the centuries: What was the nature of the alien fire that
Nadav and Avihu brought? What, specifically, was Nadav
and Avihu's sin, and why did that sin merit the death
penalty? And finally, what was the nature of the fire that
consumed them?

A straightforward reading of the text suggests that
Nadav and Avihu should not have put fire in their pans
but instead should have lit the incense by means of a fire
that descended from Heaven,[2] as the previous verse
says: "And there came forth fire from before the Lord,
and consumed upon the altar the sacrifice and the fat"
(ibid., 9:24). Perhaps, then, the sin of Aaron's sons was
a lack of faith that a fire would descend from Heaven.[3]

---

[1] Leviticus 9:1 – 11:47.
[2] This explanation of their sin is Rashbam's opinion, in his commentary
on Leviticus 10:1.
[3] See Rabbeinu Bachyay, citing Raavad.

An alternative explanation is that Nadav and Avihu's sin was that they had entered the Holy-of-Holies, the inner sanctum of the Tabernacle.[4] Consistent with this view is the Torah's later statement that God's telling Moses that Aaron may not enter the Holy-of-Holies at any time of Aaron's choosing came "after the death of the two sons of Aaron, when they came too close to the presence of the Lord, and they died" (ibid. 16:1). However, the Torah in the portion of *Shemini* does not state that Aaron's sons had entered the inner sanctum. The text here mentions only that they brought incense and an alien fire but makes no mention of where the event occurred, suggesting that it was the bringing of alien fire and not the location of the event that was the crux of their offense.

A third explanation of Nadav and Avihu's sin is that they entered the Tabernacle drunk, and the "alien fire" was alcohol.[5] The strongest support for this view is that immediately after relating the episode of Aaron's sons' death, the Torah says: "The Lord spoke to Aaron saying, 'You shall drink no wine or beer, you or your sons with you, when you enter the Tent of Meeting, so that you do not die'" (ibid. 10:8–9). Indeed, the priest must enter the Tabernacle (the Tent of Meeting) only after separating his mind from the mundane and enveloping himself in a spirit of holiness. As the next verse stresses (ibid., verse 10), there must be a firm separation between the holy and the profane. Any intoxicant disrupts a person's ability to make that firm separation.

---

[4] Ibn Ezra says this in his commentary on Leviticus 16:1, and Rashi implies as much in his commentary on 16:2. (However, in Leviticus 10:1, Ibn Ezra also says that Aaron's sons failed to wait for the fire to descend.)

[5] The opinion that Nadav and Avihu's sin was entering the Tabernacle while intoxicated is the opinion of Rabbi Ishmael in *Midrash Rabba*, and Rashi cites that opinion in Rabbi Ishmael's name.

Nadav and Avihu sinned by bringing an alien fire, and God punished them with a fire that descended "from before the Lord." But the nature of this fire was very different from that which Aaron's sons brought into the Tabernacle. As Rabbeinu Bachyay points out, the Torah states that the heavenly fire "consumed them, and they died"; but their cousins pulled their bodies out of the Tabernacle by their garments (ibid., verse 5), showing that the fire had not consumed the garments. Since the garments were made of linen (see Leviticus 6:3), any fire that consumed the bodies should have completely consumed the garments. Rabbeinu Bachyay therefore concludes that it was some kind of supernatural fire that separated their souls from their bodies but left their bodies intact.[6]

These, then, are the main interpretations of the mysterious episode of Nadav and Avihu's alien fire; and, after all has been said, their sin is still shrouded in mystery. We will, however, re-visit the issue of the priest's state of mind on entering the Tabernacle when we consider the portion of *Acharei Mot.*

---

[6] Rabbeinu Bachyay provides a comprehensive discussion of the various interpretations of the reason for Nadav and Avihu's punishment. See his commentary on Leviticus 10:2 and on Leviticus 9:24.

Parenthetically, although Rabbeinu Bachyay does not mention this, it is worth noting that we have previously seen in the Torah a supernatural fire that does not consume the physical object that we might have expected it to consume. Just as here the "fire" did not consume either the garments or the bodies of Aaron's sons, similarly in Exodus 3:2, Moses sees a burning bush, but the "fire" does not consume the bush. Rabbeinu Bachyay opines (in Exodus 3:1) that the fire of the burning bush was indeed a supernatural fire (although he does not compare it to the fire that came down from heaven to punish Aaron's sons); but perhaps these two supernatural fires were indeed similar in nature.

Tazri'a-Metzora[1]:
Leprosy

What is the mysterious affliction described in the sidrot Tazri'a and Metzora? Is it leprosy?

During the Biblical period, leprosy was a widespread, incurable, and dreaded disease; and it was particularly prevalent in Egypt.[2] The Hebrew word *tzara'at* has always referred to leprosy, and *metzora* is a person who has leprosy. The affliction called *tzara'at* as described in the Torah (see Leviticus chapters 13 and 14) bears some similarity to leprosy as we know it today; but in other ways, *tzara'at* in the Torah is quite different from leprosy. The disease that we know as leprosy is characterized by areas of skin depigmentation, often with red borders, as well as loss of sensation in the affected areas, eventual loss of fingers and toes, and mutilation of the nose.[3] The skin manifestations are described at length in the Torah; but the Torah also describes *tzara'at* of a person's house and clothing, and those features bear no resemblance to leprosy as we know it. So, we may ask, what is the *tzara'at* that is described in the Torah portions of *Tazri'a* and

---

[1] This commentary covers the two *sidrot*, *Tazri'a* (Leviticus 12:1 – 13:59) and *Metzora* (Leviticus 14:1 – 15:33), since both of these *sidrot* deal with the affliction known as *tzara'at*.

[2] See Umberto Cassuto, *A Commentary on the Book of Exodus*, on Exodus 4:7.

[3] Although in the *sidrot* of *Tazri'a* and *Metzora* the Torah does not mention the mutilation that lepers suffer, the Torah does allude to mutilation of the flesh in Numbers 12:12, in reference to Miriam's being stricken with *tzara'at*. The absence of any mention of mutilation in Leviticus chapters 13 and 14 is understandable, since here the issue is identifying the early stages of the affliction.

Metzora?   Is it leprosy (as the word is usually translated), or is it something else?

The Talmud[4] tells us that God may give *tzara'at* as a punishment for evil speech against another person.[5] When Miriam is stricken with *tzara'at* (Numbers 12:10), we learn that her affliction came as punishment for speaking badly about her brother Moses (see Numbers 12:1–2 and 8–10).   And when Moses asks God to give him a sign to prove to the Israelites that it was really God Who has sent him, God gives him two signs.   For the second one of those signs, Moses is told to put his hand into his bosom, and his hand becomes stricken with *tzara'at*—"as white as snow" (Exodus 4:6).   Rashi comments that this was a hint that Moses had spoken badly about the Israelites.

Maimonides, in his *Mishneh Torah*, says that the word *tzara'at* in the Torah refers to several different entities and that *tzara'at* of clothing and houses is different from *tzara'at* of the skin.   He doesn't commit himself regarding whether the skin manifestations are the disease known as leprosy, but he does say that the affliction of clothing and of houses that the Torah calls by the homonymous term *tzara'at* is not the same entity as the skin disease and is not a natural phenomenon; rather, it is a sign, and a miracle that was given to Israel as a warning regarding evil speech. *Tzara'at*, Maimonides says, first affects the walls of the house.   If the owner of the house heeds the warning and stops speaking evil and repents, the *tzara'at* goes no further; but if he

---

[4]   See Babylonian Talmud, *'Arakhin* 16a.
[5]   In Jewish law, *leshon hara*—evil speech (literally, "the evil tongue")— refers not only to slander (which is unfavorable words based on untruth or misrepresentation) but even to truthful statements that are spoken for the purpose of tarnishing somebody's reputation.   Moreover, the Torah forbids not only *leshon hara*, but even idle gossip about people (Leviticus 19:16).

continues to sin, the *tzara'at* progressively attacks first his garments and later his skin.[6]

Ramban is even more vague about whether he thinks *tzara'at* is a natural phenomenon and whether it is the disease known as leprosy; but he does say (on Leviticus 13:47) that *tzara'at* of a garment is not a natural phenomenon.

Unlike Maimonides and Ramban (both of whom were physicians), Sforno—who was also a physician—is much more explicit in his analysis of *tzara'at*. In his commentary on Leviticus 13:2, he says that some of the skin manifestations described in the Torah are indeed a natural disease and are a form of leprosy, but that much of what is described in the Torah is not a natural occurrence. He then goes on to list several other skin diseases from which leprosy must be differentiated, including one form of cancer.[7]

In conclusion, we have seen that the term *tzara'at* in the Torah does not refer to one entity. One of its manifestations seems to be the disease we know as leprosy, but other manifestations are of a miraculous nature. The

---

[6] Maimonides in *Mishneh Torah* (*Hilkhot Tum'at Tzara'at* 16:10), by saying that *tzara'at* of clothing and houses is different from the skin disease and is not a natural phenomenon, perhaps implies that the skin disease **is** a natural phenomenon, but he doesn't say so explicitly. However, in his *Guide for the Perplexed* (Part III, chapter 47), after summarizing the progression of *tzara'at* of houses and clothing as stated above, he says clearly that the disease *tzara'at* is a contagious disease that all people abhor and shun.

[7] Leprosy is described not only in the Bible but in many ancient and Medieval sources, and its features are consistent with the disease as we know it, with the exception that it was thought to be much more contagious than we know it to be today. Also, it is possible that some cases were misdiagnosed as leprosy. In addition to Sforno's list of conditions that could be confused with leprosy (see his commentary on Leviticus 13:2), some forms of tuberculosis, syphilis, or lupus also could have been misdiagnosed as leprosy. Nevertheless, most cases thought to be leprosy in ancient times probably were indeed leprosy.

19th Century commentator Malbim points out that in Leviticus 14:34, God says, "I shall **give** the affliction of *tzara'at* in the house ..."; and the word *venatati* (I shall **give**), he says, is used in the Torah only in a positive sense, *i.e.* as a sign of divine benevolence. But how can we consider that affliction to be a sign of God's benevolence? The answer lies in the progressive nature of *tzara'at*: the affliction of the house and then the garments coming as a warning before the person's body is affected. This is similar to what we see in the *sidra* of *Bechukkotai*, where we are given blessings and curses. If we are good, and we follow God's laws, He gives us the blessings all at once. But if we violate His laws, the curses are meted out in stages; and if we repent, we do not receive the next stage of punishment. *Tzara'at* of the house and garments, then, Malbim says, must be regarded as a miraculous gift that God gave to the nation of Israel, as a warning to correct their ways and avert being punished with the bodily affliction of leprosy.

Acharei Mot:
The Approach to Holiness

What is the most important thing for Aaron to do before entering the Holy of Holies?

In the *sidra* of *Acharei Mot*,[1] God speaks to Moses after the death of the two sons of his brother Aaron the high priest, described in the portion of *Shemini*. In the aftermath of their untimely death, God now delineates the proper manner and the proper procedure to which the high priest must adhere when entering the Sanctuary, *i.e.* the Holy of Holies, the inner sanctum of the Tabernacle.

Bezot yavo Aharon el hakodesh—"With this shall Aaron come to the Sanctuary" (Leviticus 16:3). A casual reading of the text would suggest that "this" refers to the bull and the ram that the second half of the verse instructs the high priest to bring as a burnt offering; and indeed, all translations of the Torah are consistent with that interpretation. But that reading of the text is grammatically inconsistent, since the word *zot* ("this") is feminine, whereas the Hebrew words for a bull and a ram are both masculine.[2] Furthermore, *zot* is singular, but it refers to two items, and therefore the plural form *eleh* ("these") would have been more

---

[1] Leviticus 16:1 – 18:30.
[2] Although the words *chattat* (a sin offering) and *'olah* (a burnt offering) are feminine, "this" cannot refer to those words, because it is the bull and the ram that are the appositives of "this": *Bezot yavo Aharon el hakodesh: befar ben bakar lechattat ve'ayil le'ola*—"With this shall Aaron come to the Sanctuary: with a bull for a sin offering and a ram for a burnt offering." The words *chattat* and *'olah* are merely modifiers that explain the purpose of the bull and the ram.

appropriate. Perhaps, then, the word "this" does not refer to the bull and the ram, but to some other unnamed entity with which Aaron is to enter the Sanctuary, along with the bull and the ram for sacrifice.

So, what is the mysterious "this" with which the high priest is to enter the Holy of Holies? According to the *Midrash*, it is the same "this" to which King David refers when he says, "Should an army besiege me, ... in **this** I will trust. One thing I have requested of the Lord: to dwell in the Lord's House all the days of my life, to gaze upon the grace of the Lord and to frequent His Temple" (Psalms 27:3–4).[3] The *Midrash* declares that the mysterious entity "this" to which King David refers is the holy spirit, God's Presence (the *Shekhina*), which David asks to accompany him wherever he goes.[4] With this in mind, before the priest would don his linen garments or enter

---

[3] The grammatical inconsistency (see above) of assuming that *zot* in Leviticus 16:3 refers to the bull and the ram is my own observation. While I have not seen it explicitly mentioned in the sources I consulted, I deem it likely that that grammatical inconsistency is the underlying basis for this *midrash*—and later, *Sha'arei Orah* and the Zohar (see footnote 5)— maintaining that the word "this" in Leviticus 16:3 refers to some other, unnamed, entity.

[4] The reference to *bezot* in the *Midrash* is to be found in *Midrash Tehillim* (*Shochar Tov*) on Psalms 27:3 (Psalm 27, §21), in which the *Midrash* equates King David's use of the word *zot* in that psalm with **Bezot** *yavo Aharon el hakodesh* in *Acharei Mot*. Also, in its commentary on the following verse— "One thing I have requested of the Lord ..." (Psalms 27:4)—*Midrash Tehillim* says that *Malkhut* (kingship) is what King David was requesting (ibid., §22). But the *Midrash* does not mean that David was requesting to become king. Rather, as should be evident from the phrasing of its commentary on the word *zot* and from the context of Psalms 27:3–4, what the *Midrash* means is that King David asked to partake of God's Presence on earth—the *Shekhina*—which is also known as *Malkhut*. Another example of this meaning of *Malkhut* is found in Esther 5:1, where it says that "Esther donned royalty [*Malkhut*]," and the Talmud remarks that this means she was enveloped in the holy spirit (*Megilla* 15a).

the Tabernacle to bring an offering of any kind, he had to prepare himself and put himself in the proper frame of mind. He had to separate himself from the profane and envelop himself in a spirit of holiness. That, according to this *midrash*, is the meaning of the Torah's statement, "With **this** shall Aaron come to the Sanctuary."[5]

Just as a person who enters a conflagration must first don the proper protective garments, so did the priest need to wrap himself in the spirit of holiness before entering the holy domain. And that explains the fatal flaw that led to the death of Aaron's sons: they had not entered the mental framework that was critical to their being able to approach the Lord's Presence safely. The divine Presence imparted to the area a high spiritual energy, which could be just as dangerous as a physical fire; and failing to clothe oneself in the appropriate spiritual envelope would leave a person exposed to danger. But why would Aaron's sons have been so careless as to enter the divine Presence without the proper preparation? It is likely that their behavior was, at least in part, related to their being drunk, as discussed in my commentary on *Shemini*. If they were intoxicated, that would explain why they were so careless, and it would also explain why, immediately after relating the episode of Aaron's sons' death, the Torah tells Aaron that he and his sons must not drink wine or beer just before entering the Tabernacle.

---

[5] Rabbeinu Bachyay, in his commentary on Leviticus 16:3, provides additional discussion of the word *zot* referring to the *Shekhina*. Also, the Zohar interprets the word *zot* in several contexts in the Bible as signifying the *Shekhina*, for example in Zohar III:56b (top of page), in I:72, II:57a, III:41a, and other places. And see the explanation of *zot* in the first chapter of *Sha'arei Orah*, by Yosef Gikatilla (13th Century Spain).

Kedoshim[1]:
How to Be Holy

What does the Torah mean when it tells us to be holy?
Is there some specific action to take?

The Lord spoke to Moses and told him to address the entire congregation of Israel and say to them, *Kedoshim tih'yu*—"Be holy," because I, your God, am holy (Leviticus 19:2). What does God mean when He tells us to be holy? Is there some specific action that we must take to make us holy?

Rashi maintains that the meaning of "Be holy" is to refrain from the forbidden sexual relations that were just listed in the immediately preceding section, at the end of the previous *sidra* (ibid., 18:6–30). While such a definition of being holy may seem reasonable considering that the exhortation to holiness immediately follows the list of forbidden relations, Ramban challenges Rashi's definition as being too narrow. Ramban, quoting *Sifra*,[2] says that being holy means separating oneself from all forms of defilement, including forbidden relations, forbidden foods, and other matters that the Torah forbids. Also, Ramban adds that even in activities that are permitted—whether in eating, drinking, or sexual activity—being

---

[1] Leviticus 19:1 – 20:27.

[2] *Sifra* is a compilation of rabbinic commentaries on the book of Leviticus, probably produced in the early 3rd Century. It belongs to the category of *midrash halakha*: that is, Torah commentary that concerns itself with comparison of Biblical texts and analysis of their phrasing in order to identify supporting evidence for Jewish laws that are known through the oral tradition.

holy means not going to excess. Moderation in all things is the goal.

Ramban's definition of being holy, although it does go beyond Rashi's definition, nevertheless still does not fully capture what most of us would intuitively conceive as holiness in a person. As Alsheikh points out, refraining from forbidden actions is passive, whereas the command to be holy seems to imply more than mere passive avoidance. And indeed, Ramban also intends more than his definition seems to suggest, since he later says that one must not be a vile person while staying within the confines of Torah law (*naval bir'shut haTorah*).

Perhaps a clue to how we are to achieve holiness is provided in the very next statement that the Torah makes after the command to be holy: "Each man shall revere his mother and his father, and my Sabbaths you shall observe; I am the Lord your God" (Leviticus 19:3). In this statement, the Torah likens reverence of one's parents to Sabbath observance. A person's parents teach him about humility and proper behavior; and reverence of parents (which is related to but separate from honoring them) involves obeying their instructions and thereby learning how to conduct ourselves with other people. Reverence of parents is a child's first step toward achieving holiness. Observing the Sabbath represents a person's relationship with God. But by linking Sabbath observance with reverence of parents (in verse 3), the Torah is suggesting an equivalence between reverence for parents and observance of God's commands. Moreover, as the Talmud points out, the Torah here commands reverence of parents (in verse 3); and in Deuteronomy 6:13, using similar language, the Torah commands reverence of God ("You shall revere the Lord your God, and you shall serve him"), suggesting an equivalence between the two.[3] The Torah is telling us that there should be no separation in our minds between laws pertaining to our everyday life and laws pertaining to our relationship with God. Indeed, many of the precepts listed in *Kedoshim* have no apparent bearing on our devotion to God, but pertain to mundane matters; and yet, these everyday activities are equally included in the practice of holiness.[4]

Holiness in a person is not an abstract idea but a fundamental principle of our daily lives. It is all-encompassing, including such seemingly disparate matters as reverence for parents, honesty in business, respect and love of other people, upholding equal justice for all, proper treatment of strangers, refraining from gossip, paying employees on time, keeping the laws of Sabbath and worship of God, and refraining from worship of other deities. They are all one. All of these precepts are included in the *sidra* of *Kedoshim*. They are among the core principles upon which the Torah rests, and they are all contained within the practice of holiness.

---

[3] The Talmud goes on to provide the theoretical basis for equating reverence of parents to reverence of God. The Talmud says there are three partners in the creation of a person: God, the father, and the mother. (God provides the soul, and the parents generate the body of their child.) When a person honors his parents, God considers it as though that person honored Him. See Babylonian Talmud, *Kiddushin* 30b (bottom of the page).

[4] Rashi, paraphrasing *Sifra* and the Talmud (*Yevamot* 5b) says that the Torah links reverence for parents with keeping the Sabbath to inform us that if one's parents tell him to violate one of the commandments of the Torah, he is not to obey his parents in that case, because both he and his parents are subject to God's commandments. While this is a reasonable conclusion to derive from Leviticus 19:3, Alsheikh challenges the assumption that this conclusion is the Torah's sole purpose in linking reverence for parents with keeping the Sabbath. Therefore, taking a cue from Ramban and especially from Alsheikh, I have endeavored to give a more global interpretation of verse 3 (revere your parents, and keep My Sabbaths), linking it both with the command to be holy and with the rest of the *sidra* of *Kedoshim*.

Emor 1:
Holiness and Its Antithesis

What does the law of an eye for eye have to do with holiness?

The *sidra* of *Emor*[1] begins with laws dictating the ways in which the *kohanim* (the priests) are to maintain their purity and the sanctification of their service. It goes on to discuss the holiness of the burnt offerings and how the people of Israel are to uphold the sanctity of God in their midst. Then there is a summary of all the holy days of the calendar; and finally, the high priest's obligation regarding the kindling of the Menorah (the seven-branched candelabra) and the show-bread. The concept of holiness is pervasive throughout the *sidra*, almost until the end. But, following the aforementioned topics, the Torah introduces the story of a man who cursed the name of God (Leviticus 24:10– 12 & 23). So, we may ask, what is the Torah's purpose in placing that story here, at the conclusion of this *sidra* that is so focused on purity and holiness? And, appended to the story are several laws including the so-called *lex talionis*—the law of an eye for an eye. What do those laws have to do with the story to which they are appended? In this essay, I will try to answer these two questions.

The story begins with a man of mixed lineage—the son of an Egyptian father and an Israelite mother—who fights with an Israelite man and publicly curses God by name (YHVH). Witnesses to the half-Egyptian man's blasphemy

---

[1] Leviticus 21:1 – 24:23.

bring him before Moses, and Moses has the man held under guard until God will tell him how to proceed. The story, as related in three sentences (verses 10–12), completely omits the context that would be necessary for our full understanding. We are told the name of the half-Egyptian man's mother, but there is no information about why the two men were fighting or what the fight had to do with cursing God's name. The *Midrash* fills in the background details.

There are five versions of the story, each differing slightly from the others, but all are in agreement on the basic elements.[2] It turns out that the man's Egyptian father was none other than the taskmaster whom Moses killed (see Exodus 2:12), years earlier. Each Egyptian taskmaster commanded ten Israelite officers who supervised the work of the Israelite slaves; and early one morning, when this particular taskmaster went to the home of one of his Israelite officers to order him to assemble his slaves, the taskmaster took notice of the officer's wife. She was very beautiful (according to one version), and perhaps she smiled at the taskmaster (according to other versions). The taskmaster hid outside; and as soon as the Israelite officer left his home, the taskmaster came back and raped the officer's wife, whose name was Shlomit. But the officer returned just as the taskmaster was leaving, and, realizing that he had been seen, the taskmaster started beating the officer. Just then, Moses came on the scene, killed the Egyptian taskmaster, and saved the Israelite officer from death. The officer later divorced Shlomit and married another woman. The half-Egyptian man was the son of the

---

[2] The back-story of the half-Egyptian man is related in the following five sources: 1) *Midrash Tanchuma, Emor* §24; 2) *Vayikra Rabba* 32:4; 3) *Shemot Rabba* 1:33; 4) *Pirkei Rabbi Eliezer*, chapter 48, which gives an abbreviated version; and 5) *Zohar* III:106a.

Egyptian taskmaster who had raped Shlomit (the product of that rape); and, according to the *Midrash*, the Israelite man with whom he fought was the son of the Israelite officer by the officer's second wife.

Returning to our *sidra*, we may ask: why did the witnesses to the man's blasphemy need to bring him to Moses? They themselves should have known the penalty for cursing the divine name. To this question, Abravnel answers that they knew the penalty for blasphemy committed by an Israelite, but they did not know whether the same penalty applied to a person whose father was a non-Israelite. Nevertheless, we may still ask yet again: why did Moses have to ask God what to do with the blasphemer? Surely he should have known the law! The Torah commentary *Toldot Yitzchak*[3] raises this question and answers that Moses did know the law; but Moses didn't want to be the one to condemn the man to death, because he knew there were those who would say that Moses only sentenced the half-Egyptian man to death because that man was the son of the Egyptian taskmaster whom Moses killed, and that Moses was now biased against the taskmaster's son.

So Moses asks God to decide the punishment, and God commands that anybody who curses God's name, whether an Israelite or an alien, shall be put to death (ibid., verse 16). But, returning to our initial question, why did the Torah place this story here? *Toldot Yitzchak* points out that the story follows the laws pertaining to the sanctity of the burnt offerings, the sanctification of the *kohanim* who serve in the Tabernacle, the manner in which the nation as a whole is to uphold the sanctity of God in their midst,

---

[3] A commentary on the Torah by Rabbi Isaac Karo (1458–1535). See also Description of Sources.

the purity of the oil to be used for lighting the Menorah in the Tabernacle, and a description of all the holy days of the calendar. And immediately after God gave those laws to the people of Israel, this particular man cursed God by God's explicit name (YHVH). The juxtaposition is meant to emphasize the magnitude of the man's crime—denying the holiness of the Lord, denying His presence in the midst of Israel, and denying God himself. It is a supreme act of sedition, and God tells Moses that the punishment is death.

The Torah then follows up with a series of laws whose relevance is not apparent: a murderer is to be put to death; one who kills an animal shall pay for the animal's life; and whoever injures another person, the same shall be imposed upon him—an eye for an eye, a tooth for a tooth (ibid., 24:17–21).

While in non-Jewish circles the law of an eye for an eye is controversial because it is interpreted literally, in Jewish law it was never taken literally, but it was taken to mean proportionate monetary compensation for bodily injury.[4] Enigmatically, this law and the other laws mentioned are sandwiched between the story of the blasphemer and the execution of his verdict; but most commentators ignore the connection between these laws and the story within which they are embedded.

I believe that the point the Torah is making is that these laws, taken as a group, embody the important principle of equal justice under the law. Unlike the legal codes of other nations that imposed different penalties depending on the social status of the injured person and of the perpetrator, the Torah decrees that every person must get equal justice

---

[4] The Babylonian Talmud (*Bava Kamma* 83b–84a) tells us that the law of an eye for an eye means monetary compensation for the value of the injury inflicted. See also footnote 5.

under the law.[5] The non-Israelite gets the same penalty as the Israelite. The group of laws listed between the story of the blasphemer and the execution of his verdict are very much related to the main subject of our *sidra*—the establishment of sanctity within the camp of the Israelites—since equal justice under the law is the very cornerstone of the practice of holiness. Holiness cannot be achieved in the absence of equal justice. Thus, the Torah concludes these laws with this statement: "One law shall there be for you; for the foreigner as for the citizen it shall be, for I am the Lord your God" (Leviticus 24:22).

---

[5] We must consider the law of an eye for an eye in the context of the times. The Torah phrases this law in the way it does in order to draw a contrast with the legal codes of neighboring nations, of which the Babylonian Code of Hammurabi may be cited as the prime example. Hammurabi lived several hundred years before Moses, and his legal code was undoubtedly well known throughout the ancient Near East. Paragraph 196 of Hammurabi's code states that if a seignior destroyed the eye of a member of the aristocracy, the seignior's eye shall be destroyed; and if he broke another seignior's bone, then his bone shall be broken (197); but if he destroyed the eye or broke the bone of a commoner, he shall pay one mina of silver (198); and if he destroyed the eye of a seignior's slave or broke the bone of the seignior's slave, he shall pay half his value (199). The purpose of the Torah here is not physical retribution as in Hammurabi's code, but justice in the form of just compensation for injury irrespective of the relative social status of the perpetrator and of the injured person. But the Torah purposefully uses a phrasing similar to Hammurabi's phrasing in order to emphasize its disagreement with Hammurabi's code's consideration of the relative social status of the perpetrator and the injured person in determining the penalty.

Emor 2:
The Holiday of *Shavuot*[1]

What does the holiday of Shavuot celebrate?

Each year throughout the world, Jews celebrate the holiday of *Shavuot* on the sixth day of the month of *Sivan* as the day on which God spoke the Ten Commandments at Mount Sinai. But the Torah does not give us that reason for the holiday, and nowhere does the Torah explicitly tell us that God gave the Ten Commandments on that day. So what is the true reason for the holiday? And if God's revelation at Mount Sinai did indeed occur on *Shavuot*, why does the Torah not tell us that reason for the holiday?

In the *sidra* of *Emor*, *Shavuot* is listed among the festivals that the Torah ordains (Leviticus 23:4–44). But, unlike the other holidays, the details of observance of *Shavuot* are not preceded by the statement "And the Lord spoke to Moses saying"; unlike the other holidays, the date of *Shavuot* is not given; and unlike the other two pilgrimage holidays—*Pesach* (Passover) and *Sukkot*—the holiday of *Shavuot* is not even named here. After discussing the observance of *Pesach*, the Torah tells us to count seven weeks from the day that the first grains of the spring harvest (barley) are presented, and on the fiftieth day we are to celebrate the holiday (see verses 15–21). Thus, we call this holiday *Shavuot* (weeks), and Greek-speaking Jews in ancient times referred to it as "Pentecost" (Greek for "fiftieth").

---

[1] The laws pertaining to the celebration of *Shavuot* are presented in the *sidra* of *Emor*, in Leviticus 23:15–22.

Previously, in Exodus 23:14–16, the Torah listed the three pilgrimage holidays, without giving details of their observance; and there (ibid., verse 16), the holiday is named "The Harvest Festival," during which we are to bring *bikkurim* (an offering of first produce). The holiday is mentioned in the Torah in two additional places. In Numbers 28:26, it is named "The Day of *Bikkurim*," and in Deuteronomy 16:10 it is called *Shavuot*. But even in this last source, there is no mention of any reason for the holiday other than an agricultural one, and we are told to bring an offering of our produce. So, returning to our initial question, if *Shavuot* commemorates the revelation at Mount Sinai, why does the Torah not mention that as the reason for the festival? Many of the Biblical commentators do not ask this question, perhaps because they have no satisfactory answer. And none of the commentaries that do address the issue are able to provide a fully satisfactory answer, but I want to focus on two commentators who have proposed solutions.

Rabbi Isaac Arama[2] gives an interesting explanation in his commentary, *Akedat Yitzchak*. He says that the purpose of the Israelites' redemption from Egypt was to receive the Torah,[3] as God told Moses when He first sent Moses back to Egypt to challenge Pharaoh: "When you take the nation

---

[2] Rabbi Isaac ben Moshe Arama (Spain, 1420–1494). See also Description of Sources.

[3] The statement in *Akedat Yitzhak* that God's purpose in taking the Israelites out of Egypt was to give them the Torah accords with Ramban's introduction to the book of Exodus, which I discussed in my commentary on the portion of *Pekudei*. It also accords with the usage of another name for the holiday of *Shavuot* that is frequently used in the Talmud, *Atzeret*, which means stoppage, indicating that this holiday is not an independent festival but is the completion of the process that was begun on *Pesach*. Also, it explains why the Torah fixes the date of *Shavuot* by counting from *Pesach*, and—at least in *Emor*—not giving a separate name for the later festival.

out of Egypt, you will worship God on this mountain" (Exodus 3:12). But when they left Egypt, they were still contaminated by the Egyptian religion, and God allowed seven weeks for them to remove the heathen practices from among them before giving them the Torah. This, in my opinion, is a very good explanation for the linkage between *Pesach* and *Shavuot*, and hence the reason why the Torah did not state the date of *Shavuot* but instead had us determine the date by counting fifty days from *Pesach*. But the *Akedat Yitzchak* does not provide an explanation for why the Torah doesn't even mention the giving of the Ten Commandments as a reason for the holiday.

Most commentaries, including Abravnel and *Akedat Yitzchak*, assume that God's revelation at Mount Sinai occurred on the sixth day of *Sivan*, which is the fiftieth day of the count—the day on which we celebrate *Shavuot*. But in reality, the Torah does not specify the date on which that event occurred. The actual date of the revelation at Mount Sinai is calculated from known dates that are stated in the Torah, and there is some uncertainty in that calculation. Thus, the Talmud records a dispute regarding whether God spoke the Ten Commandments to the assembled Israelites on the sixth or the seventh day of *Sivan*.[4] If the true date was the seventh of *Sivan*, then the day of *Shavuot* would be the day on which the Israelites were finally cleansed of the heathen ways of Egypt and were fully prepared to receive the laws of God. In that case, the festival would not commemorate the day of our receiving the Ten Commandments but rather, the day

---

[4] The dispute regarding whether God's revelation at Mount Sinai and His speaking of the Ten Commandments occurred on *Shavuot* or on the day following *Shavuot* is found in the Babylonian Talmud, *Yoma* 4b, *Shabbat* 86b, and *Ta'anit* 28b.

commemorating our attaining the spiritual level that would make us worthy of receiving the commandments.

In order to achieve the spiritual level to be worthy of receiving the commandments, a practice arose of staying up all night and learning Torah on *Shavuot*. That practice, which is seen as preparing a bride for her wedding (the union of the people of Israel with the Torah), is based on the Zohar,[5] and the Zohar attributes the practice to the righteous of ancient times. However, there is no other record that this was ever done before the Zohar, nor does it seem that the Zohar's recommendation was put into practice until about 1533, when Rabbi Yosef Karo[6] and Rabbi Shlomo Halevi Alkabetz[7] met together in Salonika and initiated the practice. Soon after, they emigrated to Safed, and the custom (called *Tikkun Leyl Shavuot*) became widespread in the Kabbalistic community.

---

[5] See Zohar I:8a and III:98a.

[6] Spain, Portugal, the Ottoman Empire, and Safed (Israel), 1488–1575. He is best known for his compilation of the Code of Jewish Law (the *Shulchan Arukh*). See also Description of Sources.

[7] Turkey and Safed (Israel), 1500–1576. He later composed the song *Lekha Dodi*, which is sung on Friday nights to welcome the Sabbath.

Emor 3:
The Day of Atonement and the Book of Jonah

Why did Jonah try to flee? Didn't he know it's impossible to escape from God?

On *Yom Kippur* (The Day of Atonement),[1] we read the book of Jonah. Right from the very beginning of the book, we are presented with an enigma: God speaks to Jonah, and Jonah, not wanting to receive the prophecy, "flees from before the Lord," booking passage on a ship bound for a foreign land. How can this be? Doesn't Jonah, a man of prophetic vision, understand that God is everywhere, and it is impossible to escape from God?

Before addressing that question, however, first we should consider Jonah's reason for not wanting to prophesy to the wicked city of Nineveh. A well-known *midrash* tells us that Jonah had previously prophesied to the people of Jerusalem and warned of the city's imminent destruction; but the people had repented of their sins, and God spared the city. As a result, the people of Jerusalem called Jonah a false prophet.[2] With that experience in mind, Jonah would not have wanted to repeat the scenario in Nineveh

---

[1] The laws pertaining to Yom Kippur are presented in the *sidra* of *Emor*, in Leviticus 23:26–32. The book of Jonah, which demonstrates how God rescinded His decree against the sinful city of Nineveh after the inhabitants of that city repented sincerely, ties in with the theme of Yom Kippur: God doesn't want to punish the wicked; what He wants is for the wicked to change their ways and live.

[2] See *Perkei Rabbi Eliezer*, Chapter 10.

and once again be called a false prophet. Moreover, as the text of the final chapter of the book of Jonah suggests, Jonah also felt that the people of Nineveh were so wicked that they didn't deserve God's forgiveness.

Now that we have offered reasons why Jonah didn't want to receive the prophecy regarding Nineveh, let us turn to our initial question of how Jonah could have imagined it possible to flee from God. How can we think that a prophet, a man who has first-hand knowledge of God's presence in our world, would make such a fundamental error? The Zohar considers this question and concludes that Jonah could not have made such an error.[3] Rather, Jonah may have been under the impression that prophecy could not be received outside of Israel. While it is true that there had been prophets outside of the holy land— most notably Moses—nevertheless, during the First Temple period there was no prophecy outside of the land of Israel, and it apparently was accepted teaching that, after the nation entered the Promised Land in the days of Joshua, prophecy would not occur except in Israel. Note that Jonah took a ship, and his destination was a foreign land. He had no delusion of escaping God, but he did think to avoid receiving the prophecy.

However, despite his efforts, Jonah is not able to avoid receiving the prophecy, and in the end, his worst fears are fulfilled: he delivers the prophecy, and the people of Nineveh repent. Jonah posts himself outside the city to see what will happen: will God destroy the city, or will He forgive the people and rescind His edict? When, as anticipated, Nineveh is not destroyed, Jonah is distressed.

---

[3] See Zohar I:85a. The Zohar does not explicitly state the question, but it gives the above answer to the implied question.

He cries out to God and says, "Isn't this what I said when I was still in my own land? That is why I hastened to flee to Tarshish; for I knew that You are God the merciful and compassionate, slow to anger, abundant in kindness, and relenting of doom" (Jonah 4:2). Note that the attributes of God that Jonah lists here are almost the same ones listed in Exodus 34:6–7 (after He forgave His nation for the sin of the Golden Calf and gave Moses the second set of tablets); however, in Exodus, after "slow to anger and abundant in kindness," there is yet another attribute: *erekh apayim verav chesed* **ve'emet**—slow to anger, abundant in kindness **and truth** (or faithfulness). But Jonah omits *emet*: God did not fulfill His word; He did not destroy Nineveh. Of course, God has the last word here. Yes, God is faithful to His word, but in the list of God's attributes in Exodus 34:6–7, *chesed*—mercy—precedes *emet*; and when the two conflict, it is the quality of mercy that takes priority.

Emor 4:
The Holiday of *Sukkot*[1]

What does Sukkot celebrate?

What does the holiday of *Sukkot* celebrate? I will present four answers to that question.

The first answer is given in the Torah, in Leviticus 23:42–43: "In huts (*sukkot*) you shall live for seven days. All citizens in Israel shall live in huts, so that your generations shall know that in huts I had the people of Israel live when I took them out of the land of Egypt; I am the Lord your God." But did the Israelites really live in huts during the forty years in the desert? Nowhere in the Torah's account of the Israelites' sojourn in the desert is there any evidence that they actually lived in huts. In fact, the usual abode of desert-dwellers is a tent, and the Torah on several occasions refers to the Israelites living in tents in the desert. For example, it says, "... each man would stand at the entrance of his tent" (Exodus 33:8); and Bil'am, in his blessing of the Israelites, says, "How goodly are your tents, O Jacob" (Numbers 24:5).

So if—as seems likely—the Israelites lived in tents during the forty-year sojourn in the desert following the Exodus from Egypt, why would the Torah say that we lived in *sukkot*? To answer this question, consider that the word *sukka* (the singular of *sukkot*) derives from a Hebrew word meaning "to cover" or "to shield." Therefore, in accordance

---

[1] The laws pertaining to the celebration of *Sukkot* are presented in the *sidra* of *Emor*, in Leviticus 23:33–44.

with the opinion of Rabbi Eliezer in the Talmud[2] and in accordance with the translation of Onkelos, both Rashi and Ramban are of the opinion that the Torah's statement that we lived in huts after the Exodus from Egypt should be interpreted not literally but figuratively, indicating that we were under God's protection, and we were covered by a divine shield—God's clouds of glory. Moreover, Ramban says that this figurative interpretation is the plain meaning of the text.

A second approach to understanding what the holiday of *Sukkot* celebrates is given in Exodus 23:16: "... and the harvest festival at the close of the year ...." The holiday of *Sukkot* does not actually come at the end of the calendar year, but it does mark the end of the agricultural year, as Sforno points out. In this sense, it is a holiday in which we thank God for providing for our sustenance.

A third answer is given by Shadal.[3] When the Israelites left Egypt, the first place at which they camped was named Sukkot (see Exodus 33:5). It is logical to assume that it was given that name because the Israelites dwelled in huts while at that location, and Shadal opines that it was there that the Israelites dwelled in huts (*sukkot*), and not necessarily during the entire forty years in the desert.

Shadal's proposal seems obvious, so why did none of the previous commentators even mention it? I believe that they totally ignored that interpretation because the Torah does not give the camp site of Sukkot any special importance or mention any significant event that happened there; and we remained at that camp site for only four or

---

[2] Babylonian Talmud, *Sukka* 11b.
[3] **Sh**muel **Da**vid Luzzatto, 1800–1865. See also Description of Sources.

five days at most.[4] Moreover, the Torah makes no explicit mention of our dwelling in huts at that location; we only infer that from the name of the place.

The fourth answer to the question of what the festival of *Sukkot* celebrates is found not in the Torah itself, but in the last chapter of Zekharia, the very chapter that the rabbis chose for us to read as the *Haftarah* on the first day of *Sukkot*. In that prophecy, Zekharia describes the coming of the Messianic age. In the war that will precede the coming of the Messiah, God will go to battle on our behalf (Zekharia 14:3), and we will be again under God's protection, a protection that will continue through the Messianic era itself. Moreover, as the prophet Amos tells us, "On that day, I will re-establish the *sukka* of David ..." (Amos 9:11). At that time, "the Lord will be king over all the earth; in that day, the Lord will be one, and His name one" (Zekharia 14:9). And thenceforth, all the remaining nations will come to Jerusalem once a year to celebrate the festival of *Sukkot* (ibid., verse 16). *Sukkot* will become a universal festival for all the nations of the world, and not just a Jewish holiday. What, then, does this holiday celebrate? It celebrates the ushering-in of the Messianic era, an era when all of humanity will be under divine protection and guidance, and all mankind will live under a *sukka* of peace.

---

[4] We can estimate the duration of camping at the place called Sukkot from events that occurred before and after. The splitting of the sea occurred six days after the Exodus from Egypt, and there was one additional camp site after Sukkot, before even reaching the sea; the Israelites, then, must have remained at Sukkot for not more than four or five days. It does not seem likely that a seven-day holiday would be instituted to commemorate a four- or five-day event; and, moreover, it is illogical to think that the holiday would be celebrated at a different time of the year than when the event it commemorates actually occurred.

In conclusion, which of these explanations is correct? I believe all four have merit; but in my opinion, the fourth explanation is the one that speaks to us and to our future with greatest import. Other holidays commemorate historical events: *Pesach* commemorates the Exodus from Egypt, and *Shavuot* commemorates God's giving us the Ten Commandments; but *Sukkot* presages a future event: the coming of the Messiah.

Behar:
The *Shmita* and The *Yovel*

How is the purpose of the Shmita different from that of the Yovel?

Starting from the beginning of *Behar*,[1] the Torah establishes a connection between the seventh year—the *Shmita*—and the seventh day of each week—the *Shabbat*: "When you enter the land that I am giving you, the land shall observe a Sabbath [*Shabbat*] to the Lord" (Leviticus 25:2). In the following verses, the Torah defines an agricultural cycle of seven years and forbids working the land in the seventh year. And significantly, not only does the Torah use the word *Shabbat* in reference to both the seventh day of the week and the seventh year of the agricultural cycle, but similar phrasing is used for both laws: compare "Six days you shall labor and do all your work, but the seventh day is a Sabbath to the Lord your God" (Exodus 20:9–10), and "Six years you shall sow your field, and six years you shall prune your vineyard ..., but in the seventh year it will be a Sabbath of Sabbaths—a Sabbath to the Lord" (Leviticus 25:3–4).

After giving us the laws pertaining to the *Shmita*, the Torah goes on to tell us about the fiftieth year, the *Yovel* (Jubilee). We are told to count seven cycles of seven years, and we are to declare the fiftieth year as *Yovel*—a year in which slaves are freed and real estate is returned

---

[1] Leviticus 25:1 – 26:2.

160

to its original owner. Both the *Shmita* and the *Yovel* are meant to instill in us a recognition that God is the true owner of the land, and we are merely sojourners who lease the land from Him (see verse 23). But the emphasis of the *Yovel* is on liberty: in the fiftieth year, on the Day of Atonement (*Yom Kippur*), we are to blow the *shofar* and declare liberty throughout the land and to all its inhabitants (verses 9–10).[2] Hebrew slaves are freed, because, God says, "they are My slaves, whom I brought out of the land of Egypt" (verse 42).

Besides the obvious linkage of the *Shmita* with the Sabbath day, by virtue of the use of the word *Shabbat* for each, and the sanctification of the seventh year in one case and the seventh day in the other, there is one other similarity that the commentary *Meshekh Chokhma*[3] points out: note that for both the seventh day of the week and the seventh year, the Torah says "a *Shabbat* **to the Lord**" (see above). This phrasing is to be distinguished from that pertaining to the Yovel: "And you shall sanctify the fiftieth year ..., a *Yovel* it shall be **for you**" (verse 10). The difference in phrasing, says *Meshekh Chokhma*, is very significant. The occurrence of the Sabbath day and of the seventh year are fixed times, set by God; whereas the timing of the start of the *Yovel*— just like the timing of the festivals—is set by us. The high court—the *Sanhedrin*—had the authority to declare the new moon, and the timing of the festivals was dependent on

---

[2] Significantly, the Liberty Bell, which stands in Philadelphia, Pennsylvania, bears the inscription, "Proclaim LIBERTY Throughout all the Land unto all the Inhabitants Thereof Lev. XXV. v X."

[3] A commentary on the Torah by Rabbi Meir Simcha Hakohen of Dvinsk (Lithuania, Poland, and Latvia, 1843–1926). See also Description of Sources.

the court's declaration.[4] Similarly, the freeing of slaves and the start of the other laws pertaining to the *Yovel* depended on **our** blowing the *Shofar* on the Day of Atonement (see verse 9), and on **our** declaring liberty throughout the land (verse 10). The laws of the Sabbath day and of the seventh year—the *Shmita*—apply automatically; but the laws of *Yovel* are dependent on our declaration, just as the dating of the festivals depends on our declaration of the new moon. The holiness of the seventh day stems from God's declaration of its sanctity at the completion of Creation, whereas the sanctity of the fiftieth year—and of the festivals—primarily depends on our declaration and our action. Thus, our declaration and sanctification of the *Yovel* in the 50th year— which complements the divinely-established sanctity of the *Shmita* of the 49th year—completes the fifty-year cycle. And this parallels God's creation of the world: God created the world, but He left it for humans, through our thoughts, through our words, and through our actions, to infuse holiness into the world that He created.

---

[4] The Jewish calendar is a lunar calendar. Since earliest times, the *Sanhedrin* declared the start of each month based on a sighting of the new moon. But when the land of Israel was under Roman rule, the Romans often tried to interfere with the *Sanhedrin*'s ability to publicize its declaration. Roman interference became especially intense after Rome's adoption of Christianity as the official state religion in 315 CE. Therefore, in the mid-4th Century, Hillel II used his authority as head of the *Sanhedrin* to declare the date of the new moon for the next 2,000 years. (He specified 2,000 years, because he correctly calculated that his calendar would lose one day at the end of that time.)

Bechukkotai:
The Blessings or The Curses?

Is it the blessings or the curses that are the most prominent feature of Bechukkotai?

The portion of *Bechukkotai*[1] opens with a series of blessings for those who follow and adhere to God's commandments (Leviticus 26:3–13). But it is the *tokhacha* (admonition) and its accompanying curses (ibid., verses 14–43), and not the blessings, for which *Bechukkotai* is more widely known. In contrast, Ibn Ezra asserts that this prevailing view is patently false, resulting from a simplistic and superficial understanding, and, moreover, he says that only empty-headed people focus on the fact that the curses are more numerous and more detailed than the blessings.[2] Indeed, a careful reading of the text shows that the blessings, although shorter and stated in a more general form, are in many ways more far-reaching and more profoundly transformative than the curses.

The admonitions and the curses have a stepwise progression. At first (ibid., verses 14–17), God says that if we reject His laws and His ordnances, He will afflict us with various diseases and will make us flee before our enemies. If, however, we do not heed that warning, He will inflict upon us more severe punishments (see verses 18–22); and if we continue in our wicked actions, there will be still more severe penalties (verses 23–26). Finally, if we still persist in our rebellious ways, He will lay waste to our cities and

---

[1] Leviticus 26:3 – 27:34.
[2] See Ibn Ezra's commentary on Leviticus 26:13.

exile us among the nations (verses 27–33). But, unlike, the curses, it appears that the blessings will be given to us not in stages but all at once if we follow God's commandments.

Besides the above differences in the ways in which God rewards or punishes us for our actions, Sforno points out a profound difference between our attitudes that would result in either the curses or the blessings. Whereas our following the divine commandments will bring the blessings to fruition, merely disregarding God's laws—or perhaps even intentionally violating them—will not bring the curses upon us. Rather, Sforno says, it is only if we **spurn** God's laws and **abhor** His commandments, with the intention to dissolve God's covenant, that God will bring the curses upon us.[3] And even then, the Torah says that God will not spurn or abhor us, and He will not dissolve the covenant He made with our patriarchs (ibid., verses 44–45).

In contrast to the curses, which—at least in Sforno's view—we incur only through major contempt for the divine precepts, Maimonides tells us that if we follow God's laws joyously and with attention to their wisdom, God will then remove obstacles to our performance of His commandments, such as illness, war, and famine; and He will bestow upon us various blessings—such as plenty, peace, and wealth—that will facilitate our performance of His laws.[4]

But following God's precepts will result in much more than removal of obstacles to our observance of His laws. Our following God's commandments and walking in His

---

[3] See Sforno on Leviticus 26:15–16.

[4] This opinion of Maimonides, which is based on the text of the blessings (Leviticus 26:3–13), can be found in his *Mishneh Torah, Hilkhot Teshuva* 9:1. He makes a similar statement, accompanied by a much more extensive discussion, in his commentary on the Mishnah—*Sanhedrin* 10:1 (*Chelek*).

ways will serve to elevate us and bring us closer to God. Thus, the Torah promises that God will "walk about in [our] midst" – *Vehit'halakhti betokhekhem* (ibid., verse 12); and, Sforno points out, the reflexive verb *vehit'halakhti* indicates going from place to place. God's presence will be felt not only in the Tabernacle (or later, in the Temple in Jerusalem) but will be manifest all over the land. Moreover, Maimonides stresses that our blessings will not be confined to our lives in the physical world but will extend to the hereafter, in the world to come.

We see, then, that, despite the more detailed and more lengthy listing of the admonitions and curses, it is the blessings that are the primary thrust of the portion of *Bechukkotai*; and it is the blessings rather than the curses that have the greater impact.

BOOK IV

Bamidbar (Numbers)

The fourth book of the Torah, *Bamidbar*, starts in the second year after the Israelites left Egypt and tells the story of their travels through the desert until they were on the verge of entering the land that God had promised them, the Land of Israel. The book of *Bamidbar* relates the most significant events of those years, and the laws that God gave the Israelites during their journey through the desert. Some of the highlights of the book are the census (hence the English name of the book—"Numbers"), the spies that Moses sent to scout out the land, the punishment of Miriam for speaking badly of Moses, the rebellion of Korach, the sin of Moses and Aaron, and the prophecies of Bil'am. The unrest and the internal divisions with which Moses had to contend in order to hold his newly-formed nation together are vividly presented.

Bamidbar:
The Census—Once or Twice?

Why was a second census necessary just seven months
after the previous census?

At the start of the *sidra* of *Bamidbar*,[1] God speaks to
Moses on the first day of the second month in the second
year following the Exodus from Egypt, and tells him to
conduct a census (Numbers 1:1–4).   But, if a census
was just conducted about seven months previously (see
Exodus 30:12), why was another census necessary now?

In the first census, mentioned in the portion of *Ki Tissa*
(Exodus 30:12–16), there was no direct count; rather, each
adult male of age twenty and over contributed a half *shekel*
of silver, and the number of individuals was calculated from
the amount of silver collected.   By contrast, in *Bamidbar* the
census seemingly was conducted by counting heads—*kol zakhar*
legulgelotam—"every male by their heads" (Numbers 1:2);
and the Torah indicates the military purpose of this second
census by specifying "from age twenty years and upward, all
who are fit for military service in Israel" (ibid., verse 3).

Both Rashi and Ramban maintain that the count was
done indirectly in both censuses, by collecting a half shekel
of silver from each person and tallying the silver.   Their
assumption is that this method of counting is understood
from the phrasing of Exodus 30:12, suggesting that the
indirect method was to be used thenceforth whenever
a census would be taken, and therefore the Torah did not

---

[1]   Numbers 1:1 – 4:20.

have to specify the method in Numbers 1:2. They bolster their argument by pointing to the statement that the half shekel is described as "an atonement for his soul ... in order that there be no scourge among them when they are counted" (Exodus 30:12). Counting heads directly is considered sinful and may be punished by a plague, as happened many years later when King David counted his people (see 2 Samuel, Chapter 24). Therefore, an atonement is required to forestall a plague.[2]

Abravnel, however, disagrees with Rashi and Ramban. According to Abravnel, the reason that King David's census, which was done by counting heads, resulted in a plague is that David had conducted the census on his own initiative; but the census in *Bamidbar* was being conducted at God's command. Therefore, says Abravnel, no punishment would result; and thus he maintains that the count was done directly, as the plain reading of the text (Numbers 1:2) seems to indicate. Furthermore, Abravnel says, a second census was needed a short time after the first, because the silver collected in *Ki Tissa* was for the purpose of financing the service in the Tabernacle and not for the purpose of counting potential soldiers, *i.e.* able-bodied adult Israelite men.[3]

---

[2] See Rashi and Ramban on Exodus 30:12, and Rashi on Exodus 30:15. However, Ibn Ezra, in his commentary on Exodus 30:12, quotes the Karaite commentator Yefet saying that the "scourge" (*negef*) that the half-shekel atonement-contribution was meant to avert was not a pestilence, but rather a massacre by the enemy in battle.

See "*Mattot*: The Sanctity of Life," above, for an additional explanation of the phrase "atonement for his soul" in Exodus 30:12. The reason given there is also applicable here, as an additional explanation of "atonement for his soul."

[3] For Abravnel's opinion that a plague would not ensue if the census were performed at God's command, see his commentary on Exodus 30:11–16. For his opinion explaining the reason for conducting a second census a mere seven months after the first one, see his commentary on Numbers 1:1–4, in his answer to his fourth question.

A bigger interpretive problem is raised by the results of the census: the total count of the Israelites in both censuses was identical—exactly 603,550.[4] How could that be? In the seven months between the two counts, some people must have died, and some must have turned twenty! It is unlikely that the two counts would come out the same. Rashi, Ramban, and most other commentaries struggle to explain the apparent coincidence. But in the end, such a coincidence still seems highly unlikely; and it also seems unlikely that God would work a miracle for so minor a matter as making two censuses result in an identical total.

It is most likely, then, that the count in *Ki Tissa* and the count in *Bamidbar* describe the same census and not two separate censuses. And this is the opinion of several commentators, including Yosef Bekhor Shor, *Hizkuni*, *Da'at Zekenim Miba'alei Hatosafot*, and Umberto Cassuto.[5] So, if that is the case, why does the Torah discuss the census in two separate places—*Ki Tissa* and *Bamidbar*? To answer this question, we must understand how censuses were taken in the ancient Near East. Cassuto, in his commentary on Exodus 30:11–16, describes the process. The name of each clan or family was recorded, along with the names of the members of the family. In Mesopotamia, the names were inscribed on clay tablets, and in Israel they were written on potsherds. The names of the clans, families, and individuals were needed for the military commanders

---

[4] Compare the two counts in Exodus 38:26 and Numbers 2:32.
[5] See Yosef Bekhor Shor and *Hizkuni* on Exodus 30:12, *Da'at Zekenim Miba'alei Hatosafot* on Exodus 30:16, and Umberto Cassuto's commentaries on Exodus 30:11–16 and 38:26. *Hizkuni* is the title of the Torah commentary by Rabbi Hizkiya ben Manoah (France, 13th Century). See also Description of Sources.

to assign their troops, but counting the names on the potsherds was a lengthy, exacting task. The potsherds and the half-shekel contributions were collected at the same time, shortly after *Yom Kippur* (The Day of Atonement) in the first year following the Exodus. But, says Cassuto, a detailed tally of all the names recorded on the potsherds, "by their clans, by their father's houses, **by a count of names**" (*e.g.* in Numbers 1:26), the sums of which are listed in *Bamidbar* (ibid., 1:20–47), was delayed until the month of *Nissan* in the second year, after the Tabernacle was erected. That tally was completed, as stated in verse 1, on the first day of the second month, just before the Israelites' planned entrance into the land of Canaan (which, as it turned out, did not occur as scheduled).

Thus we have explained both the "coincidence" of the two identical counts, and the reason why the mention of the same census was given at two separate times: once (in *Ki Tissa*) when the half-shekel and the potsherds were collected, and again (in *Bamidbar*) when the names were listed and tallied by tribe, clan, and family. And, not surprisingly, the total of the latter detailed count exactly matched the number calculated earlier from the amount of silver collected.

Nasso:
The Priestly Blessing and the Holy Name

Which name of God did the kohanim use in their blessing of the people?

In the *sidra* of *Nasso*[1] (the longest portion in the Torah), God tells Moses to instruct the *kohanim*—the priests—how to bless the people of Israel: *Ko tevarekhu et benei Yisrael*—"Thus you shall bless the people of Israel" (Numbers 6:23). The wording of the tri-partite blessing is then specified in the next three verses, following which, God declares, "and they shall place My Name upon the people of Israel, and I shall bless them" (ibid., verse 27). Traditionally, the *kohanim* deliver their blessing with their arms raised and their fingers spread in the form of the three-pronged Hebrew letter *shin*, the first letter of *Shaddai*—one of God's names, a name that signifies God as maker of the covenant with the nation of Israel.

The tradition of a priestly blessing did not actually begin at that time. At a somewhat earlier date—in the portion of *Shemini* (Leviticus 9:22)—we see Aaron the High Priest raising his hands and blessing the people. But, as Ramban points out, it is only here—in the portion of *Nasso*—that God specifies the words of the priestly blessing and decrees that not only Aaron himself but his descendants through the generations should continue to bless the people of Israel in this manner.[2]

---

[1] Numbers 4:21 – 7:89.
[2] See Ramban on Number 6:23.

When the *kohanim* raise their hands and deliver their blessing, they transmit God's love to the people, and the emanation of God's presence is said to flow between their fingers. Therefore it is customary not to look at the *kohanim* during their blessing. To that end, the *kohanim* cover their outstretched hands and faces with their *talitot* (prayer shawls).[3]

Verse 27 (see above) tells the *kohanim* to place God's Name upon the people of Israel. But which of the divine names were the *kohanim* to use in their blessing? Today, the name *Adonay* (The Lord) is used; but in ancient times, in the Holy Temple in Jerusalem, it was YHVH— the four-letter name—that was spoken in the priestly blessing. Later, when many people became careless with using that especially holy name, the *kohanim* swallowed the enunciation of the name so that others would not know its proper pronunciation. And after the destruction of the Second Temple, eventually the pronunciation of the four-letter name was completely lost.[4] Today, we know only the consonants of that name—YHVH—but not the vowels.

The employment of God's four-letter name in blessing was not limited to the priestly blessing. In fact, the Mishnah states that everybody was supposed to greet his

---

[3] For discussion of the priestly blessing as a transmission of God's love, see Zohar III:146a. For the practice of not looking at the *kohanim* while they are blessing the people, see Zohar III:147a.

[4] For discussion of which name of God was used in the Holy Temple in ancient times, see the Babylonian Talmud, *Kiddushin* 71a (bottom half of the page). On that page, there is also mention of God's twelve-letter name, which was known to only certain select *kohanim* and which is no longer known to us. Rashi there notes that the few *kohanim* who knew the twelve-letter name would speak it in the priestly blessing, but they would speak it indistinctly so that other *kohanim* would not perceive it and so that the singing of the other *kohanim* would drown out their voices.

friend using the divine name,[5] as we see in the Book of Ruth, where Boaz greets his workers, "YHVH be with you"; and they answer, "May YHVH bless you." And Rashi comments that this was not considered taking the Lord's name in vain.[6] But eventually over the course of centuries, the use of God's name in daily greeting of friends and acquaintances was discontinued. Nevertheless, since the Torah directs the *kohanim* to "place My Name upon the people of Israel" (Numbers 6:27), therefore one of God's names (*Adonay*—the Lord) continues to this day to be used in the priestly blessing, albeit not the four-letter name: "May the Lord bless you, and may He give you peace."

---

[5] See Mishnah *Berakhot* 9:5.
[6] See Rashi in Babylonian Talmud, *Berakhot* 54a.

Beha'alotekha 1:
The Menorah

What is the history of the Menorah?

The *sidra* of *Beha'alotekha*[1] begins with God telling Moses to instruct his brother Aaron the High Priest how to kindle the lights of the Menorah, the seven-branched candelabra that stood first in the Tabernacle in the desert and later in the Holy Temple that King Solomon built in Jerusalem. The middle light of the Menorah sat atop the central stem, while the other six branches surrounded the stem, three on each side (see Exodus 25:31–32). The stem sprouted up from a base; and the entire Menorah, including the base, was made from a single block of solid gold. It measured eighteen handbreadths in height.

The *Midrash* tells us that, of all the implements, vessels, and ornaments made for the Tabernacle, the Menorah was the most difficult to make; and Moses was confused about the instructions for fashioning it, even after God had explained it to him several times and shown him a vision of the completed Menorah.[2] But Moses's chief artisan, Bezal'el, brought the Menorah into being, and it was a wondrous piece of work indeed!

Centuries passed. In the 10th Century BCE, King Solomon built the Holy Temple in Jerusalem, and the Menorah resided there for almost four hundred years. But

---

[1] Numbers 8:1 – 12:16.

[2] For the construction of the original Menorah and the difficulty that Moses had in conceptualizing it, see *Midrash Rabba* on Numbers 8:2, and *Midrash Tanchuma, Beha'alotekha* §6.

in the year 586 BCE, the Babylonians conquered Jerusalem, plundered the Temple and burned it to the ground, and exiled the Jewish people to Babylonia. The gold and silver implements and vessels taken from the Holy Temple were brought to Babylonia, but the Menorah was not among the booty. Legend has it that the prophet Jeremiah, according to God's command, stowed the Menorah, along with several other especially holy and wondrous items, in a hidden location, there to remain until the coming of the Messiah.

Several decades passed, and the Persian Empire conquered Babylonia. The Persian King Cyrus the Great permitted the Jews to return to their land and rebuild the Temple. Probably the majority of Jews remained in Babylonia, but many did return to their ancestral land of Israel, and in the year 516 BCE the Second Temple was erected. But the original Menorah was missing, its whereabouts unknown, and a new one had to be made. The new settlers were far from wealthy, and a golden candelabra was out of the question. Therefore, the new Menorah was made of tin. Over a period of many years, the community became wealthier, and the tin Menorah was replaced by a silver one. And when their wealth increased further, a golden Menorah replaced the silver one. However, it is not clear whether the original tin Menorah was retained and covered first with a layer of silver and later with a layer of gold, or whether the silver and gold versions of the Menorah were newly made.

The Second Temple remained until the year 70 CE, when it was burnt to the ground by the Roman army under Titus, son of the Emperor Vespasian. The Roman army conquered Jerusalem and exiled the Jewish people to Rome. Titus also had the Menorah brought to Rome, and when the Arch of Titus was erected several years later to commemorate the Roman victory over the Jews, the Menorah was depicted prominently on the Arch. What happened to the Menorah of the Second Temple after it was brought to Rome is a matter of much controversy and conjecture. There is evidence that it was later taken to Constantinople, and perhaps back to Jerusalem at a still later time. But the evidence is not firm, and the fate of the Second Temple Menorah remains as much a mystery as that of the First Temple Menorah.

As mentioned, the Menorah in the Temple—both in the First Temple and in the Second Temple—had seven branches. In fact, it is a requirement that the Menorah in the Temple have seven branches. But it is forbidden to make a seven-branched candelabra outside of the Temple; and therefore depictions of the Menorah found in many synagogues have only six branches, while the menorah that is used on Chanukah has nine branches (including the *shamash*).[3]

From the above discussion it should be apparent that the Menorah was a unique and especially revered object. The Menorah of the Tabernacle and the First Temple was extraordinarily heavy and extraordinarily expensive, and the making of it baffled Moses. However, the holiness of the Menorah derives not from its physical attributes but from its role in establishing a link between our world and the spiritual world—the world above; for, as the Torah tells us, "according to the vision that the Lord had shown Moses, so he made the Menorah" (Numbers 8:4). The Menorah, then, was a physical rendering of an image derived from the upper world. And, just as God had begun the seven

---

[3] For laws pertaining to the properties of the Menorah and the proscription against making a seven-branched Menorah outside of the Temple, see Babylonian Talmud, *Menachot* 28b, and *Rosh Hashanah* 24a–b.

days of creation with the creation of light, the High Priest
lit the seven branches of the Menorah to unite us with the
divine spark that sustains the world.[4]

---

[4] Although my discussion regarding the Menorah's connection to the
spiritual world is largely my own, it is based in part on Rabbeinu Bachyay's
commentary on *Beha'alotekha* (Numbers 8:2).

Beha'alotekha 2:
The Holiness of the Menorah

How did the construction
of the Menorah reflect its holiness?

The *sidra* of *Beha'alotekha*,[1] which discusses the construction and the kindling of the Menorah—the seven-branched candelabra—is very enigmatic, and the commentaries have raised many questions about it. In this essay, I want to focus on three questions that will give us insight into the extraordinary spiritual importance that God gives to the Menorah: 1) The construction of the Menorah was such that the middle light sat atop the central stem, while the other six branches surrounded the stem, three on each side. Why did God specify that the Menorah have exactly seven branches—no more, no less? 2) The Menorah was not to be made as several pieces welded together, but was to be one solid piece of gold that was hammered into shape (Numbers 8:4). Why did God insist that it be one solid piece? 3) The oil used for lighting the Menorah had to be pure olive oil of the highest grade (Exodus 27:20). But when a person brought a *Mincha* offering, which consisted of grain mixed with oil (Leviticus 2:1), the oil did not have to be of highest grade; and yet, the *Mincha* offering was regarded as "Holy-of-Holies"—*i.e.* an offering of the highest order of holiness (see Leviticus 2:3). Why, then, did the oil for kindling the Menorah have to be of even greater purity than that of the *Mincha* offering? Is

---

[1] Numbers 8:1 – 12:16.

there a level of holiness that is still higher than Holy-of-Holies?

In our quest to answer these questions, we must first understand the nature and the symbolism of the Menorah. Light was the first of God's creations (Genesis 1:3), and the divine light illuminated and gave life to the embryonic universe. God's light symbolizes the source of life. The seven branches of the Menorah correspond to the seven days of creation, with the central branch corresponding to the Sabbath day, the culmination of creation, imbued with special holiness (Genesis 2:1–3). Thus, the lighting of the seven candles of the Menorah symbolically connected the people of Israel with the seven days of creation and, more importantly, with the Lord of creation, the source of life, the source of all that exists.

God is One, indivisible (Deuteronomy 6:4). Thus, it was necessary for the Menorah to be made as one solid piece of gold and not as multiple parts welded together, in order to fulfill its role of symbolically uniting the people of Israel with the one God.

Finally, in addressing my third question, we must consider the language of the Torah. The Torah refers to the kindling of the Menorah not as "lighting," but as "elevation": *beha'alotekha et hanerot*—literally, "When you elevate the candles" (Numbers 8:2). Why does the Torah use such an unusual phrasing? It is to call attention to the purpose of lighting the Menorah, which was to elevate the people of Israel. The purpose of lighting the Menorah was not merely to give light: it was to elevate us to the highest spiritual levels, and to connect us more closely to God. The offerings brought in the Temple in ancient times, which since the destruction of the Temple have been replaced by prayers, also served as a vehicle to approach

God, and were indeed imbued with holiness. But the particulars of the instructions given to Moses regarding the Menorah inform us that there is a still higher level of holiness than that of the holiest of offerings. The lighting of the Menorah was meant to elevate us to that higher level; and therefore, symbolically, the oil used to light the seven candles had to be of the very highest purity.[2]

---

[2] I have based the above discussion partly on my own thinking, but to a large degree on the Torah commentary by my maternal grandfather, Rabbi Shmuel Bar-Adon, in his book *Ne'umei Shmuel* (see also Description of Sources), as well as on the commentary of Rabbi Moshe Alsheikh.

Shelach:
The Narrative Thread

Spies, prostitution, and colored string. How does the Haftarah relate to the Torah portion?

The link that connects the Torah portion of *Shelach*[1] to its *Haftarah*[2] appears to be the act of sending spies. At the beginning of *Shelach*, Moses sends spies into the land of Canaan; and similarly, in the *Haftarah*, Joshua sends spies to the Canaanite city of Jericho. But the linkage between the portion of *Shelach* and its *Haftarah* goes deeper than just the act of sending spies. Two other matters bind the *sidra* to its *Haftarah*: the importance of faith, and the significance of a colored thread.

In the Torah story, ten of the twelve spies stray from the divine path. They relinquish their faith in God's guidance and protection, and when faced with the apparent Canaanite might, they are beguiled by the vision of their eyes and succumb to the dictates of their heart. They report to Moses that it would be impossible for the Israelites to conquer the Promised Land. Shortly after, God tells Moses to instruct the people of Israel to place threads (*tzitzit*) on the fringes of their garments, including one blue thread to remind them of heaven, so that they will not go astray by following the dictates of their hearts and their eyes, thereby "prostituting" themselves (as the Torah puts it—see Numbers 15:39) through their trust in false beliefs.

---

[1] Numbers 13:1 – 15:41.
[2] Joshua 2:1–24.

In contrast to the lack of faith that the spies in the portion of *Shelach* display, Joshua's spies enter Jericho and encounter a woman named Rahab, a prostitute who wants to change her life. She has heard of the miracles that God performed for Israel. She knows in her heart that God will enable the Israelites to conquer Jericho, and indeed all of Canaan; and she wants to join the nation of Israel. She hides Joshua's spies and helps them escape, lowering them from her window by a crimson cord. In return for her help, she asks that she and her family be spared. The spies tell her to leave the crimson cord hanging from her window, so that the soldiers will know which house to spare. In the ensuing battle, Joshua's army conquers Jericho. Rahab and her family are spared, and Rahab joins the nation of Israel.

The *Haftarah*, then, in many ways is the antithesis of the *sidra*. Whereas in the Torah portion, the spies abandon their trust in God's power and guardianship over Israel, thus figuratively "prostituting" themselves, in the *Haftarah* an actual prostitute rejects her former life and places her trust in God and in the oath of Joshua's spies that the Israelite army will spare her and her family. In the Torah, God commands the Israelites to wear a blue thread on the fringes of their garments to remind them of heaven and figuratively to bind them to their faith in God, lest they be led astray by the dictates of their hearts and their eyes.[3] It is a token of trust between man and God. In the *Haftarah*, a colored rope marks Rahab's house for the

---

[3] For the supernal associations of the blue thread in the *tzitzit*, see Babylonian Talmud, *Chullin* 89a (top of page), and *Menachot* 43b (bottom of page). See also Zohar II:139a (top of page). As stated in those references, the blue color of the *tzitzit* resembles the sea, the sky, the hue of sapphire, and of the divine throne.

Israelite soldiers, but it is also a mark of Rahab's faith in the honor of men and their commitment to their word. As the blue thread of the *tzitzit* is a token of man's faith in God, Rahab's crimson cord is a token of trust between man and man.

Korach:
The Man Who Would Be Priest

When Korach challenges the authority of Moses,
why does Moses respond the way he does?

The *sidra* of *Korach*[1] tells the story of a rebellion against the authority of Moses. Korach, a prominent Levite apparently motivated by jealousy, challenges the selection of Moses's brother Aaron as high priest and seeks to obtain that prestigious position for himself. Korach gathers two hundred fifty clan leaders and other notables, and confronts Moses. They say to Moses and Aaron, *Rav lakhem*—"You [plural] have too much" (Numbers 16:3). All the Israelites are holy, they say, "and the Lord is among them; so why do you place yourselves above the assembly of the Lord?" (ibid.) With these words, Korach and his mob negate Moses's role as prophet and as transmitter of God's words, and moreover, imply that it was not God but Moses who chose Aaron as high priest.

Korach's challenge undermines the authority of Moses and Aaron, and perhaps—if the entire nation is equally holy—the authority of any leader who might claim the position of prophet, king, or law-giver. It is a challenge that has to be met forcefully and in such a way that will demonstrate to the entire nation the divinely-ordained authority of Moses. So how does Moses respond? He offers a counter-challenge that, if accepted, will put the lives of Korach and all his followers at risk. Moses tells

---

[1] Numbers 16:1 – 18:32.

the rebels that in the morning each of them is to bring a pan and place incense and fire upon it; "and the man whom God will choose, he is the holy one" (verses 5–7). And Moses throws the rebels' own words back at them: *rav lakhem, benei Levi*—"you have enough, sons of Levi" (verse 7).[2]

Several questions come to mind, and I will address two of them: 1) How did the test endanger the rebels' lives, and why would they have accepted the challenge? 2) Why did Moses set the time for the test for the following morning rather than immediately?

As we saw in the Torah portion of *Shemini*, it was forbidden to bring an "alien fire" into the Tabernacle, and two of Aaron's sons had recently died by God's hand on account of that transgression.[3] And yet, Moses here proposes that Korach and his followers do exactly that! The *Midrash Tanchuma* proposes that Moses purposely scheduled the test for the following morning in order to give the rebels time to think it over and come to their senses. Moreover, the *Tanchuma* asserts that Moses made it clear that God would accept the incense offering of only one person: "and **the man** whom the Lord will choose, **he** is the holy one" (see verse 7); all the rest would incur the death penalty.[4] But the rebels numbered two hundred fifty, so the odds of coming out of the test alive would be very small. And thus, perhaps when Moses hurls the rebels' words *rav lakhem* back at them at the conclusion of verse

---

[2] Note that the word *rav* can mean "great," much," or "enough"; thus, the words *rav lakhem* can be translated as either "you have too much," (as I translated in verse 3) or "you have enough" (as I translated in verse 7). And, see below for yet another possible translation of those words.

[3] For a discussion of Aaron's sons bringing an alien fire, see "*Shemini*: An Alien Fire,"

[4] See *Midrash Tanchuma, Korach* §5.

7, those words should not be interpreted as "you have enough" as I translated above, but rather should be taken to mean "you have many" or "you are many," emphasizing the slim chance of emerging from the test alive.[5] Moses, the *Tanchuma* says, hoped that the rebels would not want to take such a risk and would back out.

Why, then, did Korach and his followers accept such a test? As for Korach himself, the *Tanchuma* offers an explanation: Korach knew through a prophecy that one of his descendants would be the great prophet Samuel, and therefore he found it inconceivable that God would not accept his offering. That perhaps could explain Korach's reason, but the reason his followers would have taken such a chance is unexplained. And so, Korach, blinded by his pride, accepted the challenge and led his followers to disaster as the earth "opened its mouth" and swallowed them up. But Moses's efforts apparently did result in at least a few of Korach's followers repenting. As the Torah tells us later (Numbers 26:11), the sons of Korach did not die, and it was from one of them that the prophet Samuel descended.

---

[5] The reinterpretation of the words *rav lakhem* to mean "you have many" in verse 7, when Moses throws the rebels' words back at them, is my own idea; but that translation is based on the language of the *Tanchuma*, and I suspect the *Tanchuma*'s view was that Moses intended exactly that reinterpretation of *rav lakhem* when he flung the rebels' own words back at them.

Chukkat:
Moses and the Rock

What specifically was Moses's sin when he hit the rock?

The Torah portion of *Chukkat*[1] contains several significant historical events, and one of the most perplexing is that of Moses striking the rock (Numbers 20:2–11). In a similar episode shortly after the Exodus from Egypt (Exodus 17:1–7), the Israelites thirsted for water in the desert, and God commanded Moses to bring forth water by striking a rock in front of the elders of Israel. Now, in *Chukkat*, about 38 or 39 years later, again there is no water. But this time, God tells Moses to take up his staff and, together with his brother Aaron, to assemble the people and bring forth water by speaking to a rock in front of the entire nation. Instead, Moses again strikes the rock, following which God declares that, in consequence of Moses and Aaron's failure to consecrate God before the entire nation, neither of them will be allowed to enter the Promised Land (verses 12–14). Aaron dies soon after (verses 22–29), while Moses continues to lead his people until just before they enter the land of Israel.

The Torah makes it very clear that Moses and Aaron sinned, but what exactly was the nature of their sin? The Torah does not clarify this point. Was it that they didn't speak to the rock?[2] But an alternative interpretation of God's command—*vedibbartem el hasela* (usually interpreted as "you shall speak to the rock")—could be that Moses and

---

[1] Numbers 19:1 – 22:2.
[2] See Rashi on Numbers 20:11 & 12, and *Yalkut Shimoni* on Numbers 20:8.

Aaron should speak to the subject of the rock, *i.e.* address the people and tell them that they will extract water from the rock;[3] and in fact they did so, just before hitting the rock: "Listen now, you rebels! Shall we bring forth water from this rock?" (Numbers 20:10.)

Perhaps, then, their sin was the act of striking the rock?[4] But it was Moses and not Aaron who struck the rock, so why was Aaron also charged with a sin?[5] Moreover, if Moses was not supposed to strike the rock, then why did God tell him to take up his staff? What was he supposed to do with the staff?[6] And finally, specifically how did Moses and Aaron fail to sanctify God? They did, after all, perform a miracle. And if they did not perform the miracle in exactly the way they had been directed to do, why did God consider that to be such a grievous sin as to merit so harsh a punishment?

Maimonides explains that calling the people rebels and striking the rock were manifestations of anger. There is no indication that God was incensed against the people of Israel at that time, so Moses's display of anger was completely inappropriate, and sinful in God's eyes.[7] But there is no evidence that Aaron was angry; so the question of why Aaron deserved to be punished still stands. Therefore, even if striking the rock was a manifestation of anger, that is probably not the full explanation for the punishment.

Ramban disputes the thesis that hitting the rock was a manifestation of anger, and he also objects that such

---

[3] See Ramban on 20:1.

[4] Rashi on 20:12. According to Rashi, Moses's failure was both in not speaking to the rock and in striking it.

[5] See Abravnel, and Sforno on 20:8.

[6] See Ramban on Numbers 20:1.

[7] See Moses Maimonides, *Shemona Perakim*, Chapter 4.

an explanation could not apply to Aaron, since Ramban cites a verse to show that Aaron never got angry in his life. Furthermore, the Torah attributes the sin of Moses and Aaron to lack of faith and not to anger: "Because you did not trust in me, to sanctify me ..." (Numbers 20:12). Ramban therefore proposes that the most likely explanation of the sin is that of Rabbeinu Chananel, who says that Moses and Aaron's sin consisted in not attributing the miracle to God but implying that it was they who produced the miracle through their own power, saying "From this rock shall **we** extract for you water?" (ibid., verse 10.)

Abravnel is not satisfied with any of the above explanations, and he offers yet another solution. According to Abravnel, the actions of Moses and Aaron in *Chukkat* were manifestations of something deeper: a flaw in their character as leaders. The flaw had also manifested itself previously. In the case of Aaron, it was in the episode of the Golden Calf, when the Torah tells us (in the portion of *Ki Tissa*) that Aaron gave in to the people's demands and built an idol for them—the Golden Calf. In the case of Moses, it was in the episode of the spies (in the portion of *Shelach*) that Moses instructed the spies to explore the Promised Land and report whether it is a good land or a bad one, whether the inhabitants are strong or weak. Indeed, God had directed Moses to send spies, but He had not told Moses to give those instructions. Moses should have stated emphatically that this was the land that God had promised, and the sole mission of the spies was to gather strategic information to enable the leaders to formulate a battle plan. In Abravnel's view, then, the episode of the rock was merely the final inciting incident but not the sole explanation for the punishment of Moses and Aaron. In fact, because of the Golden Calf, Abravnel sees Aaron's sin as the greater, and that is why Aaron did not even attempt to ask God to mitigate his punishment, whereas Moses did ask that for himself (Deuteronomy 3:23–25).[8]

Another way to look at the episode is not to view God's pronouncement as a punishment in the usual sense, although undoubtedly Moses considered it to be such. In the view of Naftali Zvi Yehuda Berlin,[9] the book of Numbers, and especially the *sidra* of *Chukkat*, is a tale of transition: the transition of the Israelites from slaves to free people, from a group of unruly tribes to a nation, from dependence—first on the Egyptians and then on God's miraculous aid—to independence and self-determination. Moses, the great leader who brought his people out of slavery in Egypt and presided over the initial stages of the transformation, now—38 years later—still regarded the people of Israel as he had when they first came out of Egypt: a difficult, stiff-necked people.[10] Moses's anger and his striking of the rock are symbolic of Moses's fossilized view of his people. But the Israelites had changed. And yet, Moses still used the same approach and the same methods that he had used with the previous generation of his people. He, and presumably Aaron also, had failed to adapt to a new reality, and therefore new leadership was necessary.

More than three millennia have passed since the events described in the portion of *Chukkat*, and over the centuries commentators have advanced many different explanations of Moses and Aaron's sin. Each explanation has a kernel

---

[8]   See Abravnel's commentary on Numbers 20:1–13.
[9]   Rabbi Naftali Zvi Yehuda Berlin, who was also known as The Netziv (1816–1893). See also Description of Sources.
[10] See the Netziv's introduction to the book of Numbers in his commentary, *Ha'amek Davar*.

of truth, but none seems completely adequate. And so, we continue to search the text of the Torah for clues. Indeed, perhaps that is the very purpose of not spelling out the sin of Moses and Aaron. God wants us to probe the characters of our greatest leaders and to identify their flaws. Even Moses, whose divine reach exceeded that of any other prophet of Israel (see Deuteronomy 34:10), nevertheless was only human, and we must never idolize him or make him superhuman in our eyes. It is the very vagueness of the Torah in identifying the sin of Moses in the portion of *Chukkat* that has spurred our exploration of his failure and has helped prevent us from attributing to him any measure of divinity.

Balak 1:
The Prophet, The Donkey, and The Angel

How could Bil'am's donkey see the angel,
but the great prophet Bil'am could not?

The *sidra* of *Balak*[1] introduces us to a most perplexing character: an Aramean prophet named Bil'am,[2] whose prophetic powers rival those of Moses;[3] and yet, for worldly honor and pecuniary gain, he tries his best to thwart what he knows to be God's will. The tale begins immediately after the Israelites' stunning military victories told at the end of the previous *sidra*. In the aftermath of those victories over three kings who attacked them, Balak, the king of Moav, still desires to make war against the approaching Israelites but feels he will need divine aid. Therefore he sends emissaries to Bil'am, a famous prophet—who, incidentally, is also known to us today from non-Biblical archaeologic sources—seeking to reward him handsomely for cursing the Israelites. Bil'am wants to comply, but God tells Bil'am that He won't allow him to curse. Nevertheless, God finally does let him go with the Moabite ministers but cautions him that he will be able to speak only the words that God wants him to say.

---

[1] Numbers 22:2 – 25:9.
[2] His name is generally given as Balaam in most English translations, but the correct name in Hebrew is Bil'am.
[3] For the rabbinic opinion that Bil'am's prophetic powers rivaled those of Moses, see *Sifrei Devarim* 357:10.

Apparently, as Bil'am travels with his two servants and the Moabite ministers on the way to Moav, he still hopes that God will relent and will let him curse. Therefore, as the group rides through a narrow pass, an angel with drawn sword blocks Bil'am's path. Bil'am's donkey—a she-ass—sees the angel and stops, but the great prophet does not see the angel. He tries to coax the beast to continue forward and strikes her three times with a stick. But the donkey will not budge. After the third beating, "God opened the mouth of the ass, and she said to Bil'am, 'What have I done to you that you have hit me these three times?'" (Numbers 22:28.)

Almost any other person would have been startled if his donkey had addressed him thus. But Bil'am merely answers the donkey as though it were a normal event for a donkey to speak. Perhaps Bil'am's lack of surprise is a function of this prophet's intimate familiarity with the supernatural. But what of Bil'am's two servants and the Moabite ministers? Wouldn't they have been startled when the donkey spoke? Rabbeinu Bachyay asks that question and answers that either they were far ahead of Bil'am and thus out of earshot, or alternatively they did not see or hear anything unusual, even though they were in close proximity. Indeed, Rabbeinu Bachyay cites an example of a similar phenomenon, where an angel appeared and spoke to Daniel: "And I Daniel saw the vision alone, and the people who were with me did not see the vision, but a great fright fell upon them ..." (Daniel 10:7).[4]

While either of the above-mentioned reasons is a plausible explanation of why the people accompanying

---

[4] See Rabbbeinu Bachyay's commentary on Numbers 22:29.

Bil'am failed to be astounded when the angel appeared and the donkey spoke, we still may ask how the great prophet Bil'am, "who knows the intent of the Most High" and who "beholds visions of the Almighty" (Numbers 24:16), failed to see the angel standing before him with drawn sword, a sight that even his donkey was able to see. Or, as the Talmud asks, he didn't even know the mind of his donkey, so how could he know God's mind?[5]

But really, it should not surprise us that someone whose vision of some things was clouded—and who failed to see a sight that even his donkey was able to see—nevertheless could have a keen perception when enveloped by the prophetic spirit. And in fact, God purposely prevented Bil'am from seeing the angel. Sforno comments that God wanted Bil'am to repent, and to realize that the donkey's strange behavior—contrary to her usual character—was a sign from God, hinting that Bil'am's going on this journey was not appropriate and was doomed to failure.[6]

The foregoing discussion assumes that the episode described on Bil'am's journey—the angel appearing and blocking the donkey's way, Bil'am's failure to see the angel, Bil'am's hitting his donkey, the donkey speaking, and Bil'am finally seeing the angel and asking forgiveness—actually took place. Maimonides, however, proposes that wherever the Torah refers to an angel speaking to a person, it is invariably in a prophetic vision or a dream. Thus, according to Maimonides, the entire story from the time Bil'am left his home with the Moabite ministers until

---

[5] Babylonian Talmud, *Berakhot* 7a.

[6] See Sforno's comments on Numbers 22:28, 30, & 32. As evidence that the donkey's behavior was contrary to her usual character, see verse 30: "... Have I ever been accustomed to do thus to you?"

his arrival in Moav (Numbers 22:21–35) occurred only in a prophetic vision or a dream.[7]

But whether the confrontation with the angel occurred in real life or only in a vision, we can have no doubt that by the time Bil'am arrived in Moav he knew that God didn't want him to curse the people of Israel. And yet, despite knowing God's intentions, Bil'am continued to harbor a hope that he could change God's mind and let him curse. Ultimately, Bil'am failed to change God's mind, and he was forced to deliver the blessings that God intended. The prophetic spirit bestows upon a prophet an ability to see and hear and feel what no other human can even imagine. But that gift comes with a cost: unlike other humans, who have free will and can choose to obey God's commandments or to reject them, the prophet cannot refuse his mission; and, while acting in his capacity as prophet and messenger of God, he loses his freedom of will. And so, all Bil'am's attempts to foil God's purposes are futile, and Bil'am speaks the message that God appointed him to speak.

---

[7] For Moses Maimonides's opinion that Bil'am's confrontation with the angel and the donkey speaking occurred in a prophetic vision or a dream, see *The Guide for the Perplexed* II:42. In fact, the Torah makes clear that God's initial instruction to Bil'am, telling him that he may go with the Moabite ministers but will be allowed to speak only the words that God will tell him, was delivered to Bil'am in a prophetic dream (see Numbers 22:19–20). The story of Bil'am's travel to Moav, including the confrontation with the angel and the donkey speaking, is placed immediately following that prophetic dream. Although Maimonides does not point out that the tale of Bil'am's journey immediately follows the prophetic dream, perhaps—consistent with the view of Maimonides—we should infer that the entire episode of Bil'am's travel to Moav (verses 21–35) is a continuation of the same prophetic dream.

Balak 2:
Can a Prophet Change God's Mind?

How did Bil'am think to circumvent God's
forbidding him to curse the Israelites?

In the *sidra* of *Balak*,[1] the Moabite king Balak sends
emissaries to the prophet Bil'am[2] requesting him to curse
the Israelites, for which service Balak is prepared to pay
the prophet a handsome fee. Bil'am wants to comply, but
first he asks God for permission. God tells Bil'am that
he may go with Balak's emissaries, but God will not allow
him to curse the Israelites. Bil'am goes anyway, apparently
hoping eventually to persuade God to allow him to curse.
In the previous essay, I touched on Bil'am's hope that
God would change His mind and allow Bil'am to curse
the Israelites. In the current essay, I will address some
fundamental questions: Why did Bil'am think God would
change His mind? Is Bil'am's premise reasonable? And,
when he finally realized the futility of trying to change
God's mind, why did he not desist, and why did he turn
toward the desert for his next prophecy?

In fact, from Bil'am's point of view it is perfectly valid
to think that a prophet can change God's mind. Perhaps
God's initial statement was just a test to see whether the
prophet will be able to adduce the proper argument to
rebut God's initial position. After all, didn't Abraham argue

---

[1]   Numbers 22:2 – 25:9.
[2]   As mentioned in a footnote in the previous essay, his name is generally
given as Balaam in most English translations, but the correct name in
Hebrew is Bil'am.

with God regarding Sodom? And didn't Moses, after the sin of the Golden Calf, successfully argue with God and get Him to rescind His initial edict against the nation of Israel? Perhaps, then, Bil'am is also prepared to argue with God; but first he tries a more positive approach: he has King Balak bring multiple sacrifices to the Lord, while he himself goes off to meditate and pray for prophetic inspiration. God, however, does not comply with Bil'am's wishes: He places a blessing in Bil'am's mouth instead of a curse.

Balak expresses his displeasure, and Bil'am tries again; but a second blessing comes from his mouth. And in that second prophecy of blessing, we find the words *Lo ish El viykhazev, uven adam veyitnecham*—"God is not a man, who lies, nor a human, who will change his mind" (Numbers 23:19). It is only when Bil'am speaks these words that he finally realizes the futility of his attempt. But Bil'am is still intent on cursing. Therefore, in his next pursuit of prophetic inspiration, Bil'am no longer turns to God but toward the desert—*vayashet el hamidbar panav* (ibid., 24:1). Onkelos interprets this as referring to Bil'am focusing on the sin of the Golden Calf, a sin that the Israelites committed in the desert many years earlier; and Rashi agrees with Onkelos.[3] But that interpretation is a stretch. Instead, Rabbeinu Bachyay explains that Bil'am, now realizing that God will not allow him to curse Israel, therefore turns toward the desert seeking prophetic inspiration not from God but from the spirit of defilement, *i.e.* the demonic realm.[4]

Indeed, while Rabbeinu Bachyay probably was unaware of the desert's significance in the pagan religions of the

---

[3] See Rashi and Onkelos on Numbers 24:1.
[4] See Rabbeinu Bachyay on Numbers 24:1.

region, he was quite correct to equate the desert with the Dark Side. The desert in Egyptian religion was the land of Set, the god of disorder, deserts, storms, and war; and notably also, the god of evil. And in other near eastern traditions, the desert probably also was considered the source of evil powers. Thus, Bil'am now seeks to receive prophecy from the demonic realm instead of from God. But God does not let that happen: the spirit of God overtakes Bil'am, and he blesses Israel yet again.

Pinchas:
The Covenant of Peace

Why does God tell Moses to grant Pinchas the priesthood? Wasn't he already a kohen?

The *sidra* of *Pinchas*[1] begins with God instructing Moses to tell Pinchas, the grandson of Aaron the High Priest, that God is granting him His covenant of peace, and that henceforth both Pinchas and his descendants will be granted the priesthood in perpetuity (Numbers 25:12–13). But why does God need to grant Pinchas the priesthood at this time? Wasn't Pinchas already a *kohen*—a priest—by virtue of his lineage? And what is the meaning of a "covenant of peace"?

One possible interpretation could be that God was here granting Pinchas the position of High Priest and not merely the title of *kohen*, which he already was. But that is not what the Torah says! Therefore, Rashi, in an attempt to make sense of a literal reading of the text, says that Pinchas was in fact not a *kohen* previously. According to Rashi, only Aaron and his sons who were anointed together with him were initially appointed to the priesthood, and it was not assumed that future descendants of Aaron would necessarily be *kohanim*.[2] But Rashi's interpretation is far from being universally accepted. And if we do not accept Rashi's position, and we assume that Pinchas was already a *kohen* by virtue of his lineage, then the original question stands: why did God now want Moses to grant the priesthood to Pinchas?

---

[1] Numbers 25:11 – 30:1.
[2] See Rashi on Numbers 25:13.

201

To answer the question, we must first consider the context of God's statement. As related in the previous Torah portion (see Numbers 22:2-7), the Moabites and the Midianites had recently collaborated in an attempt to attack and defeat the Israelites. When their attempt met with failure, the Moabites and Midianites then sent their women to lure the men of Israel, and in this they were successful. The Israelites started to go whoring with the Moabite women and to worship the idol *Ba'al-Pe'or*, for which God punished the people with a plague that killed 24,000. And one prominent Israelite, a clan chieftain, made a public display of his sexual activities with a Midianite woman. While others were appalled and apparently stunned into inaction, Pinchas seized a spear and ran them both through; and the plague ceased immediately. (See Numbers 25:1-9.) The clan chieftain's brazen act of immorality was both sinful and treasonous, and it would have incurred the death penalty, had he been arrested and tried in court. Also, the Midianite woman would have been sentenced to death as a foreigner who had lured an Israelite leader to commit treason. But Pinchas didn't wait for a court trial. This was an emergency, and Pinchas—seeing that the authorities had failed to take action—acted quickly and decisively in order to stop the plague. Under normal conditions, Pinchas's act—taking the law into his own hands—would have been condemned as criminal. But these were exceptional circumstances, and God considered Pinchas's act of zealotry to be not only justified under the circumstances, but even praiseworthy (verse 11).

Now we can address the question of why God had to grant Pinchas the priesthood at this time, following his act of zealotry. The Zohar takes up the question, and, rejecting the view that Pinchas was not already a *kohen*, the Zohar notes that under Jewish law, a *kohen* who kills someone becomes forever disqualified from the priesthood. Therefore Pinchas was now legally disqualified from continuing as a *kohen*. But God rewarded him by not only reinstating him as a *kohen* but also conferring the High Priesthood on him and his descendants.[3]

Following up on the above explanation, the Zohar remarks on the way in which the Torah reports the identity of the Israelite whom Pinchas killed: the Torah uses the passive voice, telling us "the name of the Israelite man who was killed" (verse 14), rather than saying, "the name of the Israelite **whom Pinchas killed**," in order to avoid mentioning the name of Pinchas in connection with killing. A *kohen* represents God's love for humanity in general, and for his people Israel in particular; and thus, any priest— but especially a high priest—should not be associated with killing, even a justified killing.[4]

Now we can answer my second question: what did God mean when he granted Pinchas a "covenant of peace"? In my opinion, Pinchas's act of killing another human being, even though justified, and even though it ended the plague, was nevertheless an act that disrupted the peace between God and Man and created a rift in Pinchas's bond with the Almighty. And just as God had to declare that He would reinstate Pinchas as a *kohen*, so too did He have to reinstate the covenant of peace that would affirm Pinchas's priestly function of transmitting God's love to His people.

---

[3] See Zohar III:214a.
[4] See Zohar III:221b.

Mattot:
The Sanctity of Life

After the battle against the Midianites, why did the
Israelite soldiers have to atone for sins?

In the Torah portion of *Mattot*,[1] after the Israelite army
won a battle against the Midianites, the troops were told
to cleanse and ritually purify themselves (Numbers 31:19),
as would be expected following their contact with corpses.
But then, the soldiers brought offerings of the jewelry that
they had captured from the Midianites, "to atone for our
souls before the Lord" (ibid., verse 50). For what sin were
they atoning?

Sforno opines that they were atoning for the entire
nation that had stood by without protest during the
debauchery at *Pe'or*. (See Numbers 25:1–9.) Alternatively,
the Talmud offers an opinion that they were atoning for
inappropriate sexual thoughts.[2] While that view may
seem strange to us, there nevertheless is a firm basis for
that opinion, since it was common practice for conquering
soldiers to rape the women of the conquered nation.
Thus, the inappropriate sexual thoughts to which the
Talmud refers could be thoughts about rape following the
battle; or, alternatively, the Talmud may be referring to
the debauchery at *Pe'or*.[3]

But perhaps the Torah is giving us a deeper and more
subtle message. The phrase "to atone for our souls" (as in

---

[1] Numbers 30:2 – 32:42.
[2] See Babylonian Talmud, *Shabbat* 64a.
[3] See my commentary on *Pinchas*, above.

Numbers 31:50),[4] or a variant of that phrase, is used only a few times in the Torah. The first instance is in the *sidra* of *Ki Tissa*, where each Israelite was to give a half *shekel* as "atonement for his soul" (Exodus 30:12), and a similar phrasing is used twice more in the same context (ibid., verses 15 and 16). As I discussed in my commentary on *Bamidbar*, the census described there (Numbers 1:2–3) was likely the same census described in *Ki Tissa*; and that census was a mustering of the army in preparation for battle, as explicitly stated in Numbers 1:2. Hertz,[5] in his commentary on Numbers 1:2, cites the opinion of Benno Jacob[6] that a soldier is a potential taker of life, and therefore every soldier must give a half *shekel* to atone for any lives that he may take in the course of battle.

Another example of the use of this phrase is found in Leviticus 17:11. After the prohibition of eating blood in the previous verse, the Torah explains, "For the life of the flesh is in the blood; and I have given it to you upon the

---

[4]   The Hebrew word that is translated as "to atone" (in Numbers 31:50, mentioned above in reference to atoning for one's soul) is *lekhapper*. That word is from the same root as *kofer*, which is often translated as "ransom" (as in Numbers 1:2). Thus, the word *kofer*, which can—depending on the context—denote a ransom or a security deposit, is appropriately rendered here as "atonement."

In addition to the verses cited above in which the Torah refers to atonement for a person's soul, in Numbers 35:31 the Torah tells us that we may not accept a *kofer* for the life of a murderer, "for he shall be put to death." But there, *kofer* is clearly used to mean a monetary ransom to substitute for the death penalty, and not in the sense of a spiritual atonement. This interpretation is consistent with the use of the word *kofer* in the very next verse, which forbids accepting *kofer* in lieu of a penalty of exile (ibid., 35:32).

[5]   Dr. Joseph H. Hertz (1872–1946) was Chief Rabbi of the British Empire from 1913 until his death in 1946. His commentary on the Torah is contained in *Pentateuch and Haftorahs*, London, Soncino Press, 1975.

[6]   Poland and England, 1862–1945.

altar to atone for your lives ...." In other words, even the blood of animals must not be shed except when the animals are killed in the prescribed manner and for the prescribed purpose, because all life is sacred.

Just as God enjoined the Israelites from eating blood, even centuries earlier, when He permitted humans for the first time to eat meat (Genesis 9:3) He said to Noah, "but you shall not eat flesh with its life-blood still in it" (ibid., verse 4). Cassuto remarks on Genesis 9:4 that the permission to eat meat (which God had not permitted until after the Flood) was a concession to human nature, and that concession was related to forbidding the eating of blood, in deference to the principle of the sanctity of life. Significantly, immediately following granting Noah this concession, God forbids murder and decrees its penalty in the strongest terms: "Whoever sheds human blood, by Man his blood shall be shed; for in the image of God He made humankind" (ibid., verse 6). Man, unlike other living beings, was made "in the image of God" and thus has a special place in creation, but the linkage of the prohibition of consuming the blood of an animal to the proscription of spilling the blood of a human speaks to the sanctity of **all** life.

Returning to *Mattot*, we see the soldiers bringing an offering to the Lord in atonement for the lives of their fallen enemies. Although they were enemies, they were nevertheless God's creations, and we must not rejoice at their death. Thus, the Talmud tells us that when the Egyptian army was drowning in the sea, and the angels wanted to sing, God rebuked the angels saying, "My creations are drowning, and you recite a song?"[7] And thus, even though

---

[7] Babylonian Talmud, *Megilla* 10b and *Sanhedrin* 39b.

the Midianites were enemies of Israel and enemies of God, and despite the battle against the Midianites having been waged at God's command in response to the Midianites' collaborating with the Moabites to attempt to defeat the Israelites militarily, and later undermining the Israelites' moral underpinnings by sending their women to seduce the Israelites and lead them to worship the idol *Ba'al Pe'or*,[8] even so, they too were God's creations, and their lives also were sacred. Therefore, the soldiers brought offerings to atone for their own souls, for having taken the lives of their enemies.[9]

---

[8] For God's commanding the battle against the Midianites, see Numbers 31:1–3 and 24:16–18. For the Midianites' collaboration with the Moabites against the nation of Israel, see Numbers 22:4–7. For the Midianite (and Moabite) women seducing the Israelites and leading them to worship of the idol *Ba'al Pe'or*, see Numbers 25:1–3 & 6, and 15–18.

[9] Consistent with standard Bible translations, I have translated the word *nefesh* sometimes as "soul" and sometimes as "life." The Hebrew word refers to that which gives life to the body, and the Torah uses the word to refer either to a soul or to a person's life. Therefore the word may be translated into English either as "soul" or as "life," depending on the context and on which translation fits best in English idiom. For example, in Leviticus 17:11 (quoted above), I translated "For the life of the flesh is in the blood." Translating as "the soul of the flesh" would not be as idiomatic or as euphonious.

Haftarah of *Mattot:*
The Making of a Prophet

What qualifications were prerequisite
to becoming a prophet?

And, if God chose somebody,
could he decline to be a prophet?

The *Haftarah* of *Mattot*[1]—the first chapter of Jeremiah—
introduces the prophetic mission of Jeremiah, the
prophet who foretold the destruction of the First Jewish
Commonwealth and subsequently comforted and sustained
his defeated nation. Like other prophets before him,
Jeremiah felt he was inadequate to his assigned task. But
God would accept no excuses, declaring, "Before I formed
you in the belly, I knew you; and before you emerged
from the womb, I sanctified you; a prophet to the nations
I have appointed you" (Jeremiah 1:5).

These words of God to Jeremiah raise two fundamental
questions: 1) Does a person become a prophet[2] only if
God chooses him, or can he attain prophetic vision by his
own efforts, through intensive study and self-improvement?
2) What happened to free will? Can't Jeremiah, or any
prophet, choose not to be a prophet?

---

[1] The *Haftarah* of *Mattot* is Jeremiah 1:1 – 2:3.
[2] Contrary to popular conception, the main feature of prophecy is
not prediction of future events. Although many prophecies recorded
in the Bible do contain predictions of the future, others do not contain
predictions. A prophet, then, is a person whom God has tasked with
delivering God's message. In some cases—such as Moses's prophecies
to Pharaoh or Bil'am's prophecies to Balak—the message is delivered to
a king; and in other cases—such as most of Moses's delivery of God's words
to the Israeliltes—it is for the entire populace.

On the first of these questions, Maimonides opines that prophecy is impossible without training, and it is only through intensive study and self-perfection that a person can attain prophetic vision.[3]   Nevertheless, study and training alone are not enough, and some who were adequately prepared—such as Jeremiah's secretary Baruch—never became prophets, because God had not chosen them. Study and spiritual preparation for prophecy, then, are necessary prerequisites according to Maimonides, but the aspiring prophet cannot realize his or her potential unless God selects him.[4]

A different view of prophecy is found in the philosophy of Rabbi Yehuda Halevi.[5]   According to him, God grants the prophet an inner eye, through which the prophet is able to perceive visions that are beyond the reach of other people, and it is only through this God-given faculty that a person can become a prophet. Halevi does not cite study and training as prerequisites for prophecy, and apparently they play no role, according to him.[6]

Which of these two views of prophecy is correct? The fact that prophets had disciples, some of whom were able

---

[3] For the view of Maimonides on prophecy, see *The Guide for the Perplexed* II:32.

[4] Not all prophets were male. At least three prophetesses are mentioned in the Bible: Miriam (the sister of Moses), Deborah, and Hulda. The matriarchs Sarah, Rivka, Rachel, and Leah also had prophetic powers (although the Torah doesn't actually apply to them the term "prophetess.") Also, it is unclear whether the wife of Manoah (see Judges, Chapter 13), who became the mother of Samson, should be regarded as a prophetess. It should be noted that there are several levels of prophecy, and a person who experiences one of the lower levels may not merit the title of "prophet." For a discussion of the levels of prophecy, see Maimonides, *The Guide for the Perplexed* II:45.

[5] Spain, (1075–1141). He is the author of the philosophical book *The Kuzari*. See also Description of Sources.

[6] For Halevi's view on prophecy, see *The Kuzari* IV:3, V:14, and V:16.

to prophesy,[7] provides support for the view of Maimonides. And yet, Samuel's initiation as a prophet when he was but a child (1 Samuel, Chapter 3) provides strong evidence against the contention that intensive study and training are necessary prerequisites to become a prophet. And Moses, the greatest of all prophets, had no preparation or training for his prophetic role.

I believe that the view of Maimonides is correct only up to a point. The view of Maimonides applies to many of the prophets: the hundreds or thousands who had only limited prophetic abilities and whose names we don't know. But for the greatest of the prophets, the ones who have books named after them, or others—such as Elijah—who do not have books named after them but whose prophecies appear on multiple occasions in the Bible, training was not necessary. Their inner vision—their God-given talent to perceive that which is beyond the ken of ordinary people—was so great that little or no training was needed for them. Truly, as God told Jeremiah, they were selected before they were born and were predestined to prophecy. It was not their choice, but God's.

And that brings us to our second question: what about free will? Couldn't Jeremiah, or any prophet, choose not to be a prophet? After all, the Torah tells us that Man has free will to choose the path of righteousness or the path of evil.[8] And, even for the prophet, the choice between good

---

[7] See, for example, 2 Kings 2:3 & 5, and I Kings 20:35–43. But with the exception of Elijah's disciple Elisha (see 2 Kings 2:9 & 15), it is not clear how many of the prophets' disciples were able to prophesy (or were even aspiring to become prophets themselves), and it is likely that the prophetic powers of those disciples who did prophesy (again, with the exception of Elisha) were of very limited degree, since their names are not recorded in the Bible.

[8] For a discussion about free will, see "Re'eh 1: Blessing and Temptation." See also "Nitzavim: The Power of Repentance."

and evil still applies: Bil'am, despite having been blessed with prophetic vision, chose the path of evil. Nevertheless, in the matter of delivering a prophecy with which God has tasked him, the prophet has no choice; he must prophesy willy-nilly. Jonah sought to run away from prophecy, but God would not allow it.[9] Bil'am sought to curse Israel, but God forced him to bless instead.[10] Moses, Isaiah, and Jeremiah all claimed they couldn't prophesy. But God had chosen them. He had created them to prophesy, and they could not refuse. As God declared to Jeremiah, "Before I formed you in the belly, I knew you; and before you emerged from the womb, I sanctified you" (Jeremiah 1:5). Or, as the prophet Amos puts it (Amos 3:8): "A lion has roared, who will not fear? The Lord God has spoken, who will not prophesy?"

---

[9] See "*Emor* 3: The Day of Atonement and the Book of Jonah."
[10] See "*Balak* 2: Can a Prophet Change God's Mind?"

Mas'ei:
By the Hand of Moses

The concluding verses of Leviticus and Numbers
differ only slightly. Why the difference?

The portion of *Mas'ei*,[1] which is the final *sidra* of *Bamidbar*
("Numbers")—the fourth book of the Torah—ends with the
words, "These are the commandments and the laws that
the Lord commanded the people of Israel by the hand of
Moses on the plains of Moav, by the Jordan near Jericho"
(Numbers 36:13). These words are similar to those in the
concluding sentence of the book of Leviticus: "These are
the commandments that the Lord commanded Moses for
the people of Israel at Mount Sinai." But the differences
in the two concluding sentences are significant, and I will
focus on one of the differences.

Moses is mentioned in both concluding verses; but
only here, in *Mas'ei*, does the Torah refer to "the hand of
Moses." Why? Rabbeinu Bachyay addresses this question
and offers the following answer:[2]

The first covenant between God and the nation of Israel
was made when God addressed the entire nation at Mount
Sinai. But when Moses ascended the mountain to receive
the two tablets of the Ten Commandments, the Israelites
made and worshipped a golden calf, thus breaking the
covenant. Consequently, when Moses came down the
mountain and saw what the people had done, he hurled
the tablets from his hands, and they shattered on the rocks

---

[1] Numbers 33:1 – 36:13.
[2] See Rabbeinu Bachyay on Numbers 36:13.

below. Then, on God's command, Moses carved two new stone tablets and ascended Mount Sinai, where God again inscribed those tablets with the Ten Commandments. This was the second covenant.

However, the conclusion of *Mas'ei* refers to commandments given on the plains of Moav, as the Israelites were preparing to enter the Promised Land. Now, forty years after the events at Mount Sinai, Moses is reaffirming the second covenant, which encompasses not only the commandments given at Mount Sinai but also all the commandments given during the ensuing forty years as related in the book of *Bamidbar*. This second covenant is an eternal covenant between God and Israel, never to be severed. And it is reaffirmed once more in that same fortieth year, near the end of the Torah: "These are the words of the covenant that God commanded Moses to make with the people of Israel in the land of Moav, besides the covenant that He had made with them at Horev" (Deuteronomy 28:69).[3]

So what does the phrase "by the hand of Moses" at the end of the book of *Bamidbar* signify? It emphasizes Moses's role in transmitting and executing God's fulfillment of the second covenant. Moses led his nation through the desert to the border of the Promised Land, and he taught his people the laws and precepts that God spoke to him. In the first covenant, the entire nation heard the voice of God speak the Decalogue at Mount Sinai; but God's subsequent dictates were transmitted through Moses. As we noted, the laws comprising the second covenant, in addition to reaffirming the laws contained in the Decalogue, also include the many additional laws given during the forty

---

[3] Horev is another name for Mount Sinai.

years in the desert and on the plains of Moav. Over those forty years, only Moses heard God speak, and it was Moses who transmitted God's laws and precepts to the people.[4] Thus, both figuratively and literally it was "by the hand of Moses" that God's commandments and laws were given to the nation. For it was through Moses's leadership and teaching that the people learned the way that God wanted them to live, and was literally by the hand of Moses that the Torah was written.

---

[4] See *Meshekh Chokhma* on Numbers 36:13, basing his commentary on the Babylonian Talmud, *Yoma* 4b..

BOOK V

Devarim (Deuteronomy)

The fifth book of the Torah, *Devarim*, is Moses's farewell address to his nation. He begins by reviewing the major events of the past forty years in the desert, focusing on the high points and the low points in their spiritual journey. Now, as the Israelite nation prepares to cross the Jordan River into Canaan—the land that God promised their forefathers to give to them and their descendants—Moses cautions them not to follow the heathen ways of the Canaanites and not to listen to false prophets who would lead them to forsake the laws and the practices that God has set before them. He reviews and expands upon the laws and the theological and ethical principles presented in the foregoing books. These principles include the unity of God, the principles of justice, and the roles and obligations of kings and prophets. The book concludes with a poem foreshadowing the nation's future, the blessings that Moses gives each of the twelve tribes, and finally the death of Moses, the greatest prophet and leader of Israel.

Devarim:
Words of Rebuke and Regret

Why did Moses agree to send the spies to the land of Canaan?

Devarim[1] is the first *sidra* in the final book of the Torah, containing Moses's farewell to his nation before his death, as the people prepare to enter Promised Land. Moses begins with a selective review of the last forty years since he led the Israelites out of Egypt, focusing on certain key events that changed the course of their history; and perhaps the most crucial event on which Moses casts his vision is the episode of the spies.

As told in the portion of *Shelach* (see Numbers 13:1–2), God commanded Moses to send men to "explore the land of Canaan," which God was giving to the people of Israel. After forty days, ten of the twelve spies reported that the people of Canaan were too strong, and the Israelites would not be able to conquer them. The people then despaired and demanded to return to Egypt. For this demonstration of lack of faith in divine guidance, God punished the people by condemning them to a circuitous journey of forty years through the "vast and awesome desert" (Deuteronomy 1:19) before entering the Promised Land. Now, forty years later, Moses rebukes his nation for their rebelliousness, their constant quarreling, and their lack of faith in God despite having witnessed all the miracles that God had wrought for them. (See Deuteronomy 1:9, 12, and 29–33.)

---

[1]   Deuteronomy 1:1 – 3:22.

In reading the tale of the spies as the Torah previously related it in the portion of *Shelach*, we may ask: why would God have commanded Moses to send the spies? Didn't He know what the outcome would be? But here in *Devarim*, we see that the previous account—as told in *Shelach*—begins *in medias res*, omitting the fact that God only commanded Moses to send the spies in response to a request by the people, a request that Moses himself had thought to be a good one (see Deuteronomy 1:22–23). But why would Moses have thought so?

As mentioned, the people were quarrelsome and divisive. Each of the twelve tribes had its own interests and was loath to concede anything to the interests of another tribe or of the nation as a whole. There was constant bickering, and repeated complaining about the leadership of Moses, even after he had performed miracles and brought them out of slavery in Egypt, and even after they had stood at Mount Sinai and heard the voice of God. How, then, was Moses to unite the twelve tribes into one nation with a common goal? Indeed, Moses despaired of doing so (see verses 9 and 12).

Then, as they approached the Promised Land, Moses told them that God has laid out the land before them as He promised the patriarchs; and Moses exhorted them, "Do not fear nor be dismayed" (verse 21). In response, the people **all** came to Moses and asked him to send men "to spy out the land" (verse 22). In my view, the critical words here are *kulekhem* (all of you), and *veyachperu* (and they will spy)—or literally, they will dig out—implying that they will seek to find out secrets of the Canaanites' defenses and their military capabilities.[2] Verse 22 could

---

[2] Bible translations generally do not do justice to the word *veyachperu* in Deuteronomy 1:22, translating it as "they will explore" or "they will search" or "they will scout." Those translations fall short of conveying the implication of **digging up** secrets.

equally well have been written as *Vatikrevun elai, vatomeru*—
"You approached me, and you said ...." But the insertion
of the word **kulekhem**—"You **all** approached me, and you
said ..."—is very significant and shows how Moses must
have thought about the people's request. Moses saw
that the people had become united (*kulekhem*—all of you)
around the planned conquest of the land, and, in my
opinion, it was for exactly that reason that he approved
of sending the spies.[3] But events did not work out as
Moses had hoped, and Moses came to realize that he had
been deluded about the people's motives. Indeed, at
that time, in addition to punishing the people, God also
rebuked Moses (Deuteronomy 1:37). And now, forty years
later, Moses reiterates his rebuke of the nation, but he also
admits his own fault in agreeing to send the spies.

---

[3] I have based the above interpretation of the word *kulekhem* on the
Torah commentary of my maternal grandfather, Rabbi Shmuel Bar-
Adon, in his book *Ne'umei Shmuel*. This differs from the interpretation of
Sifrei, which is that the word *kulekhem* implies a disorganized mob demand
as opposed to a formal demand by the tribal leaders. The interpretation
of *Sifrei*, however, does not explain why Moses would have thought the
request was a good one. As we see in other instances, Moses was not
prone to give in to demands of a mob. And moreover, in this instance, he
does not say that he acceded to the peoples' demand but that he thought
their request was good.

Va'etchanan 1:
The *Shema*

God is the source of good;
but where does evil come from?

The Torah portion of *Va'etchanan*[1] contains some of the central ideas of Judaism. Perhaps the idea that most distinguished the religion of Israel from the religions of all other nations of Biblical times is a single verse near the end of the portion of *Va'etchanan*: *Shema Yisrael, YHVH Eloheinu, YHVH echad*—"Listen, Israel: the Lord is our God; the Lord is one" (Deuteronomy 6:4). And it is this statement of faith, known as "The *Shema*," that Jews are commanded to recite twice every day, morning and evening (ibid., verse 7).

God's true essence is unknowable to us, and we can know Him only through His actions. Therefore we call Him by many names, each signifying a different aspect of His actions in the world.[2] Note, then, that in the above verse, two different names of the Deity are used. The first of these names, YHVH, whose root is the verb of being, signifies the Eternal, the source of all existence; and it is generally rendered into English as "The Lord." The second appellation, rendered into English as "God," is the Hebrew *Elohim*, a word signifying power and authority.

The name *Elohim*, then, refers to a God of law, of justice, and of power, the ruler of the universe, Whose will is manifest through the laws of nature. And, parenthetically, it is this name that the Torah uses throughout the account of

---

[1] Deuteronomy 3:23 – 7:11.
[2] See *Shemot Rabba* 3:6.

the creation in the first chapter of Genesis. As mentioned, the other name used in the *Shema*, YHVH, signifies the Eternal. As such, He is beyond the universe, beyond the bounds of time and space, beyond nature. Therefore He may set aside the law when He deems it appropriate, and exercise the faculty of mercy.

Thus, the two divine names YHVH and *Elohim* represent conflicting attributes. To the pagan mind, a single deity could not embody both of these conflicting attributes, these two opposite personalities. How could the same God be the source of both strict justice and mercy, of both light and darkness, of both good and evil? But, the Torah informs us, God is not a person, and neither any human attribute nor personality can we ascribe to God. As stated, we know Him only through His actions, but His true essence is beyond our ability to describe or characterize. The *Shema* tells us that He is One, the source of all: of justice and of mercy, of darkness and of light, of evil and of good.

But, one might object: doesn't Judaism have a concept of Satan, a separate spiritual entity who is the representation of evil? Indeed, Satan is mentioned in the Bible more than once. However, Satan is an angel, a messenger of God; and, as is apparent from Job 1:6–12, Satan is completely under God's control. He is not the creator of evil in the world, but merely its executor.

Evil, then, must ultimately originate from God no less so than does the good. Indeed, Isaiah puts it bluntly: *Yotzer or uvoreh choshekh, 'oseh shalom uvoreh ra'; ani YHVH 'oseh khol eleh*—"I form light and create darkness, I make peace and create evil; I am the Lord Who makes all these" (Isaiah 45:7). Significantly, the rabbis chose this verse from Isaiah as the basis for the first of the two blessings that precede the *Shema* in the morning service, although for the purposes of the morning service they emended Isaiah's words regarding God's creation of evil to read, "... Who makes peace and creates **all**," since they considered this phrasing as *lishna me'alya*—a more desirable way to sing God's praise.[3] But whether said explicitly or not, the point remains the same: both light and darkness, both good and evil, originate from God. And, in uniting polar opposites, God makes peace in His heavens as it were, creating all.[4]

---

[3] See *Berakhot* 11b.
[4] See Job 25:2, and Rashi's commentary on that verse.

Va'etchanan 2:
God's Relationship with Israel

*Which verse of the Torah best summarizes
the central belief of Judaism?*

The Torah portion of *Va'etchanan*[1] contains some of the central ideas of Judaism. In my previous commentary on *Va'etchanan*, I discussed the unity of God as presented in the *Shema*. In the current essay, I will address God's relationship with mankind in general and with the nation of Israel in particular.

If somebody who knew nothing about the Jewish religion were to ask a Jew to summarize in one sentence the central belief of Judaism, the Jew might be tempted to answer that he believes in one God, Who has no physical body and Who created the universe. While all the components of that statement are correct, such a summarization of Jewish faith would be inadequate.

When God spoke to the nation of Israel at Mount Sinai, He did not begin by saying, "I am the Lord your God, Who created the Universe." Such a representation would have been too abstract, too removed from human experience. Moreover, it would not exclude the possibility that God abandoned the universe after the creation; it does not indicate that God directs the course of history. Therefore, God began the Decalogue saying, "I am the Lord your God, Who took you out of the land of Egypt, from the house of bondage" (Exodus 20:2, and Deuteronomy 5:6). And that statement embodies the central belief of Judaism. He is

---

[1]   Deuteronomy 3:23 – 7:11.

more than the Creator of the universe: He is a personal God, Who intervenes in history on behalf of Israel[2] and to Whom we can relate through human experience.[3]

God's intervention on behalf of Israel did not end after the generation of Moses. God's attention was apparent through the leadership of Joshua and throughout the period of the Judges; and God's guidance of the nation continued to be felt through the mouths of the prophets during the almost four centuries that the First Temple stood in Jerusalem. The people of Israel—the Jews—were forcibly separated from their land when the nation was exiled in 586 BCE; but even then, God did not abandon His chosen people. Unlike the fate of other exiled nations of ancient times, the Jewish people returned to their land after seventy years.[4] They rebuilt the Holy Temple and

---

[2] In *Va'etchanan*, the Torah only addresses God's relationship with Israel and does not mention His relationship with other nations. Note, however, that God does not give His attention only to the people of Israel. As it says in Exodus 19:5, "... for indeed, all the earth is Mine"; and He has intervened in history on behalf of other nations besides Israel (see Amos 9:7). Also, God did not speak only to Israelite prophets, but also to the prophets of other nations, such as Noah, Bil'am, and Job. And yet, the nation of Israel has a special role in the world, as a chosen people and a holy nation (see Deuteronomy 7:6–8, and Exodus 19:5–6).

[3] For a discussion of the Torah's saying "I am the Lord your God, Who took you out of the land of Egypt" rather than referring to God as the creator of the world, see Yehuda Halevi's *The Kuzari* I: 25. My analysis is loosely based on the discussion in *The Kuzari*.

[4] The ten northern tribes of Israel were exiled by Assyria in 722 BCE, and only the southern kingdom—the Kingdom of Judah—remained until 586 BCE, when the Babylonians conquered them and exiled them to Babylonia. When Babylonia fell to the Persian Empire, Cyrus the Great (the Persian king) permitted the Judeans to return to their land and rebuild the Temple. Many did return, and the rebuilt Temple was completed in 516 BCE. (The ten northern tribes did not return; and thus, present-day Jews are descendants of the Kingdom of Judah, which consisted of the tribes of Judah and Benjamin, as well as Levites.)

formed the Second Commonwealth, which stood until 70 CE, when the Romans again forcibly separated the Jewish people from their land.[5] But, despite a duration of many centuries, this last exile could not be permanent either. As the *Haftarah* of *Va'etchanan* tells us, a voice from on high proclaims, "In the wilderness, make way for the Lord" (Isaiah 40:3), for those who were degraded are raised up, and God again intervenes in history to return the people of Israel to their land (ibid. 10–11).

---

[5] In the decades following the Roman exile of the Jews, the Romans tried to forbid the teaching of Torah and to suppress the Jewish religion in the Holy Land; and—in an attempt to abolish the Jewish connection to their land—they renamed the land "Palestina" (Palestine).

Va'etchanan[1] 3:
The Sabbath Day

*Why does the reason given in Va'etchanan
for observing Shabbat differ from that in Yitro?*

In the reiteration of the Decalogue as written in *Va'etchanan*, the fourth Commandment says: "Keep the Sabbath day, to sanctify it" (Deuteronomy 5:12), a statement that is similar to the formulation given in the Decalogue of *Yitro*: "Remember the Sabbath day, to sanctify it" (see Exodus 20:8). Both versions of this Commandment tell us to refrain from work on the Sabbath day; but the reason given in *Va'etchanan* for the Sabbath (*Shabbat*) differs markedly from the reason given in *Yitro*. In the Decalogue written in *Yitro*, the Torah tells us that the purpose of *Shabbat* is to commemorate God's creation of the heaven and the earth in six days and His sanctification of the seventh day when He ceased His creation (see Exodus 20:11). In contrast, the reason given for *Shabbat* in the Decalogue of *Va'etchanan* is that each of us must keep the Sabbath because we were slaves in Egypt, and God took us out of there with a mighty hand and an outstretched arm (Deuteronomy 5:15).[2] So, we may ask,

---

[1] Deuteronomy 3:23 – 7:11.

[2] Actually, the Torah pointedly phrases the Commandment in singular: "And **you [singular]** shall remember that **you [singular]** were **a slave** in the land of Egypt, and the Lord your God took you [singular] out of there ..." (Deuteronomy 5:15). But this was now forty years after the Exodus from Egypt; and Moses here was speaking to a generation of Israelites who had never been in Egypt. And yet, the Torah purposely here uses the singular, to emphasize that each of us must identify with the Israelites who were redeemed from bondage and stood at Mount Sinai. As we say on Passover, each of us should think of himself as having personally been redeemed from Egyptian bondage.

does *Shabbat* commemorate God's creation of heaven and earth, or does it commemorate God's redeeming us from slavery in Egypt?

As we saw in *Bereshit*, the Torah gives us two different accounts of creation. While both are equally holy and God-given, the first creation story focuses on what occurred in the heavenly domain, whereas the second focuses on the earthly domain and on humankind.[3] Similarly, the Torah, in its two versions of the Decalogue, presents two reasons for the Sabbath day. In both versions of the Ten Commandments, the people of Israel are to sanctify the Sabbath day, but the the two versions focus on two separate ways in which we are to do so. Both methods of sanctifying *Shabbat* are integral to the Commandment, and the two approaches complement each other.

In the Decalogue of *Yitro*, the fourth Commandment tells us, "Remember the Sabbath day, to sanctify it. ... For in six days the Lord made the heaven and the earth ..., and He rested on the seventh day; therefore, the Lord blessed the Sabbath day and sanctified it" (Exodus 20:8 & 11). We are to sanctify the Sabbath by participating with God's sanctification of the day at His completion of Creation. We participate in God's sanctification by our thoughts, and by saying the *Kiddush*, which consists of our quoting verses from the Torah referring to sanctifying the *Shabbat* and concluding with a blessing pronounced over wine or other victuals.

By contrast, in the Decalogue of *Va'etchanan*, there is no mention of God's creation of heaven and earth. In *Va'etchanan*, the reason given for *Shabbat* is based solely on an earthly event: the Exodus from Egypt. Here, we are

---

[3] See "*Bereshit* (Genesis) 1: The Creation Narrative."

not told to "remember" but to "Keep the Sabbath day" (Deuteronomy 5:12). While the intrinsic holiness of the Sabbath day derives from God's sanctifying and blessing that day at the completion of Creation (Genesis 2:3), it is the Jewish people's observance of the *mitzvot* of *Shabbat*— and our participation in God's declaration of its sanctity, both by our words and thoughts, and by our action—that cements the bond between the nation of Israel and God. As Ramban tells us in his introduction to the book of Exodus, God's purpose in bringing the Israelites out of Egyptian bondage was to bring us to Mount Sinai, to establish a covenant with us, and to forge us into a nation that would be tasked with bringing God's words into the world and facilitating the plan that God had for humankind when He created the world. The Jewish people's observance of *Shabbat* is a token of our affirming the covenant that God made with us at Sinai. Therefore, in *Va'etchanan*, the reason the Torah gives us for observing the Sabbath day is that God took us out of Egyptian bondage.[4]

We have seen, then, that there are two reasons for the Jewish people's observance of *Shabbat*, and the two reasons are intertwined. Thus, the Sabbath day exists simultaneously in two worlds—the world of God and the world of humankind. And, through its citizenship in both worlds, the Sabbath is a link connecting us to God and giving us a taste of the world above.

---

[4] Also, see my discussion in *"Behar*: The *Shmita* and The *Yovel*."

Ekev[1]:
Worship of the Heart

Upon what is the requirement for prayer based?

In ancient times in Israel, worship of God often took the form of bringing a burnt offering. However, after the destruction of the second Temple in the year 70 CE, Jews could no longer bring sacrificial offerings, and therefore the rabbis decreed that prayers would substitute for the sacrifices. They set the times of the morning and afternoon prayers (*Shacharit* and *Mincha*) to correspond to the daily sacrifices of the morning (*Tamid shel Shachar*) and afternoon (*Tamid shel Beyn Ha'arbayim*) that used to be brought in the Temple.

But prayer must not be considered only as a substitute for sacrifices. Prayer existed in the Jewish tradition long before the Torah was given. The Talmud, basing itself on various Biblical verses, states that Abraham instituted the morning prayer, that Isaac instituted the afternoon prayer, and that Jacob instituted the evening prayer.[2] Thus, verbal prayer—as distinct from sacrificial offerings—has an independent, ancient origin in Jewish tradition and did not begin only as a replacement for burnt offerings to God.

Nevertheless, even though the patriarchs initiated the three daily prayers, their practice is not necessarily the basis for the *halakhic*[3] requirement of prayer. We may theorize that in ancient times, when the Temple existed, prayer

---

[1] Deuteronomy 7:12 – 11:25.
[2] See Babylonian Talmud, *Berakhot* 26b.
[3] *Halakhic* refers to that which pertains to *halakha* (Jewish law).

independent of sacrifice was practiced only sporadically, when the spirit moved a person to pray. In that case, the current *halakhic* **requirement** of prayer is a rabbinic law that was instituted to substitute for the Temple sacrifice.

The question of whether the requirement of prayer is based on Biblical or rabbinic law was hotly debated among the *poskim*,[4] with many—perhaps most—authorities favoring a rabbinic origin for the requirement of prayer. Others, most notably Moses Maimonides, maintain that prayer is a *mitzvah de'orayta*—a Biblical precept. But Maimonides does not attribute the *halakhic* basis merely to the patriarchs' practice. Rather, Maimonides cites a verse in *Ekev* as the Biblical source for the *mitzvah* of prayer: "... and to worship Him with all your heart and with all your soul" (Deuteronomy 11:13). And, says Maimonides, what is worship of the heart? It is prayer.[5]

In the view of Maimonides, then, the requirement to pray is a Biblical law, but the Torah doesn't specify any times of prayer.[6] The **times** of prayer are of rabbinic origin; and the rabbis set those times to correspond with the times of the Temple sacrifices.

---

[4] *Poskim* are authorities on Jewish law, who render legal decisions. Also, see Glossary.

[5] See Maimonides, *Mishneh Torah, Hilkhot Tefillah* 1:1, and Maimonides, *Sefer HaMitzvot, Mitzvah* 5.

[6] See *Mishneh Torah, Hilkhot Tefillah* 1:1.

Re'eh 1:
Blessing and Temptation

How do we know that people have free will,
and that our fate is not pre-ordained?

In the *sidra* of *Re'eh*,[1] the Torah tells us that Man has a choice: "See, I am putting before you today a blessing and a curse: the blessing if you listen to the commandments of the Lord your God ...; and the curse if you do not listen ..., [and you] follow other gods that you have not known" (Deuteronomy 11:26–28). What a revolutionary idea: Man has free will! And, just as remarkably, through our choices in life, we are the masters of our destiny. For those of us who have grown up with these ideas, it may be difficult to understand how radical these ideas were in the ancient world.

Perhaps we might have expected that the idea of Man's free will would have been commonplace in polytheistic religions. After all, if different gods exist and often are in conflict with each other, couldn't a person choose to follow the dictates of one god over those of another? And yet, in the thinking of many in the ancient world, Man's free will was very limited, and he was far from master of his destiny. To the Babylonians, humans were subject to the whims of the gods; and therefore, Man always had to fear the unpredictability of divine retribution. And to the ancient Greeks, Man was caught in a web woven by the Fates; there was nothing we could do to change our predetermined fate.

---

[1] Deuteronomy 11:26 – 16:17.

But, in *Re'eh*, the Torah tells us that we—like Adam and Eve—stand before the Tree of Knowledge, and we must choose between good and evil. Oh, the choice is not so simple. Evil does not necessarily appear as evil, and temptation abounds all around us. Many of the rituals of other religions may appear beautiful and attractive to us (Deuteronomy 12:30); and a close friend or relative, or even a spouse, may speak to our hearts and entice us to follow (ibid. 13:7–8). Or a false prophet may capture our hearts with the power of his vision (ibid. 13:2–4) and lead us along the path of destruction.

However, as the *Haftarah*[2] *of Re'eh* reminds us (in Isaiah 54:16), the Destroyer is also God's creation, and, the Torah says, God is testing us (Deuteronomy 13:4). Indeed, all of life is a test, and it is our task to learn to distinguish between good and evil, and to train ourselves; for it is through training that we develop the power to resist temptation. To this end, God gives us a discipline, to keep us away from defilement and to make us holy (ibid. 14:2). One of the purposes of the dietary laws (ibid. 14:3–21), and of many of the other laws of the Torah, is to discipline us so that we will have the fortitude to control our baser impulses and resist the whisper of the serpent who calls to us from within, tempting us to taste the forbidden fruit.

Thus, it is through Torah that we are able to make the right choices, and to bring down blessings upon us from above. For, contrary to the Babylonian viewpoint, we know that God is not arbitrary in meting out judgement; we know that He has put in our hands the key to our destiny. He has placed before us life and death, good and evil. And He has instructed us: choose life (Deuteronomy 30:19).

---

[2] Isaiah 54:11 – 55:5.

Re'eh[1] 2:
The Oral Torah

Is there anything in the written text of the Torah that alludes to the existence of an oral Torah?

While the Torah is not exclusively a book of law, certainly one major purpose of the Torah is to give us a set of laws by which we are to live. But some of the laws of the Torah do not fully define their scope or do not define certain words that are critical to understanding the exact meaning of those laws. Jewish tradition has always held that, in addition to the text of the Torah that Moses wrote at God's direction, there is also an oral Torah that God gave to Moses, that interprets and expands upon laws in the written Torah; and the laws of the oral Torah have equal authority to the written text. There was an unbroken chain of transmission of the oral Torah until, early in the 3rd Century CE, Rabbi Judah the Prince recorded the core of that tradition in the Mishnah, in order to avoid a break in the chain of transmission in the face of Roman persecution.[2]

Although mainstream Judaism in ancient times accepted the authority of the oral Torah, a sect known as the Sadducees, arising during the 2nd Century BCE, rejected the authority of the oral tradition. The Sadducean sect disappeared shortly after the destruction of the Second

---

[1] Deuteronomy 11:26 – 16:17.
[2] For the chain of transmission of the oral Torah from the time of Moses down through the generations, see Mishnah *Avot* 1:1. Also, see "Mishnah" in the Glossary.

Temple in 70 CE; but in the 8ᵗʰ Century CE, Anan ben David founded a new Jewish sect, known as the Karaites, that also rejected the oral law. In modern times, Reform Judaism, as well as other Jewish movements, have rejected the oral Torah or relegated it to a position of lesser authority. So, we may ask, is there anything in the written text of the Torah that alludes to the existence of an oral Torah? Before addressing that question, I will first give two often-cited examples of laws in the Torah that call for additional interpretation.

The Torah mandates that the seventh day of the week— Saturday—be a day of rest; and we are commanded, "You shall not do any work ...," because God created the world in six days "and rested on the seventh day" (Exodus 20:10–11). But what is the definition of "work"? The Torah doesn't tell us; and the stated reason that the Torah gives us casts doubt on equating "work" with physical exertion, since God's creative acts involved no exertion but only speech. In fact, Jewish tradition tells us that the "work" forbidden on the Sabbath day does not necessarily involve physical exertion at all, but is defined as creative activity; and there are 39 specific categories of such activity.

A second example concerns the holiday of *Sukkot*. On the first day of the holiday, we are instructed to "take the fruit of a beautiful tree, branches of palms," and two other species (Leviticus 23:40). But what does the Torah mean by "the fruit of a beautiful tree"? Can it be the fruit of any tree that we consider to be beautiful, or is a specific tree intended? Jewish tradition tells us that it is, in fact, a specific fruit that we are required to take, and that fruit is an *etrog*—a citron.

In both of these examples, the written Torah omits additional details that would better clarify how to put those laws into effect; and a reader of the Torah who was unfamiliar with the traditional interpretation would have been unlikely to arrive at the exact interpretations mentioned above. And yet, those who reject the idea that God gave Moses a set of oral laws to expand upon the written text could argue that the intent of the Torah was for each person to interpret those laws according to his or her own understanding. So, in response, can we cite evidence in the written Torah for the existence of an oral law?

Indeed, there is such evidence, and it is to be found in the portion of *Re'eh*. While the Israelites were in the desert after the Exodus from Egypt, a person was permitted to eat meat only in conjunction with bringing a burnt offering of parts of the animal, and to bring such an offering a person had to be ritually pure. But as the Israelites prepare to enter the Promised Land, God decrees that eventually He will select a place in the Promised Land where offerings to God are to be brought, and thereafter it will be forbidden to bring a sacrifice at any other location (Deuteronomy 12:10–14). Will people then have to travel to that place any time they want to eat meat? No. "Whenever you desire, you may slaughter and eat meat," even if ritually impure (see verse 15). Moreover, "If the place ... is too far from you, you may slaughter ... **as I have instructed you**" (verse 21). And yet, as the Talmud points out,[3] nowhere in the written Torah are there instructions how to slaughter an animal.

The above discussion, then, shows us a specific reference in the text of the Torah to a set of laws that are not recorded in the written Torah itself. And while that does not prove conclusively the existence of an oral law that

---

[3] See Babylonian Talmud, *Chullin* 28a.

was given to Moses, nevertheless it does provide strong evidence for the existence of an oral Torah that expands upon and is coeval with the written Torah.

Shoftim 1:
In Pursuit of Law and Justice

The Torah says, "Justice, justice you shall pursue."
Why is the word justice repeated?

One of the themes that is prominent in the *sidra* of *Shoftim*[1] is the idea of justice. Right from the first word of the *sidra*, the Torah ordains that we appoint *shoftim*—judges— who will render "righteous judgement" (Deuteronomy 16:18). And two verses later, the Torah declares: *Tzedek tzedek tirdof*—"Justice, justice you shall pursue" (ibid., verse 20). The word "justice" is repeated in order to emphasize its importance,[2] to imply that every person (not only a judge) should seek justice both in words and in actions,[3] and perhaps to indicate that the human judge must seek out both the justice embodied in the letter of the law and the higher justice—the guiding principle upon which the law is based, *i.e.* both the letter and the spirit of the law. Indeed, justice is a principle that underlies all of Jewish law: as King David said, "Righteousness and justice are the foundation of Your throne" (Psalms 89:15).

But, we may ask, what is justice? In the view of the Torah, justice consists of equality of all people before the law. A judge must not give preference to anybody: "Do not pervert judgement; do not show partiality; do not take a bribe" (Deuteronomy 16:19). Impartiality must extend

---

[1]   Deuteronomy 16:18 – 21:9.
[2]   This is Ibn Ezra's opinion (one of the three explanations that he proposes for the repetition of the word).
[3]   This is the opinion of Rabbeinu Bachyay.

to all classes of people: "Do not favor the poor or show deference to the rich; judge your fellow justly" (Leviticus 19:15). And even the foreigner must be equal to a citizen under the law: "One law there shall be for you; for the foreigner as for the citizen it shall be" (ibid., 24:22). Finally, as we saw in *Emor*,[4] unlike the legal codes of other nations that imposed different penalties depending on the social status of the injured person and of the perpetrator, the Torah decrees that the penalty for inflicting an injury be determined only by the nature of the injury and not at all by the social status of the perpetrator or the victim.

The idea of equality of all people before the law stems from the creation of man: "And God created man in His image; in the image of God He created him; male and female He created them" (Genesis 1:27). And in the following verse, God tells Adam and Eve to be fruitful and multiply. Thus, all of humankind is descended from Adam and Eve; and all people—both male and female—are blessed with the divine spark in equal measure. It is for that reason that we are all equal before the Lord, and it is for that reason that we must be treated equally before the law. And that is the essence of justice.

---

[4]   See "*Emor* 1: Holiness and its Antithesis."

Shoftim 2:
Rabbinic Ordination

From where do rabbis derive their authority?

In the portion of *Shoftim*,[1] the Torah tells us that whenever there is a question of law in an individual case, the case should be brought before the *kohanim* (the priests) or the judge who presides at that time, and the ruling of those *kohanim* or judges must be followed (Deuteronomy 17:9–10). The Torah does not explicitly clarify how, in future generations, the authority of these arbiters of law is to be conferred upon them; but in Numbers 11:16–17, we are told that Moses appointed seventy elders of Israel, and God distributed an extension of the spirit that was within Moses and placed it upon them. The process by which a person in authority—in this case Moses—imparts the authority to others, with the divine stamp of approval, is known as *smicha* (ordination). And when Moses was about to die, he passed the leadership authority to Joshua in a similar manner (Deuteronomy 31:23 and 34:9).

According to Jewish tradition, *smicha*—the authority to rule on Jewish law and to apply it to specific cases—was transmitted from Moses down through the generations until the chain of transmission was broken early in the 4th Century as a result of Roman persecution of the Jews. After that time, the title "Rabbi," which formerly had been given to those upon whom *smicha* was conferred, was still used, but the title no longer signified the same degree of authority that it had formerly held.

---

[1] Deuteronomy 16:18 – 21:9.

After the chain of transmission was broken, there seemed to be no way to restore the original authority inherent in *smicha*; but the situation changed, at least in theory, when Moses Maimonides opined in the late 12th Century that *smicha* could be restored if every rabbi in the Holy Land were to agree on one person as being worthy of that authority; and that person could then confer *smicha* on others whom he deemed worthy. Moreover, Maimonides, citing Isaiah 1:26, stated that God will indeed restore judges in the land of Israel as in days of yore, and that that will happen before the coming of the Messiah.[2]

In the three centuries following the death of Maimonides in 1204, his philosophical views and many of his legal rulings—especially this one regarding restoration of the *smicha*—remained highly controversial. Thus it is not surprising that this ruling was not put into practice for many years. But in the 16th Century, Yaakov Beirav, who was the leading rabbinic scholar in the Holy Land, began to push for restoration of the *smicha* according to Maimonides's proposal. In part, Beirav's desire to do so was motivated by many new questions in Jewish law arising from *conversos*[3] who wanted to return to Judaism, but probably also in large measure due to his thinking that restoring the *smicha* may hasten the coming of the Messiah.

---

[2] For the opinion of Maimonides regarding restoration of the *smicha*, see his *Commentary on the Mishnah*, *Sanhedrin* 1:3, and his *Mishneh Torah*, *Sanhedrin* 4:11.

[3] *Conversos* were Jews who had converted to Christianity because of the intense animus and restrictions that Jews had to endure in 15th Century Spain, culminating in the Alhambra Decree of 1492, which mandated that Jews either convert to Christianity, leave the kingdom, or be killed. Many of these *conversos* secretly continued to observe the Sabbath and Jewish dietary laws, to the extent that they were able (and at the risk of their lives), even after their conversion to Christianity.

As it happened, at that time almost all the greatest Jewish legal scholars in the land of Israel lived in the northern city of Safed, where Yaakov Beirav also resided. Therefore, after convincing his colleagues in that city, in 1538 Beirav held a meeting in Safed of 25 leading rabbis of the Holy Land. The group unanimously approved his proposal, elected him as the greatest sage in Israel, and named him the first bearer of the newly-restored *smicha*. All the other rabbis in the Holy Land went along with the decision, except for one: Rabbi Levi Ibn Habib, the Chief Rabbi of Jerusalem, disagreed with the underlying theoretical basis; and, to make matters worse, he was insulted at not having been invited to the meeting. Therefore, he continued to oppose the decision of Beirav's conclave. Yaakov Beirav declared that Ibn Habib would be the first person upon whom he would confer *smicha*, but nevertheless Ibn Habib continued to object, and he declared the renewal of *smicha* invalid. In the aftermath of this dispute, Yaakov Beirav was forced to relinquish his position as Chief Rabbi of Safed and to leave the land of Israel. But before he departed Safed, he granted *smicha* to four other scholars, one of whom—Rabbi Yosef Karo—succeeded Beirav as Chief Rabbi of Safed.[4]

After the departure of Yaakov Beirav, Ibn Habib won more scholars to his opinion, and thus only Karo is known to have used his position to ordain anyone else. However, he ordained only one person, Moshe Alsheikh,[5] who later ordained Chayyim Vital. And with Chayyim

---

[4] Safed in the 16th Century was the center of Kabbalah. Both Rabbi Yaakov Beirav and Rabbi Yosef Karo were among the leading Kabbalists of Safed. But Rabbi Yosef Karo is better known today for his code of Jewish law, the *Shulchan Arukh*. See also Description of Sources.

[5] See Moshe Alsheikh in Description of Sources.

Vital apparently ends the restored *smicha*. Thus, although today's rabbis are still given something that is called *smicha*, and they are accorded the title of "Rabbi," their ordination, while it is still a mark of recognition of having attained a certain level of knowledge of Jewish law and the methodology by which the law is to be applied in practice, as well as a certain measure of authority to decide many matters in Jewish law, it does not have the same level of authority as the original *smicha*.

Thus, the great undertaking of restoring the original authority of the *smicha* came to naught. Or, as Shakespeare puts it, "And enterprises of great pitch and moment with this regard their currents turn awry, and lose the name of action."[6]

---

[6] William Shakespeare, *Hamlet*, Act 3, Scene 1.

Ki Tetze 1:
Do Not Hate an Egyptian

The Egyptians enslaved the Israelites.
So why should the people of Israel not hate Egyptians?

The *sidra* of *Ki Tetze*[1] begins: *Ki tetze lamilchama 'al oyevekha*—"When you go to war against your enemies ..." (Deuteronomy 21:10). War in the Torah's view, although it is at times necessary, must not be waged through hatred of the enemy. Moreover, even when our enemies treat us with malice, we must resist the temptation to hate them.

In the ancient world, war between neighboring nations was frequent and generally brutal. Therefore it is not surprising that the nation of Israel fought numerous wars against its neighbors. But regarding two of those neighbors, the Torah tells us, "You shall not despise an Edomite, for he is your brother; you shall not despise an Egyptian, for you were a stranger in his land" (ibid., 23:8).[2]

The people of Edom were the descendants of Esau, the brother of our ancestor Jacob; therefore it is understandable that a bond of kinship would exist between our two nations. But, since earliest times there was also jealousy and enmity: Esau plotted to kill his brother Jacob (Genesis 27:41); and centuries later, when the people of Israel approached the borders of Edom after their redemption from long years of subjugation in Egypt, the king of Edom refused to allow the Israelites passage through the King's

---

[1] Deuteronomy 21:10 – 25:19.
[2] For reasons why we might be tempted to hate the Edomites and Egyptians, see Rashi's commentary on Deuteronomy 23:8.

Road, an international thoroughfare for caravans. Instead, even after the Israelites declared they would pay for any water that they would consume, the Edomite army came out in force, threatening violence (see Numbers 20:17–21). And yet, the Torah tells us, the bond of kinship supersedes those provocations, and we must not hate the Edomites even if we go to war against them out of necessity, as occurred in later years.

But what of the Egyptians? There is no kinship between Israel and Egypt to mitigate the harsh treatment doled out to the Israelites during the many years of slavery in Egypt. The Torah commands us not to hate an Egyptian, because "you were a stranger in his land." But while we were regarded as foreigners in Egypt, the Egyptians murdered all our newborn boys by drowning them in the Nile! (See Exodus 1:15–16 and 22.) Indeed, hospitality toward a stranger is a great *mitzvah*, but was this hospitality? Must we overlook the brutal treatment we received in Egypt?

While the Egyptians did commit atrocities against the people of Israel, it was Pharaoh who ordered those heinous acts (ibid., verses 8–10, 15, and 22); and although we cannot excuse the officials and the soldiers who carried out Pharaoh's orders, it may well be that many Egyptians— perhaps even the majority—did not share Pharaoh's views. Indeed, the Torah tells us that the Lord caused the Egyptian people to "view the Israelites with favor; also, the man Moses was greatly esteemed in the land of Egypt, in the eyes of Pharaoh's servants and in the people's eyes" (ibid., 11:3). Thus, we may surmise that it was not the will of the people, but that of the tyrant who ruled them, and probably some of his government officials, that resulted in the subjugation and brutal treatment meted out to the Israelites in Egypt; and we may speculate that perhaps it was only a relatively small contingent of enforcers who were complicit in executing the Pharaoh's edict of murdering the newborns. Therefore, the Torah credits the Egyptian people with the virtue of hospitality to strangers in their land. Finally, let us not forget that prior to the ascension of the new Pharaoh in the first chapter of Exodus, the previous king of Egypt was very generous to the people of Israel, welcoming them to his country and offering the best part of his land for them to inhabit (Genesis 45:17–18 & 20). Thus, truly the Egyptian people retained great merit, and therefore—although we must also remember the suffering—the Torah commands us never to hate an Egyptian on account of our suffering while in Egypt.

As a coda to the theme of overcoming hatred, the Torah ends the portion of *Ki Tetze* with the command to abolish "the remembrance" of Amalek. This command, which is commonly misunderstood as an edict to wipe out the people of Amalek, actually instructs us to abolish senseless hatred, which was the essence of Amalek's character.[3]

---

[3] For a full exposition of this idea, see "*Ki Tetze* 3: Remember to Forget."

Ki Tetze 2:
Sin, the Nuptial Bond, and the Flight of Birds

How do the law of divorce and the law of releasing a mother bird relate to each other?

In the portion of *Ki Tetze*,[1] the Torah tells us that a marriage may be dissolved only with "a writ of divorce" (Deuteronomy 24:1). Divorce is a weighty matter, to be considered carefully, and not to be done on a whim: therefore, an official writ of divorce must be drawn up.

In numerous places, the prophets envision God as the husband of Israel; and when Israel sins, God "divorces" the northern kingdom of the ten tribes;[2] they are exiled from their land and are lost to the remainder of the Jewish people. But God stops short of fully divorcing the Kingdom of Judah: "Where is your mother's writ of divorce, that I have sent her away?" asks Isaiah, speaking for God (see Isaiah 50:1). Indeed, the Judeans—the Jews of the southern kingdom—like their northern brothers, are later also exiled from their land; but it is a separation and not a divorce.[3] After seventy years, they will return and rebuild.

---

[1] Deuteronomy 21:10 – 25:19.

[2] See Ibn Ezra's commentary on Isaiah 50:1. Also, see Hosea 2:4.

[3] For discussion of "divorce" of the ten tribes contrasted with the exile of the southern kingdom, see Radak's commentary on Isaiah 50:1. The ten northern tribes seceded after the death of King Solomon, and formed their own kingdom with their capital in Shomron (Samaria). The tribes of Judah and Benjamin remained faithful to the dynasty of David and Solomon, and their territory—thereafter called the Kingdom of Judah—had its capital in Jerusalem. For more about the exiles of both of these kingdoms, see footnote 4 in "*Va'etchanan 2*: God's Relationship with Israel."

Note Isaiah's unusual reference to "**your mother's** writ of divorce." We might readily understand the imagery of God divorcing Israel, or of expelling the people from their land on account of their sins, just as God expelled Adam and Eve from the Garden of Eden on account of their sin; but who is "your mother" in Isaiah's metaphor, and why is she sent away? Also note how Isaiah continues: "... for on account of your sins you have been sold, and through your transgressions your mother was sent away" (Isaiah 50:1), a phrasing that brings to mind *Shilu'ach Haken*—the *mitzvah* of sending away the mother bird from her nest before taking her chicks—a *mitzvah* also mentioned in the portion of *Ki Tetze*. It is not only the children of Israel who are taken from their land, but also their mother is sent away.

And so, I ask again, who is this mother in Isaiah's imagery, sent to fly away while her children are taken from their nest? Most of the commentaries gloss over that question,[4] but the Zohar has an interesting interpretation: the mother who is sent away is the *Shekhina*, the divine presence in our world. God is often envisioned as residing in Heaven, far above the realm of our existence. But God is also immanent in our world and within us. Leading a life of righteousness brings us closer to the *Shekhina*, while doing evil drives the *Shekhina* away.[5] Our sins, then, result in a two-fold exile: we are driven from our land, and the divine presence is sent away from us.

---

[4] Radak actually does address the question, saying that the mother represents the nation as a whole, whereas the children are the individuals.
[5] An example can be seen in the homiletical commentaries on the sin of Adam and Eve. As a consequence of Adam and Eve's sin, see the opening lines of *Tanna Devei Eliyahu*, where God is seen as giving Man a divorce. Contrariwise, in the Zohar it is not only God who drives Adam out of the garden, but also it is Adam who expels the *Shekhina* (Zohar I:53b, I:237a).

But the separation is not permanent. "Can one spurn the wife of his youth?" asks Isaiah in the Haftarah of *Ki Tetze* (Isaiah 54:6). "For a brief moment I forsook you, but with great compassion I will gather you back. In a flash of fury I hid my face from you a moment, but with everlasting kindness I will have compassion for you, said the Lord your Redeemer" (Isaiah 54:7–8). And when we return to God, He will return to us: "And I will betroth you forever; and I will betroth you with righteousness and justice; ... and I will betroth you with devotion and knowledge of the Lord" (Hosea 2:21–22).

Ki Tetze[1] *3:*
Remember to Forget

What does the Torah mean when it asks us
to wipe out the remembrance of Amalek?

"Remember what Amalek did to you on the way as you were leaving Egypt" (Deuteronomy 25:17). Thus the Torah, at the very end of *Ki Tetze*, begins its condemnation of the nation that attacked the Israelites without provocation or cause, but attacked out of pure malice. And, the Torah commands us, when we are settled in the land that God has given us, we are to "wipe out the *zekher* of Amalek from under the heavens; do not forget!" What does the word *zekher* mean? As it is usually translated, it means memory or remembrance. But, on the face of it, if we do as the Torah commands, and wipe out all remembrance of Amalek, how can we also remember what Amalek did?

It is therefore reasonable to conclude that this *mitzvah* of wiping out the *zekher* of Amalek does not mean what it appears to be saying. Is the Torah, then, commanding us to kill all Amalekites and utterly eliminate their physical existence? Indeed, Moses's statement in Exodus 17:16— "... it is a war of the Lord against Amalek throughout the generations"—would be consistent with that interpretation. Also, God's command to King Saul in his war against Amalek (1 Samuel 15:3) suggests such an interpretation. And yet, that is not quite what the wording of the Torah in *Ki Tetze* tells us to do. The Torah does not tell us to wipe out

---

[1] Deuteronomy 21:10 – 25:19.

the nation of Amalek itself, but to wipe out its *zekher* from under the heavens. Contrast this statement with what the Torah commands regarding a city that has utterly turned to evil (Deuteronomy 13:13–19). There, we are told to kill the inhabitants of the city "by the sword" and to burn the city down. Similarly, regarding the enemy Canaanite towns, the Torah declares, "Do not let a soul remain alive" (ibid., 20:16). But regarding Amalek, the Torah in *Ki Tetze* makes no mention of physical destruction or of killing "by the sword." What, then, are we commanded to wipe out?

As always, we must look at the context in which the *mitzvah* is presented. The commandment regarding Amalek comes at the end of a *sidra* filled with many apparently unrelated laws, including the treatment of a woman captured in war, the treatment of the firstborn son of a less-favored wife, the treatment of beasts of burden, and laws regarding rape, lending money, divorce, and many other precepts. The law immediately preceding the *mitzvah* to remember Amalek prohibits merchants from having two sets of weights and measures, so that they will not cheat their customers.

The unifying principle running through these *mitzvot* is that of equity and fairness, to prevent the stronger from taking advantage of or oppressing the weaker. And that is just what Amalek did to us. As the Torah emphasizes (Deuteronomy 25:18), Amalek attacked the Israelites when we were tired, despondent, and spiritually weak. In addition, Amalek was in no way threatened by the Israelite migration. The commentaries point out that the Amalekites came from afar to attack us, out of pure malice; and that, above all, makes their attack so despicable.

The Torah's command at the end of *Ki Tetze* regarding the nation of Amalek, then, does not tell us to repeat

Amalek's act and send our army to their distant home to wipe them out. Note that this *mitzvah* is to take effect when we are settled in our land, when we are at peace (see Deuteronomy 25:19). Surely there were Amalekites living in the Negev (see Numbers 13:29), but the primary home of the Amalekites was apparently not in the Promised Land, nor were they counted among the indigenous nations of the land of Canaan enumerated in Deuteronomy 7:1. Their principal home territory may have been in the southern Negev, which was not included in the land that God promised to the Patriarchs. By making the *mitzvah* take effect only once we are settled in peace in the Promised Land, the Torah implies that it is not physical annihilation of Amalek that is commanded here, but only the *zekher* of Amalek.

And now we come to the crux of the matter: the meaning of *zekher*. The word *zekher*, which usually denotes remembrance, in the present context perhaps is better translated as "essence." Malbim points out in his commentary on Exodus 3:15 that *zekher* may refer to "the appellations by which someone is described according to his actions"—that is, a description of his essential character. In conclusion, then, what the Torah here commands us to wipe out is not the physical existence but rather the essence of Amalek's character, which is the spirit of senseless hatred between man and man. Senseless hatred erodes the moral fabric of a nation and eventually can lead to the nation's downfall. Therefore, it is specifically and especially when we are settled in our land and are at peace that we must be sure to eliminate the spirit of senseless hatred and animosity between man and man.

Ki Tavo:
One Nation Under God

On the verge of entering the Promised Land, Moses says, "On this day you have become a nation to the Lord your God." But didn't Israel already become a nation at Mount Sinai?

The *sidra* of *Ki Tavo*[1] contains some of the final instructions, exhortations, and warnings that Moses gave to the fledgling nation of Israel as they were about to enter the Promised Land of their ancestors. Moses says, "Listen, and understand, Israel; on this day you have become a nation to the Lord your God" (Deuteronomy 27:9). But, we may ask: what does Moses mean by that statement? Didn't Israel already become a nation forty years earlier, when we left Egypt and stood at Mount Sinai seven weeks later?

Although the twelve tribes of Israel had a common heritage and a common history, until now they were just a loose association of twelve separate groups, each traveling through the desert under its own flag and with its own tribal leaders, and each having its own traditions and its own goals. Each tribe had its own desires, aspirations, and demands, and their differences led to constant strife and discontent. But now, as they were about to enter the Promised Land, they had to become a unified nation, working toward a common goal. For example, we see in Numbers 32:1–5 how the tribes of

---

[1] Deuteronomy 26:1 – 29:8.

Reuben and Gad wanted to remain across the Jordan River and not to cross the river with the other tribes. Moses had to remind them of their duty and to make their possession of the land across the Jordan conditional on their participation in the national army (ibid., verses 6–7 and 20–23).

Not only were the twelve tribes still a loose association of disparate groups, but they did not yet have a land of their own, and thus they would not have been regarded as a nation as that term was commonly understood, any more than the nomadic Bedouin tribes of the desert would have been considered a nation. But now, as the Torah states in the first verse of *Ki Tavo* (ibid., 26:1), God is giving the Israelites a land of their own, an inheritance that they shall possess, and in which they shall dwell.

Implementation of these two steps—unification of the tribes and possession of the land—would indeed transform the Israelites into a nation. But Israel was not meant to be just another nation like all other nations. As Moses said, "on this day, you have become **a nation to the Lord your God**" (ibid., 27:9). Israel was to be a nation under God, and committed to God's laws.[2]

To this end, pursuant to the command of Moses, when the Israelites crossed the Jordan River, they were to inscribe the words of the Torah on twelve large stones, and

---

[2]   When Israel stood at Mount Sinai and accepted the covenant with God, we were just beginning to become a nation. But we broke that covenant when we worshipped the Golden Calf, causing Moses to break the tablets, and our nationhood before God was thus dissolved. Now, forty years later, God reinstates the covenant, as expressed in the last verse of *Ki Tavo*: "And you shall keep the words of this covenant, and you shall observe them, so that you will act wisely in all that you will do" (Deuteronomy 29:8). See *Midrash Tanchuma Nitzavim* §3.

they were to build an altar to God with those stones.[3] Thus, the twelve tribes would be symbolically fused into one whole. The Torah will unify and bind them together, toward one goal, to one aspiration, and to one purpose, under the banner of the Torah.

---

[3] The number of stones on which the words of the Torah were to be written is not stated in the Torah (see Deuteronomy 27:2–8). But when Joshua carries out the command, he states that he collected twelve stones from the Jordan River (Joshua 4:20), and later he built the altar with the stones upon which were written the words of the Torah, in accordance with the command of Moses (ibid., 8:30–32)

Nitzavim:
The Power of Repentance

Man has free will. What, then,
happens when man chooses incorrectly?

In the *sidra* of *Nitzavim*,[1] the Torah continues its focus on man's free will—a theme that also runs through the Torah portion of *Re'eh*.[2] But in *Nitzavim*, the Torah adds a new idea: repentance.

God gave man free will, but he did not create us as infallible beings. Therefore we may at times choose wrongly. But God also provided us with a way to correct our errors. And that is indeed amazing, because it does not seem to accord with the way God made the physical world and its laws of nature. Nature seems to run by strict laws, never deviating, never repenting. And, just as God set down the laws of nature, He also gave man laws by which to live. Strict justice, then, would dictate that no extenuating circumstances should ever be considered, and no possibility to correct an error should ever be allowed.

But God created man as something more than just a mechanism, something more than just a mass of protoplasm subject to the laws of nature. When God created human beings, He breathed into us the breath of life, a spark of the divine; and thus we stand between, both Heaven and Earth reflected in our being. And, coinciding with our unique nature, God has given us the unique ability to correct our errors through repentance.

---

[1] Deuteronomy 29:9 – 30:20.
[2] See "*Re'eh* 1: Blessing and Temptation."

It is a gift that God has bestowed upon us through His love and His compassion.

Actually, the concept of repentance is not new at all: as the Talmud tells us, God created repentance before He created the world,[3] for without the ability to correct errors, we would quickly succumb to our fallibility. Nevertheless, it is not till the portion of *Nitzavim* that the Torah explicitly enunciates the concept of *teshuva* (repentance) and states it as a *mitzvah*.

The *mitzvah* of *teshuva*, however, differs fundamentally from most other *mitzvot* in that, for the *mitzvah* of *teshuva*, intention of the heart is critical to its performance. Certainly, intention of the heart is desirable for all *mitzvot*, and it is necessary for **optimal** observance of all *mitzvot*; but for most *mitzvot*, intention of the heart is not a requirement for minimum fulfillment. For example, if a person says *Kiddush*[4] without thinking about what he is saying, he has still fulfilled the *mitzvah*, although not in optimal form. Similarly, taking an example from the negative commandments, if a person has an almost-overwhelming desire to murder somebody but overcomes his desire and refrains from murder because of fear of punishment and not at all because the Torah forbids murder, he has nevertheless observed the commandment against murder.

But *teshuva* is different: like the *Shema*,[5] repentance also requires intention of the heart; and without such intention, the *mitzvah* is not fulfilled even minimally. It is not enough

---

[3] Babylonian Talmud, *Pesachim* 54a and *Nedarim* 39b. Also, *Pirkei Rabbi Eliezer*, Chapter 3.

[4] *Kiddush* (literally, "sanctification") is a blessing recited to sanctify the Shabbat or holiday. A *Kiddush* is commonly recited over wine or grape juice (although other victuals may be used instead).

[5] See Glossary. Also, see "*Va'etchanan* 1: The *Shema*."

merely to refrain from committing the same sin in the future: "... for you shall return to the Lord your God with all your heart and with all your soul" (Deuteronomy 30:10).

Continuing the theme of repentance, the *Haftarah* of *Nitzavim* tells us that when we return to Him, God will take us back fully, just as a groom receives his bride (Isaiah 61:10 & 62:5). And, as Isaiah tells us in a previous prophecy, Israel is like a dearly-beloved wife who has become temporarily estranged: "In a flash of fury I hid my Presence from you a moment, but with everlasting kindness I will have compassion for you, said the Lord, your Redeemer" (ibid., 54:8). God returns the Jewish people to the Land of Israel, God's Presence returns to Jerusalem, and the Land is no longer forsaken (ibid., 62:4–5). And, the *Haftarah* concludes: "... through His love and through His mercy He has redeemed them; He lifted them up and carried them through all the days of old" (ibid., 63:9).

Vayelekh:
Moses Passes the Torch

*Why did Moses make an ambiguous statement
when he appointed Joshua as his successor?*

In *Vayelekh*,[1] the shortest *sidra* of the entire Torah, Moses
addresses his nation on his hundred twentieth birthday,
on the eve of the nation's entry into the Promised Land.
Moses tells the people that God told him he will not cross
the Jordan River and enter the land with them, but that
the Lord will go before them (Deuteronomy 31:2–3).
Then, Moses calls Joshua and commands him before all the
people to be strong and bold, *ki ata tavo et ha'am hazeh*—
because you will go with this nation—to the land that the
Lord swore to give to them (ibid., verse 7). This phrasing
is ambiguous. Exactly what does Moses mean?

Rashi interprets Moses's statement to mean that Joshua
will lead the nation pursuant to the consensus of the elders:
i.e., Joshua will be either subservient to the elders or, at
best, the first among equals. But in contrast, says Rashi,
God's command to Joshua was **ata tavi** *et benei Yisrael*—
"You will bring the people of Israel to the land that I have
sworn to them" (verse 23), implying that Joshua will be
the commander and therefore will supersede the elders.[2]
Apparently, Rashi's position is that God's intention from
the beginning was that Joshua would be the commander

---

[1] Deuteronomy 31:1–30.
[2] The Babylonian Talmud (*Sanhedrin* 8a), which Rashi quotes, interprets
verse 23 to mean that all will depend on Joshua's command, even if the
elders disagree.

(see also Deuteronomy 3:28), and Moses altered God's instructions. Consequently, God saw fit in verse 23 to correct Moses's statement in verse 7.[3] So, if Rashi's interpretation is correct, why would Moses alter God's instructions?[4]

Could it be that Moses was jealous of Joshua? But Joshua was Moses's hand-picked disciple, whom Moses had groomed for leadership. In fact, the Talmud uses Joshua as the prime example to support its contention that a master isn't jealous of his disciple's success.[5] In contrast, however, the *Midrash Rabba* suggests that Moses was indeed jealous of Joshua, and applies to him the verse in the Song of Songs (8:6), "Fierce as death is love; hard as the grave is jealousy," referring to Moses's conflicting feelings of love and jealousy regarding his disciple.[6]

That Moses had conflicting feelings may be inferred from the phrasing of his words. "I am a hundred twenty years old today, and I can no longer go forth and come in" (Deuteronomy 31:2). Some commentators take the phrase "go forth and come in" to mean leading the nation in battle (as it is also used elsewhere in the Bible). But Rashi says it means that God has withdrawn from Moses

---

[3] *Sifrei* is unequivocal in saying that God intended to appoint Joshua as commander. *Sifrei Devarim* §29 says, "If you lead them, they will succeed; and if not, they will not succeed." And *Sifrei* brings an example of the defeat of the Israelites at Ai (see Joshua, chapter 7), when God says to Joshua, "Did I not tell Moses your teacher, 'If he leads them, they will succeed; and if not, they will not succeed'?"

[4] In verse 7, *ki ata* **tavo** *et ha'am hazeh* is universally translated as "because you **will go** with this nation." But if we want to avoid saying that Moses altered God's instruction, then we could regard *tavo* (in verse 7) as equivalent to *tavi*—"you will bring" (in verse 23), in which case verse 7 would be translated as "you will bring this nation." However, various commentators emphatically reject that translation, because *tavo* (in verse 7) is an intransitive verb.

[5] Babylonian Talmud, *Sanhedrin* 105b.

[6] See *Devarim Rabba* 9:9.

the authority to lead and has given it to Joshua. And Moses then completes his thought by adding, "and the Lord has said to me, 'You shall not cross this Jordan'" (ibid). Note that Moses doesn't simply say he will not cross the Jordan River, but he pointedly says that God forbade it. This was clearly a sore topic for Moses, and it appears that he probably appealed to God repeatedly in the past to reverse His decision (see Deuteronomy 3:23–26), to no avail. Perhaps, then, Moses does not actually have feelings of jealousy directed at Joshua, but rather resentment of the fact that he is not allowed to complete his mission as he sees it, and is compelled to leave it to somebody else. Thus, when Moses calls on Joshua and says *ki ata tavo et ha'am hazeh* ("because you will go with this nation"), Sforno stresses the word "you" ("because **you** will go"), by adding, "even though I did not merit to do so."

So Moses, understandably, has mixed feelings about transferring power to Joshua at this time; and perhaps the ambiguous phrasing that he uses in verse 7 ("because you will go with this nation") reflects his conflicting feelings. As mentioned above, Rashi opines that Moses meant to make Joshua subject to the consensus of the elders; but, as an alternative to Rashi's opinion, Moses's words instead can be interpreted—as Sforno (on verse 3) and *Or HaChayyim* (on verse 7) interpret them—to mean that God will be the actual commander, and Joshua will lead as God's agent, under God's command. This interpretation makes sense when we consider the phrasing of verse 3: That verse starts by saying, "The Lord God, He is the one Who crosses before you; He will vanquish these nations before you"; but the verse concludes, "Joshua, he is the one who crosses before you, as the Lord has declared." Who, then, will go before the Israelites? It is Joshua, acting as God's agent.

We have seen how Moses's ambiguous phrasing in verse 7 (*ata tavo et ha'am hazeh*—"you will go with this nation") explains why God had him clarify or (correct) the command, in verse 23. And perhaps the ambiguity in the initial phrasing reflects Moses's mixed emotions regarding his transfer of leadership to Joshua at this time.

Ha'azinu 1:
The Song as Witness

What is the purpose of Ha'azinu,
and why is it written in the form of a poem?

The Torah portion of *Ha'azinu*[1] is very enigmatic. It is written in the form of a poem, and it begins by calling heaven and earth as witnesses to our covenant with God (Deuteronomy 32:1). But quickly, the *sidra* launches into a condemnation of our nation as a "base and unwise people" (ibid., verse 6) who have forsaken their Lord. Consequently, we are told, The Lord spurned the Israelites, and He said, "I will hide My Presence[2] from them; I shall see what will be their end" (ibid., verses 19–20). But the closing verses of the poem tell us that just as God wounds, he also heals, and that God will wreak vengeance on His enemies and on His nation's enemies. So, we may ask, what is the purpose of *Ha'azinu*? Is it primarily a reprimand, or is it meant to uplift us?

In searching for the purpose of *Ha'azinu*, we should consider God's instruction to Moses in that regard: God commands Moses to "write this song" and to "teach it to the Israelites, and place it in their mouths,[3] so that

---

[1] Deuteronomy 32:1–52.
[2] This is Onkelos's translation.
[3] According to Ibn Ezra, "place it in their mouths" means we are to learn the song of *Ha'azinu* by heart. (Moreover, the Vulgate translates "teach it to the Israelites, and place it in their mouths" as a command to have them memorize it—*ut memoriter teneant, et ore decantent.*) Although other commentaries are silent about the matter, I believe that Ibn Ezra's interpretation is correct: every Jew must memorize the song of *Ha'azinu*; for that seems to be the plain meaning of the text. And how else will it serve us as our witness and consolation in times of distress?

this song will be **a witness among** the people of Israel" (Deuteronomy 31:19). But the Torah's phrasing of this instruction is ambiguous; and therefore, in keeping with the harsh pronouncements in *Ha'azinu*, almost all modern translations render Deuteronomy 31:19 as "… so that this song will be **a witness against** the people of Israel."[4] Thus, when God stands in judgement of the people of Israel, *Ha'azinu* is seen as a witness for the prosecution, so to speak. But significantly, the Septuagint (which is the earliest Jewish translation of the Torah)[5] translates, "… that this song may witness for me **among the children of Israel**."[6] And the Vulgate (which is probably the earliest Christian translation of the Torah)[7] translates, … *pro testimonio* **inter** *filios Israel*—"as a testimony **among** the children of Israel."

Both translations—"against" and "among"—are equally consistent with the Hebrew phrasing, but they signify very different objectives. Certainly, as mentioned, regarding *Ha'azinu* as a witness against Israel accords well with the harsh pronouncements that it contains. Nevertheless, consistent with the more favorable interpretation ("among"), the song ends on a positive note, promising that "when

---

[4] The King James Version (KJV) of the verse reads as follows: "… that this song may be a witness for me **against** the children of Israel." And almost all subsequent translations follow suit. The KJV, which was first published in the year 1611, is a Christian translation.

[5] The Septuagint is a Greek translation of the Torah, translated by a panel of seventy Jewish scholars, commissioned by King Ptolemy II Philadelphus in the 3rd Century BCE.

[6] *The Septuagint With Apocrypha: Greek and English*, English translation by Sir Lancelot C.L. Brenton, originally published by Samuel Bagster & Sons, Ltd., London, 1851. Printed in the USA by Hendrickson Publishers, 6th Printing, 1997.

[7] The Vulgate (Latin—*Vulgata*) is the Latin translation of St. Jerome. He completed his translation of the Torah about the year 405 CE. The Vulgate became the official Bible of the Catholic Church.

He sees their power is gone, and no recourse remains, ...
I will wreak vengeance on My foes, and I will repay My
enemies" (Deuteronomy 32:36 and 32:41). And finally, the
song of *Ha'azinu* promises that God will avenge His nation
(ibid., verse 43). Thus, despite all the terrible events that
are foretold for us in *Ha'azinu*, when ultimately we return
to God, He will accept us back,[8] and He will do battle on
behalf of His nation Israel. Moreover, the more favorable
interpretation is supported by Deuteronomy 31:21, wherein
God asserts that when great evil and distress will befall us,
the song—which will not be forgotten among us—will speak
up as a witness, suggesting that the song of *Ha'azinu* is to
be a consolation for the nation in times of distress. And,
in fact, it is this favorable interpretation that the Aramaic
translation of Onkelos suggests.[9] In both Deuteronomy
31:19 and 31:21, Onkelos chooses to translate the Hebrew
word *shira* (meaning song or poem) not as the Aramaic
shirata—which is equivalent to the Hebrew word—but as
tushbachta, which can mean a song but more commonly is
used to mean a praise. Thus Onkelos's phrasing seems to
suggest that the song of *Ha'azinu* acts as a witness for the
defense of Israel and not for the prosecution.

The song of *Ha'azinu* bears special importance,
concluding God's teachings to the people of Israel; and its
poetical form emphasizes its importance. So important is
Ha'azinu that it is the only part of the Torah that the people
of Israel were told to commit to memory,[10] because—even

---

[8] See Deuteronomy 30:1–3.
[9] Unfortunately, Onkelos's Aramaic translation of Deuteronomy 31:19 is
just as ambiguous (against *vs.* among) as the original Hebrew. But his
translation of the word *shira* (see the discussion above) seems to indicate
that he regarded *Ha'azinu* as a poem that, in sum, is favorable for Israel.
[10] See footnote 3 above.

though it forecasts hardship and anguish, and is fraught with warnings and admonitions—yet, its purpose is to serve as our witness of God's bond with us as protector of Israel, and to console us in times of distress.

Ha'azinu[1] 2:
The Torah and Water

Why are the words of the Torah compared to water?

In rabbinic literature, the words of Torah are likened to water. A Biblical reference for this analogy is sometimes given to Psalm 1:2–3, where a person who delights in Torah is compared to a tree planted along a stream of water. But that is a source in *Ketuvim* (The Writings). Can we find an explicit source for the analogy in the Torah itself?

The Talmud[2] states that when the Torah relates that the Israelites went three days in the desert and did not find water (see Exodus 15:22), what it really means is that they went three days without Torah. This interpretation is valid as *midrash* (allegory), but it hardly qualifies as *peshat* (the plain meaning of the text). So where in the Torah can we find the analogy explicitly stated? It is in the second verse of *Ha'azinu*: *Ya'arof kamatar likchi, tizzal katal imrati*—"May my teaching pour down like rain, my speech drip down as the dew" (Deuteronomy 32:2).

Now we have identified a verse in the Torah that compares God's teaching—the Torah—to rain. But, we may ask: in what way is the Torah analogous to rain? What is the basis for the analogy? On one level, we can say that just as water purifies and invigorates the body, so the Torah purifies and invigorates the soul. But Isaiah, who bases several of his prophecies on verses from *Ha'azinu*, explains the analogy not just for water in general

---

[1] Deuteronomy 32:1–52.
[2] Babylonian Talmud, *Bava Kamma* 82a.

but specifically for rain, as given in *Ha'azinu*: Isaiah tells us that just as the rain or the snow falls from heaven and does not return there until it has nourished the earth and made it produce vegetation, similarly God's words (*i.e.* the Torah) nourish our souls and make us grow spiritually.[3]

And so, what God, speaking through Moses, is telling the nation in the *sidra* of *Ha'azinu* is that just as the rain comes down, reviving the ground and making the grass grow, so too will God's words and His teachings stimulate the Israelites' souls and elevate their spirits as they enter the land that God has promised them.

---

[3] Paraphrased and adapted from Isaiah 55:10–11.

Ha'azinu[1] 3:
Life After Death

*Where in the Torah is there a reference
to resurrection of the dead?*

The Talmud[2] takes it as a given that the idea of resurrection of the dead derives from the Torah.[3] So where does the Torah mention resurrection of the dead? It is in the *sidra* of *Ha'azinu*: "I put to death and bring to life; I have wounded, and I will heal" (Deuteronomy 32:39). Now, you may object that the order here (putting to death followed by bringing to life) is not to be taken literally, since the order may be ascribed to poetic form. But explaining away the order is reading the verse in accordance with a preconceived notion. Indeed, why should we not read the verse literally? The poetry of *Ha'azinu* is written in parallel statements, with the second half of each verse paralleling the first half; and, as the Talmud notes,[4] the parallel statement here—wounding followed by healing—demonstrates that the order should indeed be taken literally: God puts to death, and then He brings to life. Moreover, Hanna (11th Century BCE), the mother of the prophet Samuel, in her paraphrasing of the verse in *Ha'azinu*—"The Lord puts to death and brings to life, casts down to the grave and raises up"

---

[1] Deuteronomy 32:1–52.
[2] Babylonian Talmud, Mishnah *Sanhedrin* 90a.
[3] Resurrection of the dead is mentioned in Daniel 12:13; but the Talmud's point is that the idea actually is found in the Torah and not only in a later source such as the book of Daniel.
[4] Babylonian Talmud, *Sanhedrin* 91b.

(1 Samuel 2:6)—supports the literal reading of the verse in *Ha'azinu*.

This, then, is the source in the Torah for the idea that God will bring at least some people back to life after they have died. But it is a veiled statement, and we may wonder why the Torah did not put greater emphasis on such an important concept. We may speculate that perhaps God didn't want to put much emphasis on resurrection of the dead or on life after death, specifically in order to distance us from the culture of Egypt, where the afterlife was such a central preoccupation. While we should be aware of the existence of an afterlife, the principal objective of the Torah is to teach us how to conduct ourselves in this world, the world of the present.

Vezot Haberacha:
Yeshurun—An Unusual Name
for Israel

Why is Israel called
"Yeshurun"?

In the *sidra* of *Vezot Haberacha*,[1] Moses twice refers to the nation of Israel by an unusual name—*Yeshurun*. That appellation was used only one time before in the Torah, and later it is used once more in the book of Isaiah, for a total of only four times in the entire Hebrew Bible! But what does the name signify?

Some commentators[2] derive the name *Yeshurun* from the root *yashar*—straight, or upright—indicating that the nation follows the straight and just path that God has commanded. That is the interpretation that is generally taught in modern times, to the exclusion of other interpretations of the name; and it certainly is an interpretation consistent with all the verses in which the name *Yeshurun* is used. But there is an alternative derivation of the name that, in my opinion, is even stronger.

The root *shur*—to observe, or to see—is used numerous times in the Bible (*e.g.* in Numbers 23:9 and 24:17), and it is this word that both Rabbeinu Bachyay and Sforno propose

---

[1]   Deuteronomy 33:1 – 34:12.
[2]   See Ibn Ezra on Deuteronomy 32:15, and Malbim on Deuteronomy 33:5; and see Zohar I:177b.

as the root from which the name *Yeshurun* is derived.[3] In Bachyay's view, the name *Yeshurun* refers to the entire nation's witnessing the presence of God when the Torah was given at Mount Sinai; and he supports that interpretation by noting that, in the context of *Vezot Haberacha*, the name *Yeshurun* is used immediately after Moses mentions Israel's receiving the Torah: "He [*i.e.* God] became king in *Yeshurun*, when the leaders of the nation assembled" (Deuteronomy 33:5), which, in Rabbeinu Bachyay's opinion, means that God became king of Israel when we assembled at Mount Sinai and witnessed His presence.[4] And at the conclusion of the blessings of *Vezot Haberacha*, the Torah says, "There is none like God, *Yeshurun*; Who rides through the heavens to assist you ..." (ibid, verse 26). In Rabbeinu Bachyay's interpretation, that is to say: you who have seen the glory of the Lord at Mount Sinai can bear witness that there is none like God, Who rides through the heavens to assist you.

While I think that, of all the commentators who try to explain the derivation of the name *Yeshurun*, Rabbeinu Bachyay gives the best interpretation, I propose an extension of his interpretation. Indeed, we can postulate that the name *Yeshurun* is based on the root *shur* as Bachyay proposes, but note that the name has the form of a verb in the future tense: they will see, or they will observe.

---

[3] For Rabbeinu Bachyay's derivation of *Yeshurun* from the root *shur*, see his commentary on Deuteronomy 32:15 where the Torah says that *Yeshurun* has forsaken God; and Bachyay sees this as emphasizing the magnitude of the nation's transgression: the people who witnessed God's presence at Mount Sinai have thrown off God's teachings. And see Sforno's commentary on Deuteronomy 32:15 and 33:5. (Sforno says that the name *Yeshurun* is akin to the word *ashurennu*—I behold him—in Numbers 24:17.) Finally, it should be noted that even Ibn Ezra, who prefers the derivation of *Yeshurun* from *yashar* (upright), also mentions *shur* as an alternative derivation for *Yeshurun*.
[4] The immediately preceding verse (Deuteronomy 33:4) says, "Moses commanded us the Torah, an inheritance for the assembly of Jacob."

However, the future tense in Hebrew is sometimes used to indicate an ongoing or repeated action rather than a future one;[5] and thus, Israel's name *Yeshurun* could indicate not only that we witnessed God's presence at Sinai, but that we continue to witness God's presence throughout the course of history.

I am not proposing that *Yeshurun* is being used as a verb in any of the verses where it appears, but only that it has the form of a future tense verb and that the meaning of the name somehow reflects an aspect of the nation's identity. Indeed, there are other names in the Bible that have verbal forms in future tense, such as *Yitzchak* (Isaac)—he will laugh, *Yishma'el* (Ishmael)—God will listen, and *Yisra'el* (Israel)—he contends (or will contend) with God. None of those names is ever used as a verb, despite having the form of a verb; but in each case, the meaning of the verb is somehow related to a significant identifying event or aspiration of the person who bears that name.

My proposed extension of Rabbeinu Bachyay's interpretation of the name *Yeshurun* fits equally well when applied to the first two verses in which the name is used (Deuteronomy 32:15 and 33:5). But when applied to verse 33:26, I believe that interpretation actually fits even better than Rabbeinu Bachyay's: "There is none like God, *Yeshurun*; Who rides the heavens to assist you"—Israel will continue, through the course of history, to witness God's riding through the heavens for the sake of His people

---

[5] For examples of the future tense used to indicate an ongoing or repeated action, see Deuteronomy 10:17 (*Ki YHVH ... lo yissa fanim velo yikkach shochad*—"For the Lord your God ... **shows no favor and takes no bribe**"), and Isaiah 40:26 (*hamotzi vemispar tzeva'am, lekhulam beshem yikra*—"... Who brings out their host by numbers, **and calls them each by name** ...").

Israel.   And Isaiah echoes the verse in *Vezot Haberacha* (Deuteronomy 33:26).   Addressing the nation by all three names—Jacob, Israel, and *Yeshurun*[6]—Isaiah exhorts us not to be afraid, because God, the nation's creator and protector, has chosen Israel, and Israel will continue to witness God's coming to our assistance—now and in the future.   (See Isaiah 44:1–2.)

---

[6] According to the Zohar (I:177b), the three names Jacob, Israel, and *Yeshurun* represent three levels of holiness, in that order, with *Yeshurun* being the highest.

GLOSSARY

Aggada (or *Aggadeta*): Literally, "telling." This consists of stories that amplify our understanding of the personalities of Biblical characters and add detail to Biblical events. Such stories are found in various *midrashim*, but also in the Talmud. (See also "Midrash" and "Talmud," below.)

Akedah: The binding of Isaac, told in Genesis 22:1–24. This was the tenth and final test to which Abraham was subjected. For a discussion of the *Akedah*, see "*Vayera* 2: The *Akedah*."

Amalek: A nomadic or semi-nomadic people that waged an unprovoked attack against the Israelites shortly after the Exodus from Egyptian bondage. (See Exodus 17:8–16.)

Aram: A nation situated northeast of Israel, in territory that is now part of Syria. The nation of Aram ceased to exist after the Assyrian king Tiglath-Pileser III conquered it and sacked its capital, Damascus, in 732 BCE. But the language of Aram—Aramaic—lived on for many centuries thereafter, as the official language of the Chaldean empire in Babylonia, and later as the international language in much of the Near East. (See also "Aramaic," below.)

Aramaic: The language of Aram (see entry above). Although Aram ceased to exist in 732 BCE, the Aramaic language by then had spread to other regions and was the language of the Chaldean empire. When the Chaldeans conquered Jerusalem in 586 BCE and exiled its people—the Jews—to Babylonia, Aramaic became the language of a large portion—probably the majority—of Jewish people. Even after King Cyrus of Persia conquered the Chaldean empire and permitted the Jews of Babylonia to return to Israel, Aramaic remained the vernacular among the masses in Israel, and it remained so for several centuries.

Bamidbar: The fourth book of the Torah, known in English as "Numbers." The word *bamidbar* literally means "in the desert," this being the first significant word of the book. *Bamidbar* is also the name of the first *sidra* in the book of *Bamidbar*. The reason that the book is called "Numbers" in English is that the book opens with the taking of a census.

Beracha (or *Bracha*): A blessing.

Bereshit: "In the beginning." *Bereshit* is the first word of the Torah, and it is the title of the first book of the Torah, known in English as "Genesis." While *Bereshit* is the name of the first book, *Bereshit* is also the name of the first *sidra* of the book of *Bereshit*, because both the books of the Torah and the individual *sidrot* within each book are named by the first significant word in that book or in that *sidra*.

Canaan: The territory that God promised to give to the Patriarchs—Abraham, Isaac, and Jacob—to them and their descendants, the Jewish people, as their eternal inheritance.

Chanukah (or *Hanukah*): An eight-day celebration commemorating the re-dedication of the Temple in Jerusalem following the victory of the tiny Jewish army over the mighty Greek army of Antiochus IV Epiphanes in the 2ⁿᵈ Century BCE. Candles are lit on the evening of each of the eight days of *Chanukah*: one candle on the first evening, two candles on the second evening, *etc.* (See also "*Shamash.*")

Decalogue: Literally, "Ten Words," *i.e.* Ten Statements, or Ten Pronouncements. See "Ten Commandments."

De'orayta: See "*Mitzvah de'orayta.*"

Derabbanan: See "*Mitzvah derabbanan.*"

Devarim: The fifth book of the Torah, known in English as "Deuteronomy." The word *devarim* literally means "words," this being the first significant word of the book. *Devarim* is also the name of the first *sidra* in the book of *Devarim*.

Eh'yeh: One of God's names, the meaning of which is "I will be." This is the name that God told Moses when He sent Moses to Egypt to confront Pharaoh, and Moses asked what he should tell the Israelites when they will ask what is the name of God who sent Moses. (See Exodus 3:14).

Elohim: God. The word *elohim*, however, is a generic name that can be used not only in reference to God but also to false gods, as in *elohim acherim*—other gods, or *elohei ha'amim*—the gods of the nations. The word *elohim* is also be used in the Torah in a completely secular sense, meaning a power or an authority. When the appellation *Elohim* is used in reference to God, it may connote His role in meting out stern justice or in manifesting His power.

Gemara: The part of the Talmud that consists of commentary, discussion, and debate about the Mishnah. The combination of the Mishnah and accompanying Gemara is known as the Talmud. There are two versions of the Gemara. The earlier one, which records the commentary and discussion of rabbis in Israel, was completed in the latter half of the 4th Century CE and is called the *Talmud Yerushalmi* (Jerusalem Talmud). The later one, the *Talmud Bavli* (Babylonian Talmud), which records the commentary and discussion of the rabbis of Babylonia, was completed about the year 499 CE. The Mishnah in both versions of the Talmud is the same; it is only the Gemara in which they differ from each other. Unlike the Mishnah, which is in Hebrew, both versions of the Gemara are in Aramaic. (See also "Talmud," below.)

Haftarah: A short reading taken from one of the books of the prophets, read in the synagogue each week after that week's Torah portion. Generally, there is a common theme that links each *Haftarah* with the Torah reading to which the *Haftarah* is appended.

Halakha (**or** *halacha*): Jewish law.

Hanukah: See "*Chanukah*."

High Holy Days: This is a term applied in English to *Rosh Hashanah* and *Yom Kippur*. In Hebrew, the term that is used for these two holidays is *Yamim Nora'im* (Days of Awe).

Israel: This name can refer either to the patriarch Jacob (son of Isaac) or to his descendants, the nation of Israel, the Jewish people. The appellation "Israel" can also be applied to the land of Israel, the land that God promised to the people of Israel.

Kabbalah: Literally, this word means "that which was received," *i.e.* "tradition": ideas, interpretations, customs, and laws that were transmitted through the generations. When the word *kabbalah* is used in books and commentaries up to the 13th Century, that is the only meaning of the word. In the mid-13th Century, the word *Kabbalah* also began to be applied to a system of mystical interpretations of the Biblical text; and in the course time, this latter meaning became the usual usage of the term *kabbalah*. Nevertheless, even today, the word is still also at times used in its original (non-mystical) meaning, as in the title of the 19th Century Torah commentary titled *Haketav Vehakabbalah* (*i.e.* "The Text and the Tradition").

Karaites: The Karaites are a Jewish sect that reject the existence of an oral Torah. Although there is some controversy regarding the origins of the Karaite sect, it appears to have arisen in the 8th Century CE in Baghdad, under the leadership of Anan ben David.

Kiddush: Literally, "sanctification." *Kiddush* is a blessing recited to sanctify the *Shabbat* or holiday. A *Kiddush* is commonly recited over wine or grape juice (although certain other victuals may be used instead).

Kohen: A priest who, in Biblical times, served in the Temple in Jerusalem. (Plural—*kohanim.*) All *kohanim* are descendants of Aaron, the brother of Moses. Since Aaron was a Levite (see "Levi," below), all *kohanim* are also members of the tribe of Levi; but most members of that tribe are not *kohanim*.

Levi: A Levite, *i.e.* a member of the tribe of Levi—a descendant of Jacob's third son, whose name was Levi.

Menorah: A candelabra. Specifically, in the Torah this refers to the seven-branched candelabra in the Tabernacle, which is different from the nine-branched candelabra that is used on the holiday of *Chanukah* (a holiday that did not yet exist in the time of the Torah).

Midrash: This term is applied to any of the collections of homiletic rabbinic commentaries on the Bible that were compiled during the 3rd to the 9th or 10th Centuries, primarily in Israel. (Plural—*midrashim*.) Leading examples are *Midrash Rabba* (*i.e.* "The Great *Midrash*"), *Midrash Tanchuma*, and *Pirkei Rabbi Eliezer*. These three works belong to the category *Midrash Aggada*—literally, "*Midrash* of Telling"—which includes stories that were passed down about Biblical characters, and ideas obtained by extrapolation from the Biblical text. There is also another category of *midrash*—*midrash halakha*—that concerns itself with comparison of Biblical texts and analysis of their phrasing in order to identify supporting evidence for Jewish laws that are known through the oral tradition. Examples of *midrash halakha* are *Mekhilta* (on the book of Exodus), *Sifra* (on the book of Leviticus), and *Sifrei* (on the books of Numbers and Deuteronomy). (See "*Re'eh* 2: The Oral Torah" for more about the oral tradition.)

Mishnah: The Mishnah, which is written in Hebrew, consists of rabbinic teachings of oral law that were transmitted over hundreds of years, as compiled and edited by Rabbi Judah the Prince in the early 3rd Century CE. Originally, those teachings were supposed to be transmitted only orally and were not to be written down. But, in the face of Roman persecution, Rabbi Judah the Prince decided that it was necessary to write down a concise record of those teachings, lest they be lost. After completion of the Mishnah, later rabbinic authorities published the Gemara, which is an account of the commentary, discussion, and debate about rulings in the Mishnah. The combination of Mishnah and Gemara is known as the Talmud. (See also "Gemara" and "Talmud.")

Mitzvah: A commandment. (Plural—*mitzvot*.) The Torah contains 613 commandments. (The "Ten Commandments" are actually ten statements—*dibrot*, not *mitzvot*—containing fourteen *mitzvot*.)

Mitzvah de'orayta: A *mitzvah* that comes from the Torah.

Mitzvah derabbanan: A *mitzvah* that comes from the rabbis.

Moav: A nation immediately to the east of the Dead Sea. It is called Moab in English. The people of Moav were descendants of Lot, the nephew of Abraham. The Moabite language was very similar to Hebrew, and it used the same alphabet as Hebrew.

Mount Sinai: The mountain on which God gave the Ten Commandments to the assembled people of Israel. It is also known as *Horev* (often written as "Horeb" in English).

Oral Torah (*Torah shebe'al peh*): This consists of teachings that interpret and expand upon laws in the written Torah. As the name indicates, the teachings of the oral Torah, which God gave Moses on Mount Sinai, were to be transmitted orally and not written down. See "*Re'eh* 2: The Oral Torah." Also, see "Mishnah," above.

Parasha: A section of Biblical text. (Plural—*parshiyot*.) In the traditional writing of the Torah, as it exists in Torah scrolls, the end of a *parasha* is indicated by spacing before the start of the following *parasha*. In common usage today, the word *parasha* (or *parsha*) may also be applied to the weekly Torah portion that is read in the synagogue each Saturday. However, the weekly portion is more correctly called a *sidra*. (See also "*Sidra*," below.)

Passover (*Pesach*): The holiday that commemorates the Exodus from Egypt. It is a seven-day festival in Israel, eight days outside of Israel.

Patriarchs: Abraham, Isaac, and Jacob (also known by the name "Israel"), from whose seed descend the people of Israel.

Peshat (or *Pshat*): The plain meaning of a text.

Philistines: One of the "Sea Peoples" that invaded Canaan in the 12th Century BCE. They established five cities along the southern coast of Canaan: Gaza, Ashkelon, Ashdod, Gath, and Ekron. It seems that the Philistines mentioned in Deuteronomy and in later books of the Bible were not the same as the Philistines of the book of Genesis. In the late Bronze Age, mass migrations were prevalent, and several invading peoples displaced the former inhabitants in the ancient Near East, as described in Deuteronomy 2:20–23. Deuteronomy 2:23 states that the *Kaphtorim* (Cretans or Cypriots) displaced the previous inhabitants—the Avvites—in the Gaza region. This is discussed in *Midrash Tehillim* on Psalms 60, and in the Babylonian Talmud, *Sanhedrin* 60b, as well as in Rashi's commentary on Deuteronomy 2:23. Also, significantly, the Septuagint translates "Philistines" in the book of Genesis not as Philistines but as *allophyloi*—"other nations."

***Poskim* (singular—*posek*)**: Recognized authorities on Jewish law, who render legal decisions in specific cases where no precedent exists or where prior opinions were inconclusive.

Rosh Hashanah: The festival of the New Year, celebrated on the first and second days of the month of *Tishrei* (near the end of the summer). It is regarded as a solemn holiday, a time when God judges the world and the inhabitants thereof.

Sanhedrin: The high court. Each city had a court known as the Lesser *Sanhedrin*, composed of of 23 judges. The highest court, known as the Great *Sanhedrin* (often called just *Sanhedrin*, without the qualifier), was composed of 71 judges. The head of the *Sanhedrin* was called the *Nasi* (president), and the second in charge was the *Av Beit Din*. There was only one Great *Sanhedrin* (the Supreme Court), located in Jerusalem until the year 70 CE. After the Roman conquest of Jerusalem and the destruction of the Second Temple in 70 CE, the Great *Sanhedrin* moved to Yavneh. Because of persecution by the Eastern Roman Empire, the *Sanhedrin* ceased to exist in 425 CE. One of the tractates of the Talmud is titled *Sanhedrin*, the subject of which is the details of the court system, and civil and criminal procedure in Jewish law.

Shabbat: The Sabbath day, *i.e.* the seventh day of the week—Saturday—commemorating God's ceasing His work of creation. On *Shabbat*, there is a requirement for us to sanctify the day, and certain categories of activity are forbidden.

Shaddai: One of the names of God, often compounded with *El*—another one of the divine names—as *El Shaddai*. This name, the exact meaning of which is moot, is often used in reference to the covenant between God and the Patriarchs.

Shamash: Literally, "helper." This word is applied to the ninth candle of the *Chanukah* menorah. The *Chanukah* menorah has eight candles for ritual purposes; but a ninth one, the *shamash*, which is used to light the other eight, is generally placed at a higher elevation and either in the middle (with four candles on each side of it) or not in the same row as the other candles.

Shavuot: A holiday that celebrates the wheat harvest and is also a celebration of God's speaking the Ten Commandments to the assembled people of Israel at Mount Sinai. The Torah focuses on the former reason for the holiday; but the main focus of the holiday in the last two thousand years has been the latter reason. In Israel, *Shavuot* is a one-day holiday; outside of Israel, it is observed for two days. See also "*Emor* 2: The Holiday of *Shavuot*."

Shema (or Shma): This is a declaration of faith. It consists of three selections from the Torah: 1) Deuteronomy 6:4–9, which declares that there is one God and that we are to love Him with all our hearts; 2) Deuteronomy 11:13–21, which asserts that we are to obey God's commandments; and 3) Numbers 15:37–41, which tells us not to deviate from God's path, to do all that God commanded, and to remember that God took us out of Egypt to be our Lord. The *Shema* is said twice daily (morning and evening) as part of the prayer service.

Shemot (or Shmot):   The second book of the Torah, known in English as "Exodus." The word *shemot* literally means "the names of," this being the first significant word of the book. *Shemot* is also the name of the first *sidra* in the book of *Shemot*.

Shofar: A musical instrument made of a ram's horn. The *shofar* is blown each year on *Rosh Hashanah*. Also, the Torah mandates that in the land of Israel the *shofar* be blown on *Yom Kippur* of the fiftieth year of the agrigultural cycle (the *Yovel*). And, by custom, one long blast of the *shofar* is blown each year, in all Jewish communities throughout the world, at the conclusion of the fast of *Yom Kippur*.

Sidra: One of the 54 portions into which the Torah is divided for the purpose of the weekly communal reading. (The plural form is *sidrot*.) The name of each *sidra* is derived from the first significant word in that *sidra*. Since the first significant word of each book is also, perforce, the first significant word of the first *sidra* of that book, therefore the first *sidra* of each of the five books of the Torah is called by the same name as that book. Thus, for example, the first *sidra* of the book of *Bereshit* is the *sidra* of *Bereshit*, *etc.*

Smicha (or Semicha):   Rabbinical ordination. See my discussion on the portion of *Shoftim* for further details.

Sod: Literally, this word means "secret" or "mystery." In the context of Torah exegesis, the word *sod* is applied to the mystical interpretation of the text. (See also "*Kabbalah*.")

Sukkot: A major holiday that occurs at the end of the summer or beginning of autumn, in the first month of the Hebrew calendar. It commemorates the divine protection given to the new nation of Israel after the Exodus from bondage in Egypt. Celebration of the holiday includes dwelling in *sukkot* (huts) for seven days, to commemorate the huts in which the Israelites dwelled in the desert when they left Egypt (Leviticus 23:42–43). For further discussion, see "*Emor* 4: The Holiday of *Sukkot*."

Tabernacle: A tent that served as a mobile temple, called *mishkan* in Hebrew (literally, a place of residence). The Torah also refers to it as *ohel mo'ed*—The Tent of Meeting. After the nation of Israel entered the Promised Land, the Tabernacle continued to be used until King Solomon built the Temple in Jerusalem. The Temple then replaced the Tabernacle.

Talmud: The combination of the Mishnah and accompanying Gemara is known as the Talmud. There are two versions of the Gemara: the *Talmud Yerushalmi* (Jerusalem Talmud) and the *Talmud Bavli* (Babylonian Talmud). Unlike the Mishnah, which is in Hebrew, both versions of the Gemara are in Aramaic. The Mishnah is the same in both Talmuds; it is only the Gemara that is different. The Jerusalem Talmud, completed in the 4th Century CE, records the discussions of the rabbis in the academies in Israel; whereas the Babylonian Talmud, completed about 499 CE, records the discussions in the Babylonian academies. The Babylonian Talmud is much longer and much more detailed in its analysis than is the Jerusalem Talmud. The Babylonian Talmud, including commentary thereon, is well over 5,000 pages long and is generally published in about twenty volumes. (See also "Mishnah" and "Gemara," above.)

Tanakh: This is an acronym of **T**orah, **N**evi'im ("Prophets"), **K**etuvim ("Writings"). It is synonymous with the Hebrew Bible.

Tanna: One of the rabbis of the Mishnah (see above). The plural is *tanna'im*.

Ten Commandments: This is the English name for the ten precepts that were given to the nation of Israel at Mount Sinai and which God then inscribed on two stone tablets. The Ten Commandments are often referred to as "The Decalogue." The "Ten Commandments" are called in Hebrew *Aseret Hadibrot*—"The Ten Statements." They are actually ten *dibrot* (statements), not ten *mitzvot* (commandments), and they consist of fourteen *mitzvot* (or thirteen according to some commentators).

Teshuva: Repentance. When a person realizes that he or she has sinned, the Torah requires that he not only thereafter refrain from committing the same sin, but also that he do *teshuva*. See "*Nitzavim*: The Power of Repentance" for a discussion of *teshuva*.

Torah: The five books of Moses, also known in English as the Pentateuch. These are the first five books of the Bible: *Bereshit* (known in English as "Genesis"), *Shemot* (called "Exodus" in English), *Vayikra* ("Leviticus"), *Bamidbar* ("Numbers"), and *Devarim* ("Deuteronomy"). The Hebrew name of each of these books is derived from the first significant word of that book. The literal meaning of the word *Torah* is "teaching."

Tosafot: A commentary on the Babylonian Talmud by Rashi's grandsons, often disagreeing with Rashi's interpretations.

Tzaddik: A righteous person.

Vayikra: The third book of the Torah, known in English as "Leviticus." The word *vayikra* literally means "and He called," this being the first word of the book (God called to Moses). *Vayikra* is also the name of the first *sidra* in the book of *Vayikra*.

YHVH (or sometimes transliterated as YHWH): The four-letter name of God also known in English as the Tetragrammaton. This name is never pronounced, and the pronunciation of the name has been lost to us, since the vowels of the name are no longer known. The name YHVH, which is generally translated as The Lord, derives from the verb of being and connotes God's being the source of all that exists, and His being beyond nature. The name also connotes the quality of compassion.

Yom Kippur: The Day of Atonement. *Yom Kippur* is a solemn holiday, on which Jews fast and spend the day in prayer and asking forgiveness for their sins.

DESCRIPTION OF SOURCES

Abravnel: Don Isaac Abravnel (also called Abarbanel). Portugal, Spain, Corfu, and Italy, 1437–1508. Abravnel was a financier, and he served as finance minister first to King Alfonso V of Portugal and later to King Ferdinand II of Aragon and Castile. He left Spain with the expulsion of the Jews in 1492. Abravnel's commentary on the Bible is among the most important Medieval commentaries. His approach consists of asking a series of questions at the start of each unit of text and answering them in the course of analyzing the text. His discussions are generally lengthy and include a critical review of other commentaries, often disagreeing vigorously with some of his predecessors. Unlike the practice of most Jewish commentators, Abravnel sometimes also cites Christian commentaries.

Akedat Yitzchak: A commentary on the Torah by Rabbi Isaac Arama (see below).

Alsheikh (or Alshich): Rabbi Moshe Alsheikh (1508–1593). Alsheikh was born in Adrianople, studied in Salonika under Rabbi Yosef Karo and Yosef Taitazak, and then settled in Safed, Israel. Although his main occupation was *halakha* (Jewish law), he gave sermons on the Sabbath day, and he wrote a commentary on the Hebrew Bible based on those sermons. Alsheikh's approach, like that of Abravnel, consists of asking a series of questions at the start of each unit of text and answering them in the course of his analysis of the text. His discussions, which tend to be lengthy, include the plain meaning, philosophical and ethical issues stemming from the text, as well as midrashic and Kabbalistic interpretations.

Arama. Rabbi Isaac ben Moshe Arama (Spain, 1420–1494). Arama is the author of *Akedat Yitzchak*, which is a lengthy commentary on the Torah. His discussions often include philosophical considerations, especially from Maimonides.

Babylonian Talmud: See "Talmud."

Bachyay ben Asher ibn Halawa (Spain, 1255–1340): He is also known as Rabbeinu Bachyay, Rabbeinu Bachya, or Rabbeinu Bechayei. Rather than focusing on individual words or phrases, Bachyay's commentary tends to discuss the ideas presented in the underlying text. The commentary on each verse or set of verses is divided into four distinct parts: the plain meaning of the text (*peshat*), *midrash* (a homiletic interpretation), a philosophical analysis when appropriate, and a mystical (Kabbalistic) interpretation. He often cites previous commentators, especially Ramban.

Bamidbar Rabba: The *Midrash Rabba* on the book of *Bamidbar* (the book of Numbers). (See "*Midrash Rabba*.")

Bekhor Shor: Joseph ben Isaac Bekhor Shor of Orleans (France, 12th Century). He was a disciple of Rashi's grandson Rabbeinu Tam.

Bereshit Rabba: The *Midrash Rabba* on the book of *Bereshit* (the book of Genesis). (See "*Midrash Rabba*.")

Berlin, Rabbi Naftali Zvi Yehuda: see "Netziv."

Cassuto, Umberto: Umberto (Moshe David) Cassuto (Italy and Israel, 1883–1951) was Chief Rabbi of Florence from 1914 to 1925. He was also Professor of Hebrew at the University of Florence, and later he was the chairman of Hebrew at the University of Rome. In 1938, he was forced out of his position because of antisemitic laws, and he relocated to Jerusalem, where he joined the faculty at the Hebrew University. Cassuto is the author of a commentary on the Torah. But, unfortunately, he completed his commentary only on the books of Genesis and Exodus before his death. His commentary was translated into English by Israel Abrahams.

Cordovero, Moses: Rabbi Moshe Cordovero, known as Ramak (Safed, Israel—1522–1570). Ramak was a great scholar in both Jewish law and Jewish mysticism (Kabbalah), but he is best known for his writings on Kabbalah. His major works are *Pardes Rimmonim* (first published in 1548) and *Or Yakkar*. *Pardes Rimmonim*, which was his first published book, is a systematic presentation of the main premises of Kabbalah and a discussion of their logical underpinnings. *Or Yakkar* is a 16-volume commentary on the Zohar. Ramak also authored a book on ethics titled *Tomer Devorah*, as well as several other Kabbalistic treatises. He introduced the practice of *Kabbalat Shabbat* ("Receiving the Sabbath"), consisting of the recitation of six psalms and the song *Lekha Dodi* (which was composed by his brother-in-law, Shlomo Halevi Alkabetz) at the start of the Friday evening prayers.

Da'at Zekenim: Also known as *Da'at Zekenim Miba'alei haTosefot*. It is a compilation of commentaries by several of Rashi's disciples.

Devarim Rabba: The *Midrash Rabba* on the book of *Devarim* (the book of Deuteronomy). (See *"Midrash Rabba."*)

Flavius Josephus: See "Josephus."

Gikatilla, Joseph ben Abraham: Spain, 1248 – c. 1305. His most important work, *Sha'arei Orah*, which is a mystical interpretation of the names of God, is a key book for understanding Jewish mysticism.

Guide for the Perplexed: A book of Jewish philosophy by Moses Maimonides (Rambam). (See "Maimonides.")

Haketav Vehakabbalah (*i.e.* "The Text and the Tradition") is a prominent commentary on the Torah by Rabbi Ya'akov Tzvi Mecklenburg (Germany, 1785–1865).

Halevi: Rabbi Yehuda Halevi (Spain, 1075–1141). He was a physician, Hebrew poet, and philosopher. Halevi's major philosophical work, *The Kuzari*, was written in Arabic. In 1141, he immigrated to the Holy Land, which was then under crusader rule; and he died shortly after.

Hertz, Joseph H.: Dr. Joseph H. Hertz (1872–1946) was Chief Rabbi of the British Empire from 1913 until his death in 1946. His commentary on the Torah is contained in *Pentateuch and Haftorahs*, London, Soncino Press, 1975.

Heschel, Abraham Joshua: Poland, Germany, and U.S., 1907–1972. Heschel was a rabbi, theologian, and philosopher. He was the descendant of distinguished Chasidic rabbinic dynasties. Heschel is the author of several books of Jewish philosophy and theology, including *The Sabbath*, *Man Is Not Alone*, and *God In Search of Man*.

***Hizkuni* (or *Chizkuni*)**: Composed by Rabbi Hizkiyah ben Manoah (France, 13th Century). This is an eclectic commentary gleaned from Rashi and twenty other sources, also including Rabbi Hizkiyah's original insights into the psychology of Biblical characters.

Ibn Ezra: Rabbi Abraham (ben Meir) Ibn Ezra (Spain, 12th Century). Also known in Arabic as Ibrahim al-Majid Ibn Ezra. Hebrew poet and Biblical commentator. His commentary often relies on grammar and syntax of the text in arriving at his interpretations.

Josephus (Flavius Josephus): Josephus was a Jewish historian and military leader in the 1st Century CE. He led the Judean forces in Galilee against the Roman army in the First Jewish-Roman War. After surrendering to the Romans, he was taken as a slave and translator to Vespasian (who was at that time commander of the Roman army in Judea). When Vespasian was declared emperor in 69 CE, he set Josephus free. Josephus then took Vespasian's family name, Flavius; and later, Josephus was granted Roman citizenship. His book *The Antiquities of the Jews* fills in many details of Biblical history.

Karo, Isaac: Born in Toledo in 1458, he became a rabbi and physician. In 1492, he was exiled by the Alhambra Decree of King Ferdinand of Aragon and Queen Isabella of Castile, exiling all Jews from their domain. He relocated to Lisbon, where he founded a yeshiva. But the Jews were expelled from Portugal a few years later. He died in 1535, probably in Jerusalem. Isaac Karo was the uncle of Rabbi Yosef Karo, the author of the *Shulchan Arukh* (Code of Jewish Law).

Karo, Yosef: Also spelled Joseph Caro (Spain, Portugal, the Ottoman Empire, and Israel, 1488–1575). Yosef Karo was a rabbi and one of the greatest authorities on Jewish law. He was born in Toledo (Spain) and emigrated to Portugal at the age of 4 with his family in 1492, when the Jews were expelled from Spain as a result of the Alhambra Decree. The Jews were then expelled from Portugal in 1497, and he emigrated with his parents to the Ottoman Empire, where he lived in various cities within the empire. Around the year 1535, he arrived in Safed (Israel, but at that time part of the Ottoman Empire), where he remained for the rest of his life. Rabbi Yosef Karo is best known for his compilation of the Code of Jewish Law (the *Shulchan Arukh*), but he wrote several other authoritative works including a commentary on Maimonides's *Mishneh Torah*.

Kuzari: A book of Jewish philosophy by Rabbi Yehuda Halevi (see above).

Luzzatto, Shmuel David: see "Shadal."

Maimonides: Rabbi Moshe ben Maimon, or Moses Maimonides, also known by the acronym **Ram**bam (the Hebrew vocalization of his initials)—1138–1204—not to be confused with Ram**ban** (Nachmanides). Born in Cordoba (in present-day Spain), Maimonides moved to Egypt in his youth. In Egypt, he became an authority on Jewish law, as well as being an astronomer and a physician. He served as Saladin's personal physician. Maimonides's works include *Mishneh Torah* (a systematic codification of Jewish law), *The Guide for the Perplexed* (a book of Jewish philosophy), a commentary on the Mishnah, *Sefer HaMitzvot* ("Book of the Commandments"—a listing of and a treatise about the 613 commandments of the Torah), and several other books on Jewish subjects, as well as several medical books. Most of his books, including *The Guide for the*

Perplexed, were written in Arabic. The *Mishneh Torah* and his commentary on the Mishnah were written in Hebrew.

Malbim: This is an acronym of **M**eir **L**eibush **b**en **Y**echiel **M**ikhel Wisser (Volhynia, Romania, and various cities in the Russian Empire, 1809–1879). Malbim's commentary is based on exacting analysis of the words and the grammar, and on the principle that Scripture does not use unnecessary words. In his view, there are no exact synonyms, but there is always at least a difference in nuance between words that are considered synonymous. Thus, when an apparent repetition uses a synonym, in his opinion the text is really introducing a separate idea.

Meshekh Chokhma: A commentary on the Torah by Rabbi Meir Simcha Hakohen of Dvinsk (Lithuania, Poland, and Latvia, 1843–1926). The title of the book, *Meshekh Chokhma*, means "The Pursuit of Wisdom" (referring to extracting or drawing wisdom out of its hidden depths, as in Job 28:18); but *Meshekh* is also an acronym for the author's name, Meir Simcha Kohen.

Midrash Rabba (*i.e.* "The Great *Midrash*"): A major *midrash aggada* on the Torah and the five *Megillot*. The *Midrash Rabba* on the Torah comprises *Bereshit Rabba*, *Shemot Rabba*, *Vayikra Rabba*, *Bamidbar Rabba*, and *Devarim Rabba*, on the books of *Bereshit* (Genesis), *Shemot* (Exodus), *Vayikra* (Leviticus), *Bamidbar* (Numbers), and *Devarim* (Deuteronomy), respectively. *Bereshit Rabba* was published between 300 and 500 CE. The other sections were published over the next few centuries.

Midrash Tanchuma: A major *midrash aggada* on the Torah, probably first published in the 8th or 9th Century.

Midrash Tehillim: Also known as *Midrash Shochar Tov*. It is a *midrash aggada* on the book of Psalms (*Tehillim*), probably compiled in Israel, no later than the 11ᵗʰ Century.

Mishnah: The Mishnah, which is written in Hebrew, consists of rabbinic teachings of oral law that were transmitted over hundreds of years, as compiled and edited by Rabbi Judah the Prince in the early 3ʳᵈ Century CE. Originally, those teachings were supposed to be transmitted only orally and were not to be written down. But, in the face of Roman persecution, Rabbi Judah the Prince decided that it was necessary to write down a concise record of those teachings, lest they be lost. After completion of the Mishnah, later rabbinic authorities published the Gemara, which is an account of the commentary, discussion, and debate about rulings in the Mishnah. The combination of Mishnah and Gemara is known as the Talmud. (See also "Talmud.")

Mishneh Torah: A codification of Jewish law, by Maimonides.

Mizrachi: Rabbi Elijah Mizrachi (Constantinople, 1455–1525). Mizrachi was a Talmudist, a rabbinic authority, and a mathematician. He developed a method for extracting cube roots. From 1495 until his death, he was Chief Rabbi of the Ottoman Empire. Mizrachi is best known for his major work, *Sefer HaMizrachi*, which is a super-commentary on Rashi's Torah commentary.

Nachmanides: Rabbi Moses ben Nachman. See "Ramban."

Netziv: Rabbi **N**aftali **Tz**vi **Y**ehuda **B**erlin (1816–1893). The Netziv was dean of the Volozhin Yeshiva in Lithuania (the town of Volozhin is currently in Belarus), and the author of several rabbinic works including his commentary on the Torah, titled *Ha'amek Davar*.

Ne'umei Shmuel: A book of sermons on the weekly Torah portion, by Rabbi Shmuel Bar-Adon (Poland, and Haifa, Israel), Samuel Bavli's maternal grandfather. He served as a "Talmudic lawyer" in Haifa, arguing cases before the rabbinic court. Shmuel Bar-Adon was an expert in Jewish labor law, and he was also the author of *Dinei 'Avoda*—"Labor Laws"—a case book of labor cases that he had argued before the rabbinic court.

Onkelos: A Roman who converted to Judaism and translated the Torah into Aramaic after his conversion. The Talmud says that Onkelos was a relative of the Roman emperor Titus. In some sources, he is confused with Aquila, who was also a proselyte and who translated the Torah into Greek; but Onkelos and Aquila were certainly two separate people. Onkelos is thought to have lived c. 35–120 CE. He was a disciple of Rabbi Eliezer ben Hyrcanus. His translation of the Torah, which was done under the supervision of Rabbi Eliezer and Rabbi Joshua ben Chananiah, is regarded as highly authoritative, and both Rashi and Ramban (as well as other commentators) cite his translation frequently. An interesting feature of Onkelos's translation is that in cases where the Torah's meaning could be misunderstood, Onkelos often inserts an additional word or phrase to clarify the meaning. Also, his translation goes out of its way to avoid anthropomorphisms in reference to God, and he therefore interprets rather than translates all anthropomorphisms.

Or HaChayyim: A Torah commentary by Rabbi Chayyim ben Moshe ibn Attar (Morocco, Italy, and Israel, 1696–1743).

Pirkei Rabbi Eliezer: A *midrash aggada* composed in the 8th or 9th Century, probably in Italy. Traditionally, it has been attributed to the *tanna* Rabbi Eliezer ben Hyrcanus (1st to 2nd Century). Rabbi Eliezer may have composed the core of the book, and the book perhaps was later edited and additional material inserted in the 8th or 9th Century. (See *"Tanna"* in Glossary.)

Raavad: This is an acronym of **Ra**bbi **Av**raham ben **D**avid (Provence, c. 1125–1198). He was a great commentator on the Babylonian Talmud and on the laws of Leviticus. He is probably best known for his criticisms of Maimonides's *Mishneh Torah*. In addition to Raavad's formidable reputation in the field of Jewish law, he is also regarded as one of the great leaders in the field of Jewish mysticism.

Rabbeinu Bachyay ben Asher: see *"Bachyay ben Asher ibn Halawa."*

Radak: **Ra**bbi **Da**vid **K**imchi (Provence, 1160–1235). He was a Hebrew grammarian and Biblical commentator. Radak is best known for his commentary on the prophetic books of the Bible. He was a great defender of the views of Maimonides.

Rambam: see *"Maimonides."* (The acronym **Ram**bam is pronounced with the accent on the first syllable, to distinguish him from Ram**ban**—Nachmanides—whose acronym is pronounced with the accent on the final syllable—Ram**ban**).

Ramban: Rabbi Moses ben Nachman (Spain, 1194–1270), also known in English as Nachmanides. Ramban was a physician, rabbi, and scholar of Jewish law and Bible. He was born in Girona, in Catalonia, where he lived for much of his life, eventually becoming chief rabbi of Catalonia. In 1263, Ramban debated the Dominican friar Pablo Christiani, to defend the Jewish religion.

That debate—the Disputation of Barcelona—was held in the presence of King James I of Aragon, as well as the king's court and many members of the church. Because of Christian persecution of Jews, Ramban was forced to leave Aragon in about 1264. He lived in Castile for a while, and in 1267 he arrived in Israel where he lived until his death. Ramban is best known for his commentary on the Torah, in which he frequently disagrees with Rashi on the plain meaning of the text. After discussing the plain meaning, Ramban often also discusses or hints at a mystical interpretation.

Rashbam: This is an acronym for **Ra**bbi **Sh**muel **b**en **M**eir (France, c. 1085 – c. 1158). He was a grandson of Rashi. In his commentary, Rashbam tries to adhere to the plain meaning of the text (the *peshat*). He often disagrees with Rashi's interpretations.

Rashi: This is an acronym for **Ra**bbi **Sh**lomo **Yi**tzchaki, *i.e.* Shlomo, son of Yitzchak (Troyes, France, 1040–1105). His commentary on the Torah and other books of the Bible is concise and directed to presenting what he regarded as the plain meaning of the text. Also, Rashi's Torah commentary often includes homiletic excerpts from the *midrash* and the Talmud wherever there are gaps in understanding the plain meaning, and where he considered that these homiletic passages would illuminate the understanding of the text of the Torah. Rashi's commentary is generally the first Torah commentary that children learn in elementary school.

Sefer HaChinukh (*i.e.* "The Book of Education"): A 13th Century book published anonymously and attributed to Aharon ben Levi, but the identification of the author is uncertain. The book discusses the 613 *mitzvot*, based on the enumeration of Maimonides, and listed in order of their appearance in the Torah. The discussion of each *mitzvah* includes the philosophical basis of that *mitzvah* and the particulars of its observance.

Septuagint: The Septuagint is a Greek translation of the Torah, translated by a panel of seventy Jewish scholars, commissioned by King Ptolemy II Philadelphus, in Egypt in the 3rd Century BCE.

Sforno: Rabbi Ovadia Sforno (Italy, 1475–1550). He was a physician, rabbi, and philosopher. He wrote commentaries on the Torah and on several other books of the Bible. His commentaries tend to be concise and focused on the plain meaning of the text, although he does occasionally deviate into philosophy when there is an especially important point to be made. Sforno draws upon other commentaries (although, in keeping with the trend in his generation, he doesn't reference his sources). Often, he gives original interpretations, which in some cases differ significantly from those of other commentators.

Shadal: This is an acronym for **Sh**muel **Da**vid **L**uzzatto (Italy, 1800–1865). Besides his commentary on the Torah, he composed a book on Hebrew Grammar (written in Italian), a commentary on the books of Isaiah and Job, Italian translations of Isaiah and Job, and a large number of articles in various periodicals and scholarly correspondences in Italian, German, and French.

Shemot Rabba: The *Midrash Rabba* on the book of *Shemot* (the book of Exodus). (See "*Midrash Rabba*.")

Sifra: This book is a *midrash halakha* on the book of Leviticus, probably produced in the early 3rd Century. (See "*Midrash*" in Glossary.)

Sifrei: This refers to two books of *midrash halakha*, on the books of Numbers (*Sifrei Bamidbar*) and Deuteronomy (*Sifrei Devarim*), dating from the period of the Mishnah, around the 2nd Century. (Also, see *"Midrash"* in Glossary.)

Talmud: The combination of the Mishnah and accompanying Gemara is known as the Talmud. There are two versions of the Gemara: that of the *Talmud Yerushalmi* (Jerusalem Talmud) and that of the *Talmud Bavli* (Babylonian Talmud). Unlike the Mishnah, which is in Hebrew, both versions of the Gemara are in Aramaic. The Mishnah is the same in both Talmuds; it is only the Gemara that is different. The Jerusalem Talmud, completed in the 4th Century CE, records the discussions of the rabbis in the academies in Israel; whereas the Babylonian Talmud, completed about 499 CE, records the discussions in the Babylonian academies. The Babylonian Talmud is much longer and much more detailed in its analysis than is the Jerusalem Talmud. The Babylonian Talmud, including commentary thereon, is well over 5,000 pages long and is generally published in about twenty volumes. (See also "Mishnah," above.)

Tanna Devei Eliyahu: This is a *midrash aggada* that is mentioned in the Talmud, but the final redaction was probably in the 10th Century. The theme of this *midrash* is the evolution of the world. The first half of the book deals with the period from the creation to the expulsion of Adam and Eve from the Garden of Eden, and the second half deals with the period from the expulsion from the Garden of Eden until the Flood.

Toldot Yitzchak: A commentary on the Torah (completed in 1517) by Rabbi Isaac Karo (see above).

Tosafot: A commentary on the Babylonian Talmud by Rashi's grandsons, often disagreeing with Rashi's interpretations.

Vulgate (Latin—Vulgata): This is the Latin translation of St. Jerome. He completed his translation of the Torah about the year 405 CE. The Vulgate became the official Bible of the Catholic Church.

Vayikra Rabba: The *Midrash Rabba* on the book of *Vayikra* (the book of Leviticus). (See "*Midrash Rabba.*")

Zohar (literally, "Radiance") is regarded as the central book of Kabbalah. Written in a composite dialect of Aramaic, it is a commentary on the Torah. Its approach is primarily mystical, but there are also homiletical interpretations, and often highly original insights into the plain meaning (*peshat*) of the Torah. The Zohar was published in installments, by Rabbi Moshe deLeon, in Leon (Spain) in the last two decades of the 13th and the first decade of the 14th Century. Traditionally, it was attributed to Rabbi Shim'on bar Yohai (Israel, 2nd Century), but many have questioned that attribution since shortly after its initial appearance and continuing to the present time. The first printed editions were published in Italy in the 1550s; and the standard edition today, in three volumes, follows the format of the Mantua edition of 1558, such that all page references are to that edition.

ACKNOWLEDGEMENTS

I want to thank my father Hillel Bavli, who inspired my love of the Torah and gave me an intimate knowledge of and proficiency in Biblical Hebrew. My father, although mainly known as a Hebrew poet, had a vast knowledge of the entire Hebrew Bible. He and my mother, Rahela Bavli—also a Hebrew poet—spoke to me only in Hebrew when I was little, thereby imparting to me a sensitivity to the nuances of the Hebrew language.

Also, I thank my uncle Aaron Bar-Adon, who recently died shortly before his 99th birthday. He had an extensive knowledge of Biblical Hebrew usage and was on the faculty of the University of Texas in Austin, where he taught courses in Hebrew, Arabic, and linguistics. On many occasions, I called him to discuss Biblical phrases. He was always a great help, and he will be sorely missed.

And above all, I thank my dear wife and soulmate Madeline, who was a sounding-board for many ideas and helped me tremendously in editing this book.

PRAISE FOR
THE LIGHT OF THE TORAH

"I have very much enjoyed reading Dr. Shmuel Bavli's essays on the *parshiyot ha-shavua*. Written very clearly and drawing upon a wide range of sources—from Talmudic through modern times—Dr. Bavli has brought new insights to paths well-trodden, providing creative interpretations for many biblical narratives and laws. I have learned a lot from his thoughtful and most interesting perspectives. All will benefit from these reflections, beginners and scholars alike."

—Rabbi Dr. Jacob J. Schacter
University Professor of Jewish History and Jewish Thought, Yeshiva University, New York, NY

"Dr. Samuel Bavli is a lover of Torah. Throughout a life of devotion to medicine as an esteemed endocrinologist, he nurtured his passion for scripture by regular study and by writing well-researched essays on the weekly portion. He has now made these available to the public, to the delight, enrichment and inspiration of us all."

—Rabbi Haskel Lookstein
Rabbi Emeritus of Congregation Kehilath Jeshurun, New York, NY

"I am pleased to offer high praise of Dr. Samuel Bavli's wonderfully engaging and deeply insightful work, *The Light of the Torah*. It reflects the remarkable breadth of knowledge of my friend and colleague, in both the Torah and our contemporary reality. Dr. Bavli has truly provided us with insight and wisdom that is so valuable for the thinking Jew of today. Kol Hakavod!"

—Rabbi Kenneth Hain
Rabbi, Congregation Beth Sholom, Lawrence, NY

ABOUT THE AUTHOR

Samuel Bavli, professionally trained as a medical doctor, has been a lifelong writer. Dr. Bavli comes from a long line of rabbis; and his father, the Hebrew poet Hillel Bavli, instilled in him a love of literature, a love of the Hebrew Bible and a sensitivity to the nuances of Biblical Hebrew. For several years, he taught a class on the book of Isaiah; and for ten years, he taught a class on the Zohar at the Orthodox synagogue where he is a member. Drawing inspiration from the numerous Jewish physicians who, through the course of Jewish history, wrote commentaries on the Torah and devoted themselves to the exposition of Jewish thought and theology, Dr. Bavli decided to write this book, which is the fruit of his many years of delving into the in-depth analysis of major concepts in the Torah. He is also the author of two books of historical fiction. Dr. Bavli is now retired from medicine, and he devotes much of his time to writing and to studying Torah.

Made in the USA
Monee, IL
28 December 2022

c401c9a6-5ce2-4e31-8c92-a50130c1c473R01